DIARY
of a
CONGRESSMAN

To H. Reid, a faithful friend and a great guy. With very best regards —

Bill Whitehurst

November 9, 1983

DIARY
of a
CONGRESSMAN

G. William Whitehurst

THE DONNING COMPANY
Publishers
Norfolk/Virginia Beach

The Donning Company/Publishers
5659 Virginia Beach Boulevard
Norfolk, Virginia 23502

Library of Congress Cataloging in Publication Data

Whitehurst, G. William
    Diary of a congressman.

    1. United States. Congress. 2. Legislators—
United States. 3. United States—Politics and
government—1945-   I. Title.
JK1041.W47   1983   328.73'092'4   83-16523
ISBN 0-89865-336-3
ISBN 0-89865-355-5 (pbk.)

Printed in the United States of America

Dedication

To J. Pierrepont Moffat, whose example moved me
to keep this journal, and to my wife Janie,
who willingly and faithfully transcribed it.

Foreword

When Bill Whitehurst came to Washington nearly sixteen years ago, he brought with him two assets developed in his first career in academe: the ability to witness world events with the dispassionate but trained eye of an historian, and the necessary discipline to chronicle them for future generations.

In a few years, I suspect, Bill will have earned his "leave" from the halls of Congress to resume the academic life he loves so dearly. His loss to the Congress, where he has always been held in the highest esteem by all—especially for his intellect and understanding of education and national defense issues—will be sorely felt.

In a state that prides itself for its ties to the founders of America, Bill Whitehurst deserves to be associated with Virginia's many great statesmen. He is a Virginia treasure all of us can take pride in for the standard of excellence he has set for those who aspire to public and political careers.

In this first volume, which I hope will be followed by a second, Bill has given us a rare insight into the inner workings of the Congress as witnessed by one with a feeling for their place in history. *Diary of a Congressman* traces the years 1972-1977 and allows us to walk by the side of a senior Representative into the halls and chambers of our nation's legislative body and eavesdrop on discussions from presidents and world leaders to freshmen Members of Congress.

The importance of a historical document such as *Diary of a Congressman* is that it gives us a permanent record of the events that helped shape the nation and our neighbors in the world community.

"History," as no less a thinker than Cicero observed over 2,000 years ago, "is the witness that testifies to the passing of time; it illuminates reality, vitalizes memory, provides guidance in daily life, and

1

brings us tidings of antiquity." With pen and notepad constantly in tow, Bill Whitehurst has given us an insider's view of history in the making during some of the most tumultuous years in our country's brief history.

Besides being a serious historian, Bill is a fine writer who has not failed to capture in humorous detail some of the more tedious moments in every Congressman's life. On one occasion, Bill and other members of the Armed Services Committee found themselves straining to maintain their interest in the unveiling of a portrait of a former committee chairman. During one particularly long-winded speech honoring the late chairman, Bill discovered that he wasn't the only one in the room squirming in his seat, observing: "One woman in the front was in tears, but a hell of a lot more were glancing at their watches."

My friendship with Bill goes back to the beginning of his congressional career in 1969 when I was Under Secretary of the Navy. It was evident from his first term when he took his seat on the Armed Services Committee that he would develop a mastery of national defense issues with the same scholarly determination that marked his years as a college professor. In times of considerable opposition to increasing defense spending, Bill has been one of the few leaders in Congress consistently able to take the long view and not be persuaded to stray from a course that ensures our national security.

Although this volume covers only one segment of his lengthy career, Bill's complete diary will no doubt be regarded as an invaluable resource for generations to come. To date, Bill has chronicled the careers of five presidents who have occupied the White House; witnessed a nation and Congress torn by a war in Southeast Asia; agonized with other Members of Congress over the possibility of impeaching Richard M. Nixon; shared the elation over the Camp David Accords; endured the grueling months following the takeover of the United States embassy in Iran; and participated in some of the most dramatic battles in Congress between liberal and conservative forces with the arrival in Washington of Ronald Reagan.

Diary of a Congressman represents one more achievement in a remarkable career in Congress that has been characterized by Bill's unswerving devotion to his country and its people. He is truly a unique individual who has enriched us all with a work that will endure long after he has passed from the scene.

SENATOR JOHN W. WARNER
UNITED STATES SENATE

Introduction

Subjective as they are, diaries nevertheless offer an insight into history that makes them unique. Samuel Pepys, for example, affords us a view of seventeenth-century London that is without parallel. Scholars have traditionally sought out diaries when researching a particular era. They bring to life individuals who have long departed the stage of history. Documents and state papers provide the official basis for historical facts, but diaries and letters of the principals are the flesh and blood of the past.

Diaries are also very personal. Few diarists have kept their journals for the express purpose of publication. Most have done so in order to preserve their memories for their families and friends, and, in the case of public figures, to ensure that their side of the story is told for posterity's sake. For historians, diaries, whether they were the property of the famous or the obscure, are a rich lode, and the chronicle of the past would be a barren record without them.

All of this leads me to the explanation of why I began keeping a diary when I was first sworn in as a Member of the 91st Congress in January 1969. I did so to repay a historical debt. In 1959, I was deep into research on my doctoral dissertation, which centered on the initial attempts of President Franklin Roosevelt to lead America down the path of collective security in the years preceding World War II. In the course of my research, I stumbled upon the diary of an American diplomat named J. Pierrepont Moffat. The published version of the diary was limited and severely edited. I knew that if I could gain access to the original diary it would be a gold mine of information for me. Learning that the manuscript was at Harvard University, I wrote to the librarian and ultimately, through the courtesy of Moffat's widow, I was able to examine the original diary.

For the better part of a week in August 1959 I read and took notes from the diary of a man whose diplomatic career had ended suddenly with his death in 1943. Now, sixteen years later, I was combing the daily record of his activities in the year 1937. One afternoon, after spending hours with Moffat's journal, I suddenly felt a hand pressing on my shoulder. I turned immediately to see who it was, but there was no one there. Except for another graduate student at a nearby table, the room was empty. Instinctively, I felt that Pierrepont Moffat had stepped from the pages of his diary. Aside from telling my wife that evening, it was years before I would confide this story to anyone else. I have never had another experience like it, before or since.

Running for Congress was the furthest thing from my mind in 1959. I was intent only upon completing the work toward my Ph.D. and resuming my academic career at Old Dominion University, where I taught history. But fate deemed otherwise, and in 1968 I was elected to my first term to represent the Second District of Virginia. Frankly, I did not expect to enjoy so long a congressional career, and I thought that the voters would probably return me to the academic world within a few years. However, shortly before I came to Washington, I remembered how valuable Pierrepont Moffat's diary had been to my research, so I decided that I ought to repay my debt to Moffat by keeping a journal of my own, an account of my activities, the people I met, my impressions, and the host of personal experiences that fill our days.

As I stood in the House of Representatives in January 1969, neither I nor any of those taking the oath of office with me would have dreamed of the events that were to take place in the decade ahead of us. I heard Lyndon Johnson deliver his last State of the Union Address on the eve of his leaving office and sensed the drama of the end of a turbulent political career. My appetite to set down these feelings was whetted, and thus began countless hours at my typewriter after the House adjourned.

The single most important virtue necessary for keeping a diary is discipline. Several times during my first six months in Congress I nearly abandoned it. There were many evenings when I simply did not feel like giving the time to writing, and I was tempted to put it aside. But down deep I knew that I enjoyed a rare privilege. Fewer than 11,000 Americans at that time had ever served in the Congress of the United States. Only a very small number of them had kept a record of their service. I rightly suspected that few of my contemporaries were bothering to set down their daily observations, and I wanted to create a dimension for my congressional career that would be of my own making. I also still felt that debt to Moffat. Finally, a pattern developed. Not every day was event-filled. Many were insignificant and merited little more than a few lines. Others were more interesting, and a few were special.

The reader will notice that some of the entries cover several days. The reason is that I have not always been able to record my impressions at the end of each day. Often my wife and I were out for an evening, or the House remained in session late. Occasionally I have been too tired to put in an hour or so on my diary. When that happened, I would simply scribble a few notes and save them until I had the time and was mentally alert.

Over the years, I have worked out the following routine: I first type a rough draft, usually before or after supper at home in Arlington. The next morning, before leaving for the Hill, I will edit the previous night's work, and after I am satisfied with it I give it to my wife, who then types the finished product, making changes in grammar, syntax, or punctuation as necessary. Sometimes, when we have shared an experience, she will add her own remarks to mine, so the journal reflects our joint career. The pages are then numbered and inserted in a binder for the current calendar year. In January of each year, we begin a new volume.

When the opportunity was presented to publish my diary, I considered selecting entries beginning with my first year. In reviewing those, however, I was struck by the paucity of events of any real significance. I was also just beginning to learn what to look for, to observe with a discerning eye, and to see beyond the superficial. Quite honestly, I was so in awe of my surroundings that I felt overwhelmed, and it shows in those early pages. I'm not certain that I want anyone to read those first entries and have kept them from even my publisher.

So I decided to begin the published version of my journal with 1972, the year when the seeds were sown for the most serious constitutional crisis our nation has faced in this century: Watergate. The reader will note that the first reference to Watergate does not occur until some weeks after the initial news of the break-in. I was tempted to go back and insert an entry on that date, because I recalled the morning when the *Washington Post* headlined the story. What made it memorable was the fact that I recognized one of the men who was arrested and later convicted. His photograph, along with those of the others who had been apprehended, appeared on the front page of the *Post*. He was identified as Frank Sturgis, but I remembered him as Frank Fiorini, who had been enrolled in my European History class in the early 1950s at the college where I taught in Norfolk, Virginia. His academic career was short-lived, and I recalled his being in and out of the news for a few years thereafter. But aside from this personal connection, I attached no particular importance to the break-in at the Democratic headquarters as far as President Nixon was concerned.

Not until well into summer, after Watergate had ceased to be referred to flippantly as a "caper" and my colleagues began to speak of it in more sober terms, did I begin to mention it in my diary. Thus the reader will not find any reference to it in the early entries for 1972. But as the event began to reach crisis proportions, scarcely a week went by without my detailing some conversation or a Watergate-related development in my chronicle. The reader will observe my personal metamorphosis from disbelief, to suspicion, to final realization of the truth of the President's role in the cover-up that followed the break-in. The diary reveals the depth of the anguish that I, and many of my House colleagues, felt as impeachment loomed in the summer of 1974.

There are, of course, other stories on these pages. There is much more besides Watergate. There are profiles of my colleagues, some of whom the reader can readily identify and others less well known. The House, after all, has 435 Members and turns over a number of them every two years. It is not a refuge for anonymity, but neither is it a body that spawns household names. Those who seek more exclusivity usually run for the Senate, always referred to in the House as "the other body," a term that acknowledges a physical presence on the other side of the Capitol but little else.

The reader will also travel abroad with me and share face-to-face meetings with heads of state and political leaders in other countries. Such trips are often described as "junkets" by the media. Some are, but most are useful, interesting, and helpful in the discharge of a Member's responsibilities. One always returns more knowledgeable and with a deeper understanding of American interests and problems overseas, and such missions should be neither discouraged nor misunderstood.

Finally, half the fun in a diary is the trivia that one finds in it. I hope that this one is no exception. Heaven knows, there is plenty of it in these pages, and I trust that the reader will be as amused as I was by some of the events. One question remains to be answered: Why does this volume stop with the year 1977? The answer is simple. Had the publisher produced a book that embraced twelve years instead of six, the book would have been at least twice as long, and its size would have discouraged all but the most determined of readers. However, should this book enjoy some modest success, a second volume will be forthcoming.

Now, please turn the page and join me in the Congress.

Prologue: 1969 to 1972

I am sure that no newly-elected Member of Congress will ever forget his first exposure to the majesty of the Capitol. Mine came about two weeks after my initial election in November 1968. I had driven to Washington to see Gerald Ford, then Minority Leader of the House, to make a personal appeal for appointment to the House Armed Services Committee, an assignment that I knew would be important for my congressional district and my own political future. I also had to interview several prospective members for my staff.

The Minority Leader's office is located on the second floor of the Capitol, not far from the Rotunda. I recall walking down the main corridor, where the statues of the states' most honored sons and daughters stood on their pedestals. The echo of my footsteps on the marble floor had a dreamlike quality. I could scarcely believe that I was soon to become a part of this august assembly.

Incredible as it may seem, although I had been to Washington many times, I had never been inside the House of Representatives. When my meeting with Gerald Ford was over, I walked back toward the House side of the Capitol and decided that I shouldn't leave without getting a view of the House Chamber. Since the Congress had adjourned *sine die* prior to the election, there were few people about. After some searching, I found the Speaker's Lobby, where doors lead into the chamber itself. There were two Capitol police officers on duty. I introduced myself as a Member-elect and asked if I could go in and look around. Immediately, they rose and pushed the doors open for me, and I went in. Obviously curious to watch my reaction, both of the officers followed me into the Chamber. "Well, what do you think of it, Congressman?" one of them asked. I hesitated before saying anything, then replied, "I don't want you to get the wrong impression, but it's smaller than I thought it would be." They laughed and said, "That's because you are looking at the Chamber from the Floor. From the gallery it looks larger." "That's probably just as well," I commented, "because that's where the public sits."

It was awesome, all the same, but later on, after I had spent many hours listening to my colleagues, I recalled what Harry Truman had said about his initiation into the U.S. Senate back in the 1930s. He said that for the first six months he wondered how he had ever gotten there. The second six months he wondered how the others had gotten there. Nevertheless, standing in the House of Representatives that November morning, I could not imagine the events to which I would be a witness in the decade ahead. When I was sworn in just a few weeks later, not only was I baffled by parliamentary intricacies, but I became lost in the tunnels that connect the Capitol with the House office buildings. Between all the various votes that were called that day and my wanderings in the halls, I missed practically all of my own swearing-in party back in my office; there was no food left when I finally got back and most of the guests had gone home.

A two-year term of office provides a newly-elected Member with little more time than to merely "learn the ropes." If his constituents are reasonably satisfied with the record of an incumbent, they ought to send him back for a second term. I remember telling my wife that one evening in 1970, when we were leaving the office. I said that I really felt that the voters should reelect me, or they would waste two years training someone else. She knew that I did not mean it boastfully; there is so much to learn during the first eighteen months of office and by the middle of the second year most Members are obliged to turn their attentions to their political careers.

Looking back over nearly eight full terms, I know now how naive I was at the outset about the role of a congressman, but also how quickly I began to learn to serve effectively. I also realize what an absolute adventure it has been. I have had a ringside seat in the greatest legislative body in the world, and been a witness to, and indeed a participant in, some of the richest drama of the twentieth century. There are a few brief episodes from the early period which are worth including here. The first dealt with my appointment to the Armed Services Committee, which I had so actively sought.

Soon after President Johnson's farewell State of the Union Address, I was seated in one of the easy chairs in the Republican lounge just off the floor of the House, having my usual tuna fish sandwich for lunch. I was vaguely aware that just behind me Jerry Ford, Les Arends (then the Minority Whip), and one or two others in the Republican Leadership had gathered and were talking in low tones. I wasn't paying any attention, until I heard my own name; my ears pricked up at that, and I eavesdropped without really intending to. It was obvious that they were discussing committee assignments, with much give and take, until Gerry Ford finally said, with some asperity, "I don't care what you say—I think we should give it to the kid from Norfolk!" It was then that I learned that I had succeeded in my quest.

I did my best to remain invisible, because it would have been embarrassing for all concerned if the group had realized that I was there. But I will always be grateful to Jerry Ford for keeping his word to "the kid from Norfolk."

The second episode occurred on January 14, 1969. Officially, it was the State of the Union Address, but a better title would have been "Lyndon Johnson's Farewell," a last opportunity for a President with only six days left in his term of office to summarize his achievements and restate his priorities. But LBJ was incapable of confining his remarks to the customary review of his tenure in the White House. We were treated instead to a nostalgic recollection of his early career in this very body, and, at the end, the emotional personal wrenching of a man for whom politics was a consuming passion.

It was my introduction to this unique constitutional institution. Hardly any President since Woodrow Wilson had passed up the chance to appear personally before the Congress to deliver this mandated address. Johnson would have invented an opportunity had the Constitution not provided one.

It began when Fishbait Miller, the squat, jug-eared Doorkeeper of the House, announced in his stentorian voice the arrival of the United States Senate. At once the members of the other body walked down the center aisle and took their seats at the front of the Chamber. They were then followed in succession by the members of the Diplomatic Corps, who took their places in the bank of seats to our extreme right, then the Supreme Court and the Cabinet, all of whom were placed in the front row. The First Lady and their two daughters, Lynda Bird and Luci, along with Muriel Humphrey, the wife of the Vice President, entered the section of the gallery reserved for the First Family. They were greeted with prolonged applause. Seats everywhere were at a premium; even the aisles were filled.

I had attended a dinner with some of my Virginia colleagues earlier in the evening and almost didn't get back to the House in time. When I reached the Speaker's Lobby, I found that every Member was being challenged to show his ID card to the Capitol police. Mine hadn't been issued to me yet, and on impulse I pulled out my new Western Union credit card. It was the most official-looking thing that I could find in my wallet. When I flashed it at the officer, he did a double-take, but the officer next to him laughed and said, "Let him in. Anybody who'd show that kind of card has to be a new Member."

At length, when all of our official visitors had been seated, Fishbait announced, "Mr. Speaker, the President of the United States," and the audience as one rose to its feet and applauded. Many of the Democrats cheered, giving Lyndon Johnson his last hurrah. To this tumult, he strode down the aisle to the podium below Speaker John McCormack and the Vice President. He savored every moment of it.

Overwhelmed by the drama, I was surprised by the unfriendly comments by some of the Republicans around me. H. R. Gross of Iowa said, "Well, I wonder what Old Cornball is going to spring on us tonight." LBJ, of course, heard none of this. He spoke easily and forcefully, his voice showing no strain. Not surprisingly, he put the best possible face on his Administration, glossing over his failures. The omission of these brought some audible comments from the Republican side of the aisle. Toward the end, Johnson began to reminisce about his first days in the House some thirty-seven years before. He said that he had begun as one of the Doorkeepers, which prompted solitary handclapping by Fishbait. Someone near me quipped, "Fishbait shouldn't get his hopes up. He'll never make it to the White House." Somebody else said, "He didn't begin on the door. He was an elevator operator, and that's where the SOB should have ended up." Generally, however, there was a deeper well of charity toward the President.

LBJ wasn't through, though. He wallowed in handing out favors, and even though they were the verbal kind, he wasn't going to be denied tonight. He showered compliments on practically everyone—first his Vice President, then Mike Mansfield, and then McCormack, who was so pleased that he almost squirmed in his seat. Then Johnson started on our side with Everett Dirksen and Jerry Ford, raising the decibel level among the Republicans.

When there was no one left to hail, the President seemed to realize at last that his departure could no longer be prolonged. With a sigh that was nearly audible, he slapped his hands against the sides of the podium in a gesture that seemed to say, "This is it." None of his critics disturbed his momentary reverie, but listened quietly while he expressed his gratitude for the long service that he had been able to give. There was a moment of silence before the audience realized that he had finished, and then stormy applause with everyone rising to their feet. But Lyndon Johnson appeared oblivious to it. He turned and looked up at the gallery where Lady Bird sat watching him. For a few seconds they held each other's gaze, clearly realizing that they had come to the end of a long road together, and then the President wasted little time in leaving the Chamber, pausing only briefly to shake an outstretched hand.

Finally, there was a day in March 1970, when an afternoon in the Armed Services Committee ended with some mild horseplay at my expense. I was wearing a pair of loafers which had become quite loose on my feet. After taking my seat, I slipped them off and wriggled my toes in my socks. Becoming fully engrossed in the briefing that was going on, I failed to notice that John Hunt, who sat next to me, had pushed one of my shoes over to Ed Foreman, who in turn passed it along to someone else. Later, when I noticed that one of my loafers was missing, I turned to Hunt, who feigned ignorance. Foreman shrugged his shoulders, and I knew then that I was a victim of a conspiracy. Then I noticed that Russ Blandford, our chief counsel, who normally had a serious mien in committee hearings, had a broad grin on his face. There was nothing for me to do but wait patiently for the meeting to end. When it did, I limped on one shoe along the lower tier of seats, which the junior Members occupy. As I passed the chairman, Mendel Rivers, he asked me, "Are you missing a shoe?" "Mr. Chairman," I replied, "when I came on the Committee, they told me that I would have to stay on my toes. That's what I was doing today when somebody took my shoe." Mr. Rivers chuckled and walked away. At least I was sure he didn't have it. I found it later in the wastebasket on the top tier, which meant that it must have passed through the hands of at least ten of my Democratic colleagues en route.

If the voters knew that this kind of nonsense went on while we were taking up the nation's defense, I'm sure that all of our seats would be forfeit.

1972

Wednesday, February 16, 1972

The most interesting development during the day was the meeting of the Wednesday Group* in Orval Hansen's office. Herm Schneebeli, the ranking Republican on the Ways and Means Committee, gave us a report on the formidable Wilbur Mills, who has apparently been bitten decisively by the Presidential bug. Herm said that despite Wilbur's public pronouncements about not campaigning actively, he sees a definite change in Committee activities and doesn't look for any major work to emerge this session. He even doubts that there will be a health care bill, which has been much touted. The others agreed that Mills isn't the unassailable lion of the past. In the words of Chuck Whalen, "He's lost his objectivity."

Peter Frelinghuysen, whose mind and rhetoric I have come to appreciate, gave us a summary of an Anglo-American meeting he attended in Bermuda. He complained about the price of the rooms, $70 a day, which he felt was outrageous, even though it included meals. However, he reserved his choicest barbs for Wayne Hays, who was a source of embarrassment to one and all.

According to Peter, Hays showed up with two girls, either from his staff or from the Foreign Affairs Committee, one of them a platinum blonde. He was apparently just as abrasive and sarcastic at the conference as he is on the Floor of the House, leaving the British somewhat nonplused and the Americans fuming. Peter swore up and down that he would never attend another conference with Hays and declared that he did not know how Hays got invited to these powwows.

---

* The Wednesday Group is an informal association of about thirty Republican Members of the House of Representatives. It is generally regarded as the moderate wing of the Republican Membership. I joined it during my second term.

12

We had an executive session this week of the Armed Services Committee to hear from Admiral "Ike" Kidd on the LHA and DD963 programs at Litton Shipyard in Pascagoula, Mississippi. The LHA is a landing ship of a new design, which also has a helicopter deck. It's the kind of vessel that is needed for landing assaults in the future, a self-contained vessel of great versatility. Originally, nine of these ships were to have been built, but cost factors reduced the number to five. Technical problems have developed in the new automated construction techniques in the Litton yard.

Litton has gotten itself in a bind. They've spent about half the money and will need at least another half billion dollars to complete the program on the LHAs. They've also had a hard time recruiting workers to come to Pascagoula, where living conditions aren't very satisfactory. Eddie Hébert held up an ad offering a $1,000 bonus for skilled workers. We went round and round on the matter. Ike declared that we need the ships. The Russians are sailing rings around us in the Med and elsewhere. Many of our destroyers are handicapped by age and can't begin to compete with the Russians. The LHAs are unique. The Russians have nothing like them. We got into a discussion of cancelling the contract. Ike said that if we cancel, we still end up paying Litton for what they've done. In addition, they'll make a $40 million profit. Bill Nichols of Alabama said that we had farmers we paid not to grow crops. If we paid Litton that money and got no ships, it struck him that we were funding a "seagoing soil bank." His remark got the only laugh in an otherwise grim session. Both Sam Stratton and Otis Pike wanted to know why we couldn't charge Litton with defaulting on the contract by not delivering the ships when they were due. Ike said that it was damned hard to get this kind of decision. At this, Sam became peeved and declared the shipyard was overdue already. "How much longer do we have to wait before they *can* be charged with defaulting?" Bill Dickinson came down on a familiar theme of his: the Navy's consistent under-estimation of the inflation factor in awarding contracts. We build in a sure cost overrun by doing this.

No final decision was forthcoming on the meeting on Monday. However, on Friday, Charlie Ill, who is assistant secretary of the Navy for installations and logistics, dropped by my office for a chat, and I brought the matter up. Charlie said that it was a bad situation all right, and he wasn't sure how they were going to resolve it. He alluded to a renegotiation of the contract and also made it clear that Litton was going to have its feet held to the fire. I told him that if I had known that we were going to be asked by Litton and Grumman (who are seeking renegotiation of their F-14 contract) to bail them out with more money, I would have voted against giving Lockheed a guaranteed loan. I said that maybe we ought to let one of these companies go under, then the rest of them might employ better management procedures. Charlie partly agreed but declared that the real problem is that when new weapons systems are being developed, it's just impossible to calculate down to the last dollar what costs are going to be. He said that for an overseas project he always allows a 25 percent contingency. If he had had the same percentage in the case of Litton, there would have been no problem. Congress, of course, won't allow this practice at home. The nub of it is that we need the ships, so we're between a rock and a hard place.

Monday, April 24, 1972

I had a meeting of the Armed Services Committee this morning, which was a continuation of the painful postmortem on the Litton contract on the LHAs and the DD-963s. Several conclusions were officially reached, and a couple of unofficial ones, by some of the members. First of all, the Navy made a horrendous blunder in estimating the ability of Litton to build a new shipyard, which it did at Pascagoula, complete with automated techniques for ship construction, and to build these vessels within the time frame specified. It is obvious that shipbuilding requires the greatest kind of design and engineering coordination. It's like assembling a football or basketball team. They need to play together for a year or so before they become effective. In starting from scratch, Litton could not possibly complete the contract. Apparently the Navy was enamored of the idea of automated ship construction, which has taken hold in Europe, and Japan, and especially the USSR. On this premise all other calculations rested.

The more the Members dug into it, the worse it looked. Poor Ike Kidd manfully faced up to it, even though he hadn't made the decisions that got us into this situation. The unspoken aspect, at least on the record, was the role of John Stennis, the powerful Senator who chairs the Senate Armed Services Committee. If I recall the testimony correctly, the House had wanted the project to be divided among three yards, but it was on the insistence of Stennis, in the House-Senate conference on the bill, that it went to one—the one, as it turned out, that was in his state, Mississippi. Going over to the House at noon, both Bill Randall and Alton Lennon of the Democratic side of the Committee made reference to Stennis' role. So did Carleton King, in the Republican lounge, when I went in for lunch. I am very much afraid that all of this will hit the press, and it will put the C-5A controversy in the shade. Only Lockheed will be happy about that.

By far the most remarkable part of these few days was the SALT briefing at the White House on Thursday morning. About 100 Members from five committees were there, representing the House and Senate Armed Services Committees, the Senate Foreign Relations Committee, the House Foreign Affairs Committee, and the Joint Committee on Atomic Energy. Chairs had been set up in the State Dining Room. I got a seat on the second row, next to Walter Powell, one of our new Members on the Armed Services Committee. The front row was held for some of the Senate power structure. Senator Fulbright was directly in front of me, along with Gale McGee and John Stennis. Others present from the Senate were Pastore, Jackson, Harry Byrd, and Percy, to name just a few. We had good representation from the House.

The President walked in about 9:20, having been preceded by Henry Kissinger, who engaged in some brief banter with several of the Members. We stood and applauded for the President when he came in, and then he went to the podium which had been set up in front and began to speak without notes. He indicated that his own remarks would be short because he had to welcome the President of Mexico, who was due to arrive at 10:00, on the South Lawn of the White House.

The President made it clear that Dr. Kissinger would be speaking for him, that he would answer questions, and would be available within the limits of executive privilege in the future to answer any questions the Members of Congress might have. The President then made a plea for the treaty and the agreements he had made in Moscow, saying that he wanted not a rubber stamp on his efforts, but a "follow-through" on the part of the Congress. He emphasized that there were no winners or losers in the agreements. Nixon felt that both sides, and the world, had won. Since there were advantages in it for both sides, both had a vested interest in keeping the accords. Then he noted that presidential intervention had been necessary to complete the work begun at Helsinki and Vienna, because agreements affecting the vital security of a nation like Russia are handled only by the top leaders, so his own presence was required. He went on to say that the second round of negotiations would begin in October, and therefore he hoped the Congress would give its approval to the treaty and agreements by September 1.

The last point the President made in connection with what he had done was that we should now go forward with those areas of defense that were not covered by the agreements. He said that Premier Brezhnev told him that the Soviet Union intended to proceed with defense programs, and it would be dangerous for us not to do so. He declared that if we wanted the follow-on agreements, we have to take two steps: "First to approve these agreements; and second, we need a credible defense position so that the Soviet Union will have an incentive to negotiate a permanent offensive freeze. That is all we want."

15

Following these thoughts, the President made reference to the past. He said that he was an admirer of Woodrow Wilson, and that the Treaty of Versailles and the League of Nations failed because of ineffective consultation with the Senate. "We, of course, do not want that to happen. We have appreciated the consultation we have had up to this point, and we are now going forward with this meeting at this time." And then he recalled what Wilson had said when he was traveling the country during the debate on the league and the Versailles treaty. "My clients are the children. My clients are the future generations." The President then urged those present to be reminded that "our clients are the next generation," and that by approving the treaty and agreements, we would do our duty "by our clients, which are the next generation." For an off-the-cuff speech, it was very effective. Still, the best part of the morning was yet to come.

I will say now what I said to my staff when I got back to the office: Henry Kissinger has to be the most articulate and intelligent man I have ever heard. He had a prepared address, which took about thirty minutes to read. It was an eloquent statement, analytical but incisive. When he began, he surveyed the historical setting for SALT. It was interesting, but I thought that he might achieve the unsought result of making his audience feel they were being given a lecture. Such was not the case. It was only an introduction to the comprehensive survey and analysis of what was actually negotiated.

His analysis made clear the unique nature of the power relationship we have with the Russians. The determination of national power, he said, has changed fundamentally in the nuclear age. Both we and the Soviets "have begun to find that each increment of power does not necessarily represent an increment of useable political strength." And later, this statement: "We hoped that the Soviet Union would acquire a stake in a wide spectrum of negotiations, and that it would become convinced that its interests would be best served if the entire process unfolded. We have sought, in short, to create a vested interest in mutual restraint."

He warned that the two powers should not let the opportunity slip away from them by "jockeying for marginal advantages." And he summarized by saying, "We must not develop a national psychology by which we can act only on the basis of what we are against, and not what we are for."

Anticipating some of the criticism made of the agreements, Kissinger noted that while the Russians had an advantage on mega-tonnage, we had one in warheads. He pointed also to our superior bomber force and the better quality of our weapons, and he told us something that we had not heard: the freeze on ICBMs and on submarine-launched missiles was our idea, not the Russians'. They had been reluctant to include them in an agreement.

In the question-and-answer period which followed, Kissinger showed himself a master, fielding the questions or counter-statements with assurance and ease. No one was able to score a point at his expense. Fulbright, as dean of the Senate delegation by virtue of his chairmanship of the Foreign Relations Committee, spoke first. He said that he was in complete agreement regarding the treaty and arms limitation agreement the President had made, but he had reservations about pushing ahead with accelerated development of other weapons. I thought it was a shallow observation. Kissinger gave him the obvious answer: that only if we pushed forward would we be able to negotiate a meaningful second phase. Fulbright should have recalled the President's words, when he declared that only because we were in a position of strength did the Russians agree to reduce their defense effort, too. This was surely the case of the ABM authorization in the United States.

Scoop Jackson spoke critically of "ambiguities" in the agreements. He felt the limitation on land-based missiles was not solid. Kissinger replied that he saw no such interpretation. The Russians were entitled to 1,618 ICBMs. If they exceeded that number, the agreement would be in question. John Stennis announced that he was going to support fully the ULMS (now Trident) program and not give it limited support as he had originally intended.

On the basis of what I saw, I am convinced that there will be little effective opposition or delay to the treaty and agreement negotiated by the President. I wouldn't be at all surprised to see him get his September 1 deadline, too.

I left at 11:30, taking several of my colleagues back with me. President Echeverria of Mexico spoke to the House at 12:30 before a joint meeting. I got a seat near the aisle beside Earl Ruth. Manuel Lujan of New Mexico joined us and was then surprised to hear the Speaker call his name as one of the Members to escort the President of Mexico into the Chamber. Manuel, who is nearly always cheerful, stood up with a broad grin, not certain of where he should go. Some of the older Members told him to go out into the hall and wait with the others. Later, when they marched in, he was bringing up the rear, grinning for all he was worth. Several of the fellows shouted, "Olé, Manuel!"

President Echeverria did not deliver the usual "I'm glad to be here, and ours is a beautiful friendship" speech. He was cordial, to be sure, but he had brought with him a list of grievances, and he wanted to make sure that Congress got the message. We did, although a number of the Members didn't like it. Doc Hall and H. R. Gross were sitting in front of me, and they began to look at each other when Echeverria mentioned the need for the United States to pay attention to its neighbors and some of the weaker powers of the world, who were poorer. He recited a specific list of ills that he wanted discussed and solved. At some points, he was interrupted by applause, but much of it was spotty. Doc and H.R. didn't clap until he had finished, and then not enthusiastically. I was selective in my own appreciation, but I wasn't offended. Quite frankly, I appreciated President Echeverria's candor. Being a great power requires a measure of patience. I believe that he is in fact a friend, and friends should not be offended by frankness.

He had a translator, who repeated the speech in English at the end of each paragraph. It was time-consuming, but effective. When the President had finished his prepared speech, he laid the script aside and went on for another five minutes or so extemporaneously. By this time, some of the Members were getting restless. Earl, always a wit, leaned over and said quite audibly, "I wonder if he knows how to 'revise and extend' his remarks." It produced a ripple of laughter around us.

Monday, July 17, 1972—Tuesday, July 18, 1972

Senator McGovern and his followers may be whistling up optimism for the fall campaign, but it certainly isn't reflected in the opinions of the House Democrats. I haven't canvassed an awful lot of them, but the few I have heard from are not happy about McGovern's nomination. Bob Steele told me that he had asked Mo Udall what McGovern's chances were in Arizona. Mo said that the best thing McGovern could do would be to fly over the state and wave. He said that every time McGovern landed and made a speech the Democrats lost three more seats in the state legislature. Considering the fact that Stewart Udall is a McGovern advisor and Mo is pretty liberal in his own right, that's a rather pessimistic reaction. Jim O'Hara, who played an active role at the Democratic Convention, said that McGovern hasn't got a chance of carrying Michigan.

Of the three Virginia Democrats running for reelection, only Tom Downing has an opponent. He told the press that he wasn't running with the Senator or against him; he's just running his own campaign for reelection. Tom said that he had made a visit to the Northern Neck of Virginia, a rural area that will be added to his district. The first question he was asked was, "Are you a McGovern Democrat?" He has gone to some length to deny that he is. In fact, he told a reporter that his position was 360 degrees apart from Senator McGovern. The next day a NASA employee called him and said, "Congressman, you may be a pretty good politician, but you're a lousy mathematician." Only then did Tom realize that he had come full circle in his statement.

I was walking through the tunnel to the House with Jack Brinkley of Georgia, and he said that he went to the Convention, and he faulted others from his party in Congress who wouldn't go. He felt that if enough of them had gone, they might have been able to block McGovern's nomination.

The Republicans, by and large, are pleased with the nomination, but there is a mood of no-nonsense about what lies ahead. All are aware that McGovern put together a winning combination in the face of seemingly insuperable odds. To lay back on the oars at this point would be foolhardy. Indeed, the feeling is that if we turn to, we can pick up some seats. No one feels that we have a very good chance of capturing

18

Congress, but the margin could be diminished.

Wednesday, August 9, 1972

B ill Dickinson called for a meeting of Southern Republicans in Les Arends' Whip Office off the floor this afternoon. He had Harry Dent from the White House over to speak. Scores of conservative Democrats are loudly declaring their support for the President, but in the same breath are making it clear that they are not supporting Republican candidates in the House and Senate.

Bill singled out Connally in particular. He said that in four years the President would be gone and he wanted to know how the rest of us felt about keeping the Republican Party growing and strong. He said that we ought to be encouraging the Southern voter to join our party and he had a mock-up of a billboard with some people pictured on it and the words, "Republicans Are Our Kind of Folks." Bob Wilson spoke up to say that there is a good chance that some of the Southern Democrats will come over. Harry let everyone talk, but he didn't seem to offer any hope that the White House was going to jump in and start urging its new-found Democratic friends to endorse Republican Congressional candidates.

Charlie Jonas asked Harry about the Watergate fiasco. The morning paper had revelations which make it clear that someone from the Committee to Reelect the President did, in fact, finance the caper. Harry obviously knew more than he was willing to tell. He said that they hoped that they could keep it as far away from the President as possible but he betrayed his fears by noting that the attorneys down at the Justice Department "are hostile bastards who are hangovers from the Johnson Administration."

Wednesday, September 13, 1972—Monday, September 18, 1972

S even weeks to go till the election, and construction crews are already beginning to assemble the scaffolding for the inaugural platform and stands.

That nobody is safe any more was reflected in the results of two primaries held last Tuesday. John McMillan of South Carolina was defeated after having been here since his election in 1938. Wayne Aspinall also lost his bid for renomination in a Colorado primary. Aspinall was singled out by the conservationists as one of the "dirty dozen" congressmen who had voted consistently against conservation and anti-pollution legislation. McMillan lost in a runoff after being charged with making a deal with the third man in the previous election. When seniority like that can be overturned, it serves as a grim reminder that no seat is safe.

Bill Fitts Ryan died last night (Sunday) in New York. This comes as no surprise, considering how badly he has looked for the last few months. The Democrats can nominate his successor by committee, and that person will be the automatic winner since the Republicans don't have a candidate. The likeliest candidate is Bella Abzug, but she could be denied a shot at it, considering the fact that she made a lot of Ryan's supporters mad by going after Bill's seat last spring and forcing him to expend so much effort to hold it.

The past few days covered by this entry have been interesting. We began with a Republican conference in the House Chamber on Wednesday morning at 9:30. The item that got the most attention was the Nader investigation of the Congress. A number of the Members voiced their anger at the distortions and even mistakes in their profiles. Apparently no one has been spared, conservatives and liberals alike. According to one fellow, Henry Reuss grew almost violent in denouncing the report on himself, shouting that he had been a friend of Nader's cause and that the profile was misleading and false. He said that the Nader representatives sought to calm Henry and told him that it would be changed. Bill Widnall, who was visibly agitated, took the microphone to ask who had authorized Nader to have a room in the Cannon Building. Jerry replied that the Speaker had taken the decision on himself and had not consulted the Republicans. "Was he sober?" somebody asked. This brought some snickers and comments about the Speaker's accident two weeks ago, when he struck two cars over in Georgetown outside the Zebra Lounge.

At the Wednesday Group meeting that afternoon, I heard more about the Nader profiles. Howard Robison apparently got unusually severe treatment, with some old Drew Pearson charges that had long since been refuted included in the report, without the accompanying refutation. All of this produced a decidedly uneasy feeling in me, because my own profile was to be made available to me for examination on Thursday afternoon.

Burnett had gone to Norfolk to make a speech for me, so I took Buddy and Janie along with me to examine the profile. It was neither as bad as I feared, nor as fair as I thought it should be. It was also shorter than the average, being some fourteen pages in length, as opposed to the average of thirty for most of the Members. It began with a look at my financial campaign in the past and made the point that we would not release our list of contributors to them.

Most offensive was the summary of my votes on certain conservation issues. The votes were selective and the comment was blatantly slanted. Nothing was said about my wildlife legislation. I got a favorable mark for my trip to Germany last year, where I spent considerably less than the $50 a day allowed for Congressmen. Some glaring errors were included: for one thing, Janie and I were listed as having been married for twenty-two years, instead of twenty-six. Since our children are twenty-five and twenty-three, we noted this correction at the top. While

I have occasionally been called a bastard, it seems a bit unfair to imply that my children are, too. They also had my rank on the Committee wrong. I didn't make a big fuss about it, but I hope that I can get some revision to put my record in a clearer perspective.

I got amused at Ed Koch, who was reviewing his profile in another part of the room while I was looking at mine. Obviously upset, his face flushed, he was pacing up and down like an expectant father. If I didn't know better, I would swear that Nader was trying to wipe the Congressional slate clean by getting rid of all of us.

1973

Tuesday, January 16, 1973

The major event was a visit from Charlie III in the morning. He told me a week ago that he wanted to come in to give me the lowdown on the Gordon Rule business.* When I saw his name on my appointment card, I figured that he had arranged to talk to me about that. I could tell that he was disturbed when he came in, but I learned after we were in the office that it was not the Rule case that had upset him. Essentially, he repeated what he had said on the phone before, that Rule wasn't a team player and, indeed, was not to be trusted, because he was constantly running off to the press, or even to the Secretary. Charlie said that while Rule could pick out the flaws in a contract he showed little disposition for positive thinking. Then Charlie dropped the bombshell. He said that as of 11:00 that morning it was being announced that he had resigned his post as Assistant Secretary for Installations and Logistics. "But why?" I asked. "Two and two still equals four, Bill," he replied. It does, but I still didn't understand. He went on to

---

* Gordon Rule was one of the Navy's most critical cost-cutters. In December 1972 he was director of the Procurement Control and Clearance Division of the United States Navy. One of his duties was to act as a watchdog over naval contracts. Testifying before a Senate subcommittee, chaired by Senator William Proxmire, he was outspoken in his criticism of cost overruns by Litton Industries in the construction of amphibious assault ships. He also told the subcommittee that President Nixon had made a mistake in appointing Roy L. Ash, the former president of Litton, as director of the Office of Management and Budget. The following day he was asked by Admiral Isaac Kidd, chief of the Navy Materiel Command, to retire. Rule refused and was transferred to a lesser job out of the Pentagon. But Congress and the press came to Rule's rescue, and on March 23, 1973, after a series of Senate hearings on the Rule case, Admiral Kidd notified Rule that he was being returned to his old job. As the years passed, Admiral Kidd and Gordon Rule became fast friends, and Kidd hailed him for his work. Rule crossed swords with other Navy and defense figures throughout the 1960s and 1970s. He died in Arlington, Virginia on August 10, 1982, an iconoclast to the end.

point out how he had fought Litton on its contracts at Pascagoula. Charlie said that where the Navy had ordered specification changes he felt that there was an obligation to adjust contracts, but he contended that Litton had made some bad managerial mistakes in their new yard at Pascagoula and were trying to get the government to pick up the bill by claiming that they had created a new national resource with a yard that could build ships in a more modern and efficient way. Charlie wouldn't buy that idea. He said that when Richardson was appointed as the new Secretary of Defense, Richardson had said not once but twice that he wanted Charlie to stay. As late as last Monday, Charlie said, Richardson had called him to repeat it. Then Charlie got a call from some major at the White House telling him that his resignation had been accepted. Since Ash, the president of Litton, had been appointed director of OMB (Office of Management and Budget) by the President, Charlie said that it was obvious where the pressure had come from to oust him. Worse, he said that it could mean that OMB would now attempt to control the Department of Defense from their end. "The government is too goddamned big for a single agency to make that kind of decision," Charlie said. "You've got to delegate authority." He went on to review the excellent record of Mel Laird and Dave Packard, who he felt had kept a responsible hand on the Department of Defense and had absolutely refused to permit any politics to be played with contracts. Charlie said that he could no longer be sure that that would be done.

I asked him what he was going to do. "I've got a few bucks in the bank," he replied, "but I've got four daughters to get through college." He mused about his background, when he was vice president of Page. "I've gotten used to the big time. I can't get away from it," he said. I reassured him that private industry would certainly snap him up because of his talents. "Don't be so sure," he answered. "The President let me go. Who would want to hire me under this cloud?" I really felt sorry for him. He has so much integrity. I recall my own calls to him in the past, when I wanted a favor. He was always straightforward and laid matters on the line. Sometimes I got what I wanted and sometimes I didn't, but I always had confidence in him. Today I wrote the President to tell him how sorry I was to see Charlie let go, that I felt his dismissal was unnecessary and unwise. Nothing will come of it, of course. I have no standing at the White House, but I felt that somebody on the Hill ought to say a word on Charlie's behalf.

Tuesday, January 23, 1973—
Wednesday, January 24, 1973

Last night the President made the speech that the nation has been waiting for for four years. He announced a ceasefire in Indochina and the return of our prisoners within sixty days. During the day the announcement came that the President was going to speak that evening, and it was generally felt that since Dr. Kissinger had met only briefly with Le Duc Tho in Paris and was flying home, an agreement had been reached. The speech was brief, but the form was good. The President left the details of the agreement for a briefing by Kissinger today (Wednesday). He emphasized that we had attained "peace with honor," a nebulous phrase around here, one that has been open to a lot of interpretation for some time. My own judgment is that Nixon got far more than anybody had thought he could get just a few months ago. We're out of the war, and the prisoners are coming home. Thieu still remains as chief of state of South Vietnam. A ceasefire of sorts has been agreed to, and if there is any chance for it to last, there is a large enough supervisory team on hand to determine infractions. I had lunch today with a Cambodian official named DyBellong, who is close to Lon Nol and has been in America arranging aid to Cambodia. He returns to Pnom Penh at the end of this week. I asked him through an interpreter what he thought of the peace accord. He replied that he had mixed feelings but that he hoped for a lasting peace. I think the essential thing is that most Americans feel that we have done all we could on behalf of the South Vietnamese. For us, peace with honor implies just that. Having discharged our obligations to them as an ally, we have left them with a situation that is largely stalemated. They have the military means at their disposal to defend themselves in the event the war is resumed. Whether they have the will is up to them. We can't ship that to them.

I told a reporter last night that I had a number of thoughts about the end of the war. Certainly I am thankful that it has come to an end and that our men will be returned to their families, especially those men who have been prisoners. I added that the war was like an ulcer. We have suffered from it for so long—ten years now—that it was going to take awhile to get over it. We were going to have to adjust to living without it. I then said that many people have come to blame a host of our problems on the war. It has been a convenient whipping boy for other ills. Now those problems will have to be faced on their own merits, and we will have to devise solutions without the luxury of blaming the war if we can't find them.

In the evening, Janie and I went to the Capitol Hill Club for dinner. Rog Morton, Secretary of the Interior, was there by himself, and before leaving he came over to our table to chat for a few minutes. We talked about President Johnson's sudden death, and Rog told us that he had been down to the LBJ Ranch less than two weeks ago, when the National Park Service had taken over the property. According to Rog, when the project was under discussion Johnson had said, a few weeks before, that, "You had better hurry up and get this done, because I won't live more than another month or two." Rog said that Johnson had looked terrible, but he hadn't expected him to go this soon.

I asked Rog if he was going to hear the President's speech. He said that he was about to leave for the White House to join the other Cabinet members. I became curious, and he went on to say that after the speech he would be given a list of a dozen people to call, several dozen, in fact, to ask them what they thought of the speech. He said that he's done this in the past, and by calling people in the West last, he could contact quite a large number well into the small hours of the morning because of the time difference. It was a shrewd political move on the part of the White House to use Cabinet members in this way. "Who do you call?" I asked. "Governors, Republican leaders in various states," he replied.

This afternoon I attended the memorial services for President Johnson in the Capitol Rotunda. While I've only been in Congress for four years, I must confess that this was the most mixed assemblage I've seen at one of these things. Those present ran the gamut from Van Cliburn to Mayor Daley of Chicago. I really cannot do justice to the scene. Someone with a keener eye and a feel for the occasion could give a better summary. The House Members were grouped in a semicircle on the House side of the Rotunda. On the west front side stood members of the Army Chorus. Then toward the other side were the Diplomatic Corps, and next to them the Supreme Court, with the Cabinet behind them. There was a break to form an aisle to the door leading to the Senate wing, and beyond it stood the Senate and an assortment of individuals, some of whom I could not identify. Among them was Al Lowenstein, whose presence remained a puzzle to most of us. It was he who had led the "Dump Johnson" movement back in 1968. Someone remarked that maybe he had come to make sure LBJ was really dead. Next to the Senate was a podium with a small area for the members of the Johnson family. Around on our side was room for the Texas delegation and the Joint Chiefs. The press occupied a raised platform behind those on the west side of the Rotunda. The klieg lights were on throughout, and the heat from these plus the crush of the crowd made everyone hot and uncomfortable.

Services were supposed to begin at 2:30, but were delayed an hour. Animated conversation, greetings, and the like consumed much of the time. The House Members enjoyed picking out the Senators and commenting upon them, although I would suspect that the Senate felt exclusive enough that they wouldn't bother to identify House Members, not when there are only 100 of them and 435 of us.

Among the diplomats I picked out my friend Rolf Pauls, the German ambassador, and also Dobrynin, the Soviet ambassador. He's much taller than I had realized from seeing him in the House, truly a big man. Of that group the Japanese ambassador Ushiba and his wife got the most attention, primarily because she was wearing the traditional Japanese kimono, gray with a broad black sash. She remained composed throughout it all, never varying her posture, while her husband suffered visibly from the heat of the lights and kept mopping his face with his handkerchief.

Not only were the current Supreme Court Justices present, with Burger and Douglas being clearly identifiable, but former Chief Justice Warren was also there. It became a kind of "old home week" for many of them, greeting their former friends and colleagues. I don't know how many former Cabinet officers were present, but Dean Rusk was there and gave one of the two eulogies. General Westmoreland, now retired and in civilian clothes, was standing near the East Front door. Former Speaker McCormack came. I heard someone in back of me comment on how badly he looked. Someone else piped up, "He always looks that way."

Relatives of President Johnson began to arrive shortly after 3:00. I recognized his brother, and I believe he had a sister there. Assorted nieces and nephews filled out the group.

A twenty-one-gun salute sounded outside, and shortly afterwards the color guard came in, posting themselves at the west end of the black catafalque which has supported the caskets of presidents and other notables in the Rotunda since it was built for the coffin of Abraham Lincoln. Finally came the procession out of the corridor leading to the Senate, the Joint Chiefs in front, followed by the pallbearers carrying the casket, and behind them Johnson's immediate family and President and Mrs. Nixon. All of the somber ceremony, which has now become familiar, was played out in front of us, the faultless placing of the casket, the mournful slow salute of the pallbearers, and their silent departure. It was a moving scene, as it always is, and never fails to transfix those who witness it. Our foreign guests were particularly keen in their interest in this American ceremony.

The two eulogies were spoken by Jake Pickle, the Texas congressman who represents Johnson's old congressional district, and former Secretary of State Dean Rusk. I will not try to recapitulate their addresses here. Both were personal, Pickle's the more so, since he identified with Johnson as a fellow Texan and close friend. Lady Bird Johnson was composed, and her face wore the slight smile of approval that she frequently has. When her eyes watered at some emotional reference to her late husband, it was momentary. Lyndon would have been proud of her. The two Robb grandchildren were present, and the youngest, a little girl, proved too restless. Her father held her for a while, and then her mother, and for an instant she held her grandmother's hand, but soon she got underfoot, and was passed back to some of the relatives to hold. All of the family controlled their feelings, although Lynda Bird nodded assent and silently mouthed approval at some tribute made to her father's memory.

I thought that both eulogies were fairly spoken. No attempt was made to hide Johnson's role in the Vietnam war, but emphasis was placed on the social programs he had initiated and the civil rights laws passed at his urging. I am sure that everyone present was mindful that if a dramatic script had been written, the cast and the events of the past two days could not have been more powerful than the real one played before us. We were burying the war with LBJ.

At the conclusion of the eulogies, the President placed a wreath at the foot of the casket, stepped back, and closed his eyes in prayer. The

House and Senate wreaths were placed on either side of his, and the Army Chorus sang two hymns, one of which I recognized as the Navy hymn "Eternal Father, Strong to Save."

At the end, the President turned to Mrs. Johnson and shook hands with her and the other members of Johnson's immediate family. He had stood beside Lady Bird throughout the service. Mrs. Nixon also bade goodbye, as did the Nixon girls, and then it was all over. Tomorrow there's a church service in Washington, and then LBJ will make his last trip home to the Pedernales. He died at a dramatic moment, one that he would probably not have chosen willingly, because his own political career fell victim to the war he could not win or end. Dying when he did, he seemed twice a victim of that war.

Tuesday, January 30, 1973

We had a Republican briefing this morning by Roy Ash, the new director of the Office of Management and Budget. The attendance was pretty good. I think that most of the Members came out of curiosity to see what Ash was like, and also there's been a lot of flak over the hard line the President is taking with respect to holding the line on spending. There doesn't seem to be any flexibility at all.

Although I haven't been happy about Ash's appointment, I must admit that he handled the situation well at the briefing. He used some simple charts to illustrate how the budgets have grown in the last three years, the direction our spending has taken, and why the ceiling recommended by the White House ought to be observed. He seemed sure of himself in answering the questions that were raised and succeeded in not antagonizing anyone, which was something of a feat in itself. H. R. Gross took a swipe at foreign aid and wanted to know "why the gizzard wasn't cut out of that," in order to cut back on spending. Then he raised a more cogent point in asking whether or not we were going to be called on to vote for funds to rebuild North Vietnam. A murmur of discord ran through the group, but Ash sidestepped the question by replying that no decision had been made and mentioning the nebulous wording in this regard in the agreements signed in Paris. It is clear that an outright vote for such funding would be overwhelmingly defeated.

Tuesday, February 27, 1973

The switching of parties by Don Riegle has brought the usual round of jokes. Wayne Hays took the floor last week to ask the Republicans to try to dissuade Riegle from making the move. "We in the majority have treated you fellows pretty nice since I have been here," he said, "so I do not see why you would want to inflict him upon us. You know, after all is said and done, we have enough troubles of our own, and I do not think you ought to send any of your troubles over on our side." Riegle was not around to reply, but he would be best served by keeping silent, anyway. Nobody in the House can match Hays for pure venom.

Monday, March 26, 1973

Dan Daniel said that he was in Lynchburg on Sunday and was disturbed to see so much ill feeling toward the Republicans because of the Watergate business. One man told him that unless Nixon spoke up, he wasn't going to vote for any Republicans this year. Considering the fact that no Republicans are candidates for federal office, that's a pretty strong stand. Bob Daniel said that he had heard there will be some revelations before the end of the year that could lead to impeachment charges. That's just too farfetched for me to believe, but the odor growing stronger here every day simply reinforces my conviction of last year when the thing first broke, that the White House made a mistake by not cleaning its own house right away. I strongly suspect that John Mitchell knew and countenanced it.

On the way back from lunch, Joel Broyhill fell in step with me and began to talk about what Dan had said. He remarked that he was disgusted by people who manifest outrage over what happened at the Watergate, because these same people come to us and ask that traffic tickets be fixed or that they receive some other favor to which they would not ordinarily be entitled. "You're right," I replied, "there is a certain curious double standard in this country, but that doesn't mean that we should countenance dishonesty or unethical behavior." All of us practice a degree of hypocrisy, some more than others. This journal certainly reflects my own share of it, but I would hope that if a member of my staff or anyone involved in my campaign were mixed up in something which was wrong, I would have the good sense as well as the moral resolve to clean it up myself. It is the only ethical reservation I have about Nixon's stewardship in the White House, and no satisfactory explanation has been forthcoming from him as to why he has remained silent.

Tuesday, March 27, 1973

It's a good thing there was no business in the House today because it seemed that I spent all of my time in one conference or another. First thing this morning I had a visit from a member of the Philippine National Assembly. In view of the proclamation of martial law in the Philippines by President Marcos, he has decided to remain in the United States rather than return home to certain civil restriction. He has a daughter here with whom he has been visiting. Naturally, he didn't come to make social small talk. He tried to persuade me to use my influence to deny military and economic aid to the Marcos government so that martial law will be ended, and above all so that free elections will be held when Marcos' term expires at the end of the year.

Yesterday I was visited by two Pakistanis, now living here, who asked me to speak out against the continued confinement of over 90,000 Pakistani prisoners of war by India. All of these foreign nationals form quite a little lobby in Washington, acting either on their own or at the behest of their embassies or political organizations. This year I have been contacted by Greeks who are disaffected with the junta there. Nationalist China has its own group of apologists here on the Hill, most of whom are strongly conservative Members. Last year several of them circulated a joint happy birthday letter to Chiang Kai-shek. Those felicitations must have been small comfort to the Generalissimo, considering the friendly greetings that Richard Nixon and Mao Tse-tung were exchanging in Peking earlier.

I spent the better part of an hour with a group of Catholic clergy and laymen from Virginia, who were in town to see the Virginia Members about amnesty, the cut in social welfare programs, and related subjects. Since I had the time, and they also invited me to go to lunch with them, I enjoyed the dialogue. It proved to be a good mental exercise, although no conclusions were reached. Like so many of these folks, they believed that the cuts in the social programs could be made up out of the hide of the defense budget. The only thing they agreed with the President on was his recommended total ceiling on spending. In other words, they liked the size of the pie, but not the size of their piece of it. They made reservations for lunch at the Rotunda, which is just off the Hill but is not the cheapest place to eat. When the bill was presented to Father Schmied at my table, he raised his eyebrows and exclaimed, "This will break the diocese!" I suggested that next time we arrange for something in one of the House dining rooms.

In the middle of the afternoon I attended a meeting of interested Members regarding the proposed closure of the Public Health Service hospitals. Paul Rogers of Florida chaired the meeting, and Harley Staggers came in for awhile to listen. Aside from making a lot of noise and then getting the Secretary of HEW before Paul's subcommittee later on this spring, there doesn't seem to be much chance of saving them. HEW has had the axe out for the hospitals for several years. They just want to get out of the health service business altogether. I believe the policy is unwise and fiscal nonsense. The hospital in Boston is being ordered closed, but $7 million is included in the budget for it this year to restore the buildings so that a local authority will take it over! That decision must have originated in the ward at St. Elizabeth's Hospital.

Monday, April 2, 1973

The showdown between the President and the Congress over his first veto this year will occur tomorrow. The betting is that the Senate will vote to override him while the House will sustain. On Wednesday the twenty-eighth, we had a Republican conference to review the matter. The floor was taken primarily by those who will stand by the President on the question of the Vocational Rehabilitation Bill. Jerry Ford made a strong statement, and Jack Kemp, who voted for the bill on final passage, said that he "had seen the light" and knew that if the budget line was to be held he would have to reverse his position. He sounded like a sinner confessing in church. The best pitch for the President was made by Wilmer Mizell, who compared the situation to his days with the Cardinals playing against the Giants in the Polo Grounds. Will said that Durocher always had his pitchers dust off the leading Cardinal hitters, so Stanky, the Cardinal manager, made Mizell dust off the Giant pitcher and lead hitter. He said that if he didn't do it, the Giants would blank the Cardinal hitting, and he emphasized that the President was "our number four batter. If they knock him down on this one," Will said, "we won't have any runs at the end of the game." The Members gave him a rousing cheer.

The Wednesday Group had Bob Haldeman as its guest last week. He looks the part of Nixon's hatchet man. His eyes are a pale blue, utterly without warmth. I suppose that sounds a little dramatic, but he certainly comes across as a cold fish. The meeting itself was something less than sensational. I thought that we might get into the Watergate business right away, but Howard Robison, who chaired the meeting, apparently wanted to confine discussion to the issue of better liaison between the White House and the Republican Members. So for the better part of an hour the conversation centered on the gripes of those who felt that the White House ignores the Members or doesn't indicate ahead of time what its policies are going to be.

I had to leave just after 6:00, but Al Bell told me the next day that Watergate was brought up and that Haldeman said that the White House has nothing to hide. Haldeman declared that the President was helpless to defend himself against unfounded accusations and that he wasn't going to reply to wild statements. I told Al that explanation just didn't stand up. The statements that have been made by McCord are very serious, and I think that the President's silence is hurting him.

Thursday, April 12, 1973

We have just returned from one of the most pleasant weekends we have had in a long time. Yesterday afternoon (Saturday), after having office hours in Norfolk and a luncheon speech to the humane society people at Virginia Beach, we drove up to Brandon, the eighteenth-century home of Bob and Sally Daniel on the James River, and spent the night, coming back here in the middle of the day. I had heard what a beautiful place Brandon is, but I was not prepared for the gracious charm that such a home can project. The grounds and the majesty of the house itself easily cast a spell over every visitor. Thad Murray, Bob's administrative assistant, and his wife Nan were overnight guests, along with Lin and Jinks Holton. The Saturday night dinner guests included some of the Fourth District politicos, plus several couples who are friends of the Daniels. We were pampered as we've seldom been and enjoyed the height of luxury by going to bed with a fire in the old fireplace in our room, which was in one of the two wings built in the eighteenth century, before Jefferson planned the rest of the house. This morning the wives were served breakfast in their rooms while the men had theirs in the dining room. I found the table discussion as enjoyable as the breakfast itself. Lin told us that he had been talking to John Connally of Texas recently. John brought up the move of Mills Godwin toward the Republican ranks. Lin said that we had been working on Mills, and then we were going to start working on Connally. His reply was, "Well, I'll be ready for you, but this Watergate thing has got to be settled first." Lin then said that he and Connally explored it in earnest. Connally used some Texas prose to describe his own view. "Somebody will just have to belly up and admit he's responsible." Lin agreed and then became reflective with the three of us at the table. He said that he could not possibly tell the President this, but that John Connally could. Indeed, said Lin, Connally was probably the only man who could tell Nixon to do it.

It's Lin's opinion that John Mitchell is involved in it, and Maurice Stans, too. "How can you pay six people to plead guilty and have all that money changing hands?" he asked. He added that he never could understand why Nixon placed his campaign in the hands of a claims attorney. What was only a distant rumble of discontent a few months ago has turned into a thunder of discontent in Republican ranks. John Anderson used his best evangelistic style in the House last week to denounce Dick Kleindienst's claims of executive power and privilege. Jerry Ford has called for the appearance of the White House aides before Senator Ervin's committee. The ripple extends to the Virginia gubernatorial race. Mills Godwin said yesterday that he will have to reassess his own position with regard to the Republican Party unless this thing is cleared up.

The interesting thing is that I still am not getting a lot of mail on the subject. Most people are concerned with the problems that personally confront them, such as rising prices and their desire for controls. But Watergate compounds the President's difficulties. Unable to solve the economic question, he is made to appear as a villain by the sordidness of Watergate. The political consequences of this aren't lost on anyone who wears the Republican badge. Both the press and the voter have a degree of honor that is often self-serving. The laws of economics quite often fail to respond to executive or legislative nostrums. It isn't Nixon policies that have led us to the present economic state, but he's taking the brunt of the blame for failing to come through with a solution. If he fails to show candor in dealing with the Watergate business, then hostility toward them will be cloaked in a crusade of righteousness, which could well be directed against all Republican candidates next year because they will be the most easily available targets of wrath.

Tuesday, April 17, 1973

This morning I drove over to Crystal City for breakfast with Charlie Ill at his office. He'll be leaving on the fifteenth of May, forced out, as he confirmed, by Roy Ash. I had written a letter to the President on Charlie's behalf some months ago when Charlie first got word that he was getting the axe. His act today was a gesture of thanks for my futile efforts on his behalf out of friendship.

I asked him what he was going to do when he left. He said that he was going to take the summer off to sail and spend time at his place on Maryland's Eastern Shore. It was his intention to do the same thing back in 1968, but he got involved in the President's campaign, which is something of an irony. This morning he was in a relaxed mood, having gotten over the initial bitterness at being sacked by Ash. Our conversation covered a number of subjects, several of which are worth recounting here.

I told him that I had heard privately that Newport News Ship-building and Drydock Company was having growing pains and would like to know if it was true. He confirmed that it is. "No company can grow from 18,000 to 27,000 in so short a time and not have problems," he said. I nodded and mentioned that this was part of Litton's trouble in Pascagoula, although they seemed to have worked themselves out of the worst of this. Then he told me what a fit Rickover was giving Newport News Ship. He said that Rickover moves in when he wants to take over, clearing out everybody who might get in his way and putting his own people in place of them. Charlie declared that Rickover wants to make Newport News his yard, where their total program will be geared to satisfying his wants. The officials at Newport News want plenty of Navy business, but not to the exclusion of everything else. Recently, they got contracts for three large tankers to carry liquid natural gas. Charlie said that Rickover was so determined to block them from building those ships that he went downtown to try to get their subsidy cut off. Apparently Bud Ackerman, chairman of the board at Newport News Ship, has been having a real go-around with Rick-over. Charlie himself has tilted with the old man. In fact, Charlie said that the day before Rickover had his heart attack a few months ago, the two of them had a real shouting match in Charlie's office which could be heard at the far end of the building. When news came in the following day that Rickover had been felled by a heart attack, Charlie said his calls were split between those who felt he had caused unnecessary strain on Rickover's heart and others who were anxious to know if he had "finally gotten rid of the S.O.B." Another bit of Rickover lore, I thought, and then, irony of ironies, this afternoon a brown envelope marked "Personal" was placed on my desk. Inside was a sheet of paper with two quotations from one of the early Christian fathers on the meaning of Easter. It was from Hyman Rickover, and on Passover, no less.

Charlie touched briefly on the base closings. He said that the only way to make a real saving is to cut out something big, not just trim here and there. He told me that every damned base we have has fat in it. "We've got to have a store for Momma to shop in, clubs to take Momma to, and every other convenience you can think of," he said. I think that Charlie was just unloading some of the frustration he's built up from living with the military for the past four years, nearly two of which have been as an assistant secretary of the Navy. As we left the table, I shook his hand and wished him well. He is a competent and energetic fellow who has been the victim of the kind of vendetta that is all too commonplace around here. He nailed Litton on their failure to meet their contracts with the Navy, and Ash of Litton in turn has nailed him. And people in the country wonder why more public servants are unwilling to rock the boat.

Wednesday, May 2, 1973

The most absorbing aspect of the day was at the Wednesday Group meeting in Larry Coughlin's office. Aside from the usual reports, we had a discussion of the Watergate business. The greatest revelation to me was Pete McCloskey's statement that he and John Ehrlichman had been on the Stanford Law School debate team back in the early '50s. Apparently they had been fairly close. Pete said that when the Korean War came along, he was called to duty with the Marine Corps while Ehrlichman remained at Stanford. This whole business has shaken Pete. He declared that John Ehrlichman was about the last person in the world that he would have suspected of doing something illegal, or covering up for a crime such as the break-ins of the Ellsberg files by Liddy and Hunt. The weird thing is that he thinks that Nixon is perfectly capable of committing such an act, but not one of his chief lieutenants.

Pete brought up the possibility of impeachment, which he thinks is very real. Down deep, he believes that Nixon knew about and countenanced the cover-up. "You only have to look at his record," he said, "to see two things. He has always taken secret money from big business, and he has fought dirty campaigns." Pete noted that a California court had taken Nixon to task for a particular campaign tactic. He asked us what our reaction was to the President's speech of Monday night, indicating that he was very skeptical about the President's words. I spoke up to say that I didn't read it that way, that if the President said that he didn't know anything about it, then I was disposed to take him at his word. Several others spoke up to affirm the same thing.

Attention then turned to Richardson's appointment as Attorney General and whether or not he could undertake the kind of investigation that would be credible, or whether there ought to be a special prosecutor appointed, as a number of congressmen and senators are now calling for. I joined John Dellenback in holding that Richardson ought to be given a free hand. John heatedly declared that it was unthinkable that Nixon, having giving Richardson a free hand to act, would then attempt to control him. Stu McKinney said that he had confidence in him, too, and that furthermore, he felt that after the Navy cutbacks in New England this offered Richardson the only chance to recoup his political fortune by conducting a vigorous investigation. It was an angle I had never thought of and whose validity I would question.

The issue of impeachment was explored, and several said they shared Mel Laird's view that if the President had committed an illegal act, they would not want to know about it, because they felt that the harm done to the office would be irreparable. Pete rebutted this by making the point that the President could not be above the law. "Who is going to question him?" someone asked. That, of course, is a good question. Certainly he is unlikely to appear before the grand jury or Senator Ervin's committee. I suppose the answers of his staff and others involved will provide the answer to whether or not the President told the truth to the American people on Monday night. I still believe that he did.

Earlier in the afternoon, Wayne Woodlief, a reporter from home, called me to get some thoughts on the possibility of impeachment, reminding me that several columnists had raised the matter. I replied that I thought it unwise and unfair to the President to speculate on such an event in view of the fact that there was no hard proof that he was guilty of any wrongdoing. I added that to speculate on impeachment on the basis of rumor and more speculation had the appearance of a lynching party. For those reasons, I just wasn't going to make a statement that would give rise to any implication on my part that the President had done anything less than tell the truth when he said that he had no prior knowledge of the break-in, and believed that none of his staff was involved when he was told so last summer.

Wayne went on to ask what the consequences would be if impeachment did occur. I said that the damage done to the government would be incalculable. I noted that the Constitution was a unique thing, providing us a delicate balance within the government, and that the consensus whereby we are governed flows from all three branches, although not simultaneously and sometimes with more force from one branch than from another. If the Executive arm were discredited, this sensitive balance would be seriously jeopardized. I also said that there was something else, an intangible aspect of our nation that had been important in our development. Americans have always believed that their system offered the best way for human progress. We have always regarded our system as an experiment, one that is ongoing, adaptable from generation to generation. Undergirding this belief has been a lasting confidence in the government itself. The Presidency, the most respected office of all, has called not a few men to greatness, has survived some mediocre ones, but has never been used as an instrument of corruption.

I went on to say that as remote as the possibility was in my mind, if impeachment became a reality, it could cause paralysis of the government, immeasurably deepen the national disillusionment caused by the Vietnam war, and deprive the free world of confidence in its strongest power. In short, the complications which would arise from such an event were almost endless. That is why I have refused to join in any public speculation on impeachment. I concluded by telling Wayne that I hoped never to live long enough or be a member of this body to have to consider a motion to impeach.

In the midst of all this grief, John Connally became a Republican today. That has to be counted as good news, and it confirms his reputation for gutsiness.

Monday, May 7, 1973

The Republicans of the Virginia delegation met in the Whip's office about 2:00 p.m. at the behest of Joel Broyhill. Joel had worked up a proposed joint statement offering a course for handling the Watergate investigation. He said that it would take the entire matter out of the hands of the Senate Committee and the government itself. Joel suggested that a twelve-man special court of inquiry be created, composed of six state supreme court judges appointed by six Democratic governors and six by six Republican governors, one from each state. These in turn would hold secret sessions to interrogate witnesses, out of the limelight of the press. Joel said that the precedent for such a special court could be found in the commission which investigated the Kennedy assassination as well as the special commission that investigated the Pearl Harbor attack in 1941.

Few of the group were enthusiastic about Joel's scheme. Most felt that events are moving too fast to warrant a joint statement right now. I noted that Richardson said today that he was going to appoint a special prosecutor, that if we threw in another formula at this point it would appear that we were just trying to get our oar in the water. I reiterated what I said Sunday, that the President needs our support right now and that I for one would be willing to see us make such a gesture. It would mean a great deal to him. This got a little warmer reception, but the view that we should sit tight prevailed. We agreed to meet again in a few days, perhaps by Thursday, to reconsider what should be done.

Tuesday, May 8, 1973—Wednesday, May 9, 1973

There just doesn't seem to be any let-up. The week started out busy and continues that way. I've just looked at Thursday's schedule, and it's filled, too. What I feared late in the winter has come to pass. Our delay in taking up the defense budget has caused us double Committee sessions each day this week. On Tuesday morning, we squandered two hours on another one of those resolutions seeking information on the bombing of Cambodia and Laos—how much tonnage dropped, how many sorties flown, what losses in men and planes, the cost, the number of American personnel in both countries and their functions, etc. Deputy Assistant Secretary Doolin was back and did his usual superb job fielding questions.

The principal discussion fell on the authority of the Administration to carry out offensive air operations in Laos and Cambodia. Doolin pointed out that the North Vietnamese were in clear violation of Article 20 of the Paris accords by maintaining forces in both Cambodia and Laos. They have 8,000 troops in Cambodia and are directing the operations of the Khmer Rouge, the insurgents who are endeavoring to bring down the government of Lon Nol. Doolin said that if the North Vietnamese withdrew there would be an immediate ceasefire, because the Cambodian communists could not carry on the fight.

The resolution was initiated by Bob Leggett with a group of cosponsors, none of whom bothered to show for the hearing. Bob got support from Otis Pike and several others, including the new Members, Pat Schroeder and Ron Dellums. I thought that Pat was weak. She was not knowledgeable enough to ask a really searching question, and Doolin went through the motions of explaining patiently why the bombing was being carried out. Dellums wasn't much better. He had some of his staff running in and out with messages, but he failed to make a dent. I told Janie later that these people make a fundamental error: they try to base their arguments on the same legal grounds that the Administration witnesses use, and they end up frustrated. The simple fact is that the North Vietnamese have violated the Paris agreement. Dellums tried to steer the argument over to the point that the Senate had not actually ratified the Paris agreement, so the Administration was acting illegally. Both he and other critics of the bombing would have done better if they had simply denounced the whole business on the grounds that the United States has gotten the best it could from a bad situation and should therefore avoid any further involvement, the Paris accords notwithstanding. Such a position would have a certain appeal to common sense, while ignoring the technicality of the Administration position. But for some reason they feel that they have to find some grounds to show that the Administration is acting illegally or unconstitutionally.

Tuesday, May 15, 1973

The Committee met today to hear Deputy Assistant Secretary Doolin appeal for an authorization of $2.5 billion to provide arms for the South Vietnamese and Laotian forces. There was a corporal's guard present to question him, but he got some heavy going from an unexpected quarter, Bill Dickinson of Alabama. Bill has always been a supporter of the President in Indochina. Today he gave vent to his doubts about the wisdom of pumping in that kind of money. He feels that Thieu ought to be able to make a go of it without that kind of sustaining aid. Doolin replied that this grant was necessary to replace losses and ensure that the South Vietnamese would have sufficient materiel to defend themselves. In answer to a personal question as to whether or not he thought that this kind of an appropriation would be requested again next year, Doolin paused and then said carefully that he did not. At this, Les Arends spoke up to commend Doolin for being circumspect in giving that kind of answer, rather than being categorical or dogmatic. Les said that he had been reading *The Best and the Brightest,* and remembered when Bob McNamara had sat at Doolin's chair at the witness table in 1965 and had stated flatly that the war would be over by the end of the year. Doolin made it clear that his estimate was a purely personal one. I hope he's right. Now that the prisoners are back, it's just amazing how quickly support of any kind for Vietnam has begun to evaporate. It leads me to believe that the President could suffer another setback in the House on this issue like the one last Thursday in the vote to cut off funds for the bombing of Cambodia.

Wednesday, May 30, 1973

At the Wednesday Group today there was some discussion of the impact of Watergate on Republican stock. Garner Shriver said that in a poll he had taken among his constituents, the same percentage that had voted for Nixon supported him in his Watergate statement and felt that the investigation was taking a proper course. Others disputed this. Al Bell declared that Bradley's victory in the Los Angeles mayoral election was partly due to Watergate, that he had charged Yorty with Watergate tactics. I thought this was far-fetched. More telling was a statement by Mark Andrews, who said that a poll in North Dakota showed that of those who reflected party affiliation, the Republicans were down by 10 percent and the Democrats up by 9 percent. My personal view is that Watergate will not be the decisive factor in next year's election, but the economy will, and right now it doesn't look too good.

Tuesday, June 26, 1973

This week promises to be even busier than last, with another Friday session before we go on a week's vacation for July 4. Yesterday we voted on the critical amendments with respect to funding for the continued bombing of Cambodia. It was a bad day for the President's cause. The Eagleton Amendment from the Senate carried by a fairly safe margin, but then there was an amendment by George Mahon which would have permitted bombing until September 1. It lost on a tie, 204 to 204, the most dramatic vote we've had this year. The amendments were part of a Supplemental Appropriation conference report which included a number of diverse items, but this was the featured one. Today there were some futile attempts to save the day for the Administration, but all failed. The President now has the choice of vetoing it, although a number of agencies will have to have the money by the end of the month or they will run out of funds. Jerry Ford said that Nixon would indeed veto it, so I joined over eighty others in voting against it.

Wayne Woodlief called me to ask why I had voted to continue funds for the bombing. I replied that the President's policies had led us out of Vietnam, had brought a ceasefire in Laos, and had gotten our prisoners back. Not to back him now would be a vote of no-confidence at the last minute, and I felt he ought to be given every opportunity to see if he could bring pressure on Hanoi and its communist allies in Cambodia to make peace.

If this wasn't bad enough for the President, the testimony of John Dean before the Ervin Committee has cast the darkest shadow of all. There was a television set in the Republican lounge today, but the audience was not as enthusiastic as it has been when we've watched the World Series in there. A kind of resigned gloom pervaded the place. There wasn't much conversation, only an occasional mutter of "the son of a bitch." Dean has done the President considerable damage. If his testimony were to be corroborated by any of the other White House people, the President would be in an untenable position. So far, Dean appears to be the only one willing to indict the President. Unless he gets backed up it's unlikely that a resignation or impeachment will be forthcoming.

Last night Janie and I attended a dinner party at the F Street Club given by Cynthia Newman. Among the guests were Congressman Bob Wilson, Bill Steiger, Rog Morton of Interior, and Bo Callaway, the new Secretary of the Army, along with Harry Fleming, formerly of the White House staff, and several others. Watergate came up, and I was interested in some comments Bob Wilson made. He used to be chairman of the Republican Congressional Committee but was forced out, largely by the machinations of Haldeman. Bob said that after the 1968 election he had made an innocent statement about why the Republicans had not captured the Congress, and Haldeman had called him the next day to ream him out for it. Bob said that Haldeman was behind the sacking of Lee Potter over at the Congressional Committee. Haldeman told him that he wanted Potter fired. Bob said that he wouldn't do it, that Lee had done a great job raising money for candidates and ought to stay on. In the end, Haldeman got his way. Harry declared that Haldeman's behavior was one of the reasons he left, and now he's congratulating himself on his good luck in getting out when he did. As badly as all of them feel about the impact of Watergate on the President, none of them have shed any tears about the fall of Haldeman. I got an interesting postscript at dinner. I sat next to Mrs. Callaway. She told me that she and Bo are renting the Haldeman house over in Georgetown. She said that they didn't know when they went to see it that it was Haldeman's house, having made arrangements through an agent. She said the house is beautiful, but there is an air of tragedy about it. The furniture is all in place, and everything is in excellent taste. It's as if the occupants had had to flee and leave everything behind them. She added that there are no ashtrays. The Haldemans are Christian Scientists and don't smoke.

The final blow to fall on the President this week will come in the form of the War Powers Resolution. There was general debate on it last night, and we vote on it tomorrow. I can't help but be suspicious about the resolution's being scheduled for this week, with the Dean testimony being taken over in the Senate. I have serious reservations about the resolution, but if some amendments are added which would change the direction in which it's now heading, then I might be disposed to vote for it. The critical feature of it states that if, after 120 days following the President's commitment of American armed forces abroad to engage in combat, Congress has failed to come forward with a declaration of war or resolution of support, then the President must withdraw them. The salient point of it is that the President will have to act if there is congressional inaction. John Buchanan and Chuck Whalen have an amendment which would require the Congress to act within that time frame, so that each Member would have the responsibility of voting to support or not support what the President had done. In spite of all this, I have misgivings about our passing this kind of legislation in the climate of disillusionment that persists in the wake of the Vietnam war. We are reacting to our frustrations, rather than conceiving legislation under normal conditions.

Wednesday, June 27, 1973

The big issue in the House this afternoon was the vote on the President's veto of the Second Supplemental Appropriation Bill, which contained the ban on the use of funds for bombing Cambodia. It missed the necessary two-thirds majority by more than thirty votes. Having stuck by the President when the bill was first before us, I stood with him again. What followed was an angry outburst by the majority, led by Bob Giaimo of Connecticut. George Mahon said that his Appropriations Committee would go back and bring out a "sanitized" bill without the offending feature that had prompted the veto. This only enraged those who want all bombing ended immediately. Giaimo accused the President of defying the will of Congress and hinted that he was willing to cut off necessary funds for the conduct of the government to get his way. Al Cederberg jumped up to challenge him, making the point that if they wanted to stop the bombing of Cambodia, they ought to treat it as a separate matter and not tie it to an appropriations bill with a host of other unrelated subjects. It was a fierce display, and not a pleasant one to watch. Later in the afternoon, I heard that there are such strong feelings to force the President's hand on this that the Eagleton Amendment is going to be attached to the Debt Ceiling Bill in the Senate and every other measure that comes up. In the House, they are already talking of remaining here next week if necessary to vote on a possible veto of the Continuing Appropriation Bill which we passed yesterday with the Eagleton Amendment attached. Aside from the determination to end completely all involvement in Indochina, the contest represents a showdown between the President and Congress, a reaction to the frustration that the Democrats in Congress have endured and the defeats they suffered at Nixon's hands earlier this year. With Dean singing away over at the Senate, they are really getting in their licks.

The only break the President got today was the announcement by the leadership that the War Powers Resolution has been pulled off the calendar and won't be brought up again until mid-July. With the Interior Appropriations Bill on today and a series of delaying quorum calls in the middle of it, the leadership knew that they were in for another session that could conceivably run until tomorrow morning. They wisely withdrew it. Most of the Members breathed a sigh of relief. We were able to adjourn by 7:00 this evening, so we have the unexpected bonus of being home tonight.

Wednesday, September 5, 1973

The Wednesday Group has a tentative social meeting set up for next week with Vice President Agnew at Peter Frelinghuysen's home. Apparently Agnew has accepted pending a definite date being settled upon. Someone quipped that it would be fed to the press as a going-away party. There's no question about the fact that the Vice President is under fire right now, although I haven't talked to anyone who seriously believes that he took a payoff while serving as governor of

Maryland.

Ham Fish told us that the Judiciary Committee, of which he is a member, got Drinan's motion to impeach the President the week before we adjourned for the recess, and the Republican Members tried to get the chairman to hold hearings and throw the thing out quickly so that Drinan wouldn't have a month at home to tell everybody about his effort to impeach Nixon. However, the Democrats weren't interested in touching it and probably never will be.

Wednesday, September 19, 1973

I went to my subcommittee, where we started to cut up the military construction budget in earnest. Our staffer, Jim Shumate, had about $100 million in Army and Navy projects that he had already singled out, and we approved most of these in about forty-five minutes. However, we want to make a cut of over $300 million, and that isn't easy. We'll have a whack at the Air Force tomorrow. After we finished with what Jim had listed, we took a few amendments for add-ons. Jack Brinkley had one for a barracks in Fort Benning which amounted to over $9 million. It provoked some opposition from Charlie Bennett, Bill Bray, Charlie Wilson, and Otis Pike. Their position was that if one Member asked for something, it would be hard to turn down others. They gave Jack a hard time, but in the end his add-on was sustained by a five to four vote. After this, Charlie Bennett brought up several projects that Bob Sikes of Florida wants in his district. Charlie said that he didn't have his heart in it, but Bob had asked him to do it. He added that Bob was a tough individual who had a memory for those who crossed him. As a member of the Appropriations Committee, Bob could be in a position to be particularly rough on someone who bucked him. Since I had a small project of my own, I wasn't about to vote No on Bob's requests. Only Otis, Bill, and Charlie Wilson voted No on them.

Then it was my turn, and I made a pitch for the Navy to buy up the leaseholds of the clothiers and tavern owners who operated on the former railroad property outside the main gate of the Naval Station in Norfolk. I really didn't make my initial arguments very well, and Charlie Bennett and Bill Bray started in on me about why the Navy hadn't had it in their initial budget. I explained that it was an oversight, and that the matter had come to a head because the merchants themselves were now anxious to get out. I tried to say that this move would make the original sale a "clean" one by tidying it up, and then I mentioned the saving we would make by doing it now rather than putting it off until later, when relocation costs would be higher. They didn't know anything about relocation costs, and until I read them the law on it, they denied that there was one.

I could tell from the drift that it was going poorly, and had I known I would get such a challenge, I would have gone to them all beforehand to

41

get their consent, plus preparing a little fact sheet. I naively had thought that they would consent on the grounds of courtesy to a fellow member of the subcommittee. So I learned another lesson. When the vote was taken, mine passed by the same margin that Jack had won his by. Afterward, I shook his hand, and we thanked each other. I also thanked Robin Beard. His feeling was the same as mine, that one always looked after a colleague if his request was reasonable, and all of us know that there are certain requests that are important to a Member's district. "That's what it's about, isn't it?" I said to Robin. "It is as far as I'm concerned," he replied.

After that nonsense ended, we stewed over the total amount of the budget, and Charlie Wilson, who occasionally acts like an old woman in these sessions, threw up his hands and said that we might as well repeal our intent to cut the budget and just go to the floor with the bill and let the House cut it. Instead, Otis declared that the Army had all of its projects in order of priority, and it might be well if we just began at the bottom and worked up. The subcommittee latched on to that, and off we went, hacking away at the bottom of the Army requests. We had whittled off over $11 million worth when Otis decided to call it a day. Jim didn't have the Air Force cuts ready, and we felt it might be best to wait until we had acted on those before going back and cutting on the Army some more. It was as crude a piece of financial surgery as I ever expect to see, but I'll be damned if I know of a more scientific way to trim a budget. I got fractured at Otis. He smells an angle everywhere. As we began to lop off the items of lowest priority, he observed that most of them were not the really expensive projects, and he wondered out loud if the Army hadn't planned it this way so that we would leave the more expensive ones at the top of the list alone.

The House met on the veto of the minimum wage, but the result was pretty much of a foregone conclusion. There just wasn't the same suspense as last week. This time the Administration had the horses. The entire Virginia delegation voted to sustain. I got tickled at Bill Wampler. He waited until thirty seconds before the time ran out to punch his card in. I asked him why, when he was going to vote to sustain anyway. He said, "I just want them to see my name blank up there until the last minute. That way they appreciate me more."

While we were sitting there, Bob Daniel got us in a huddle to tell us confidentially that he had talked to Bill Ruckelshaus over the weekend and was told that Vice President Agnew is expected to resign. There's been a lot of speculation about it this week, complete with a headline in the *Washington Post*. At noon today there was a daffy picture in the Republican lounge of a cat hanging by its front claws to a crossbar, with the words underneath, "Hang in there, baby." Attached to its was a large card for Members to sign. The whole thing is to be presented to Agnew as a token of support by his friends in the House. I had signed it before hearing Bob's story, but he exercised some prudence and didn't. After Bob's revelation, we began to speculate on who Nixon might appoint to succeed Agnew. Stan Parris said that no matter what happened, it would result in a donnybrook. It seems that the entire House and Senate voting together would vote on whether to approve or not approve the President's choice. All of this really makes me wonder what else can happen to rock the boat in this country.

Thursday, September 20, 1973— Monday, September 24, 1973

My subcommittee has finally concluded its work on the military construction legislation. Following my narrow victory with my amendment on Wednesday, I was chagrined to come to the committee room on Thursday morning and find a Navy civilian representative there to tell me that the $1.8 million that we had earmarked the day before for picking up the leaseholds was not enough and that the proper figure was $3.4 million. This meant I had to go back and ask for a larger sum. I mentally cursed the Navy for not having given me the figure earlier. At the proper moment, I asked for unanimous consent to revise the amount upward to $3.8 million. Otis gave me a hard time and wanted to know if I would be willing to cut something else in the budget to offset it. Given the opportunity, I said that I would. Charlie started up again about the Navy not being able to take the leaseholds, but when I began to rebut him, he declared that he really didn't want to argue about it, so there was no objection to my motion. A few minutes later we took up the Navy's budget requests and reached a project in excess of $4 million for pollution abatement at Mare Island, California. It was obvious that Otis was waiting for someone to offer a motion to cut it, so I volunteered, and made up for the $3.4 million add-on in Norfolk. I replied that I could stand the smell from California a lot better than the noise I would get from Norfolk. Subsequently I did agree to several cuts in requested project approvals in my district. Charlie Bennett told me today that I had made a believer out of him in agreeing to those cuts. Fair is fair, I thought. Even so, I came out of the subcommittee with about $20 million in appropriations for military construction in my area, and that's pretty high.

We got into a minor struggle over dependent housing. Robin Beard and I held that the Defense Department is not allowing enough money per unit. They asked for $27,500 this year, up from $24,000. Jim Shumate said we ought to increase it another thousand dollars, but Robin and I contended that you can't build a decent house for that amount. I have agitated for a visit to several of our bases to look at dependent housing, because I've gotten a lot of complaints from officers about the shoddy construction and poor accommodations just as Robin has. He's seen some of the housing and has substantiated my own statements, but somehow we just haven't gotten through to the others, with the exception of Carleton King, whose son is a naval officer. Today (Monday) we lost on an attempt to increase the authorized sum for a unit to $30,000, which I offered as an amendment. To keep the total cost down, I suggested that we authorize only 7,000 units out of the 11,000 asked for. It didn't have a chance. We went with Jim's figure and 9,000 units. Ironically, this afternoon Jim passed around a speech that Senator Stennis had made today in the Senate, in which he gave the results of some interviews he had had with soldiers and officers of the Ninth Division in the Northwest about the all-volunteer Army. One of their chief complaints was about housing. I'll be damned if I know why the others on the subcommittee are so adamant. The cost of housing has skyrocketed in the past six months. Excluding the cost of land and taking advantage of a common building plan, it just isn't possible to build a decent house with four bedrooms for $30,000. I think we've made a terrible mistake by being penny wise and pound foolish.

Tuesday, October 2, 1973

The Agnew business has gotten considerable comment from the Members, especially in view of Carl Albert's decision not to take up Agnew's request that the House investigate his case. Ed Hutchinson, the ranking Republican on the Judiciary Committee, said that such a hearing could be accomplished in about a month, but of course, the Democrats want nothing to do with it. Some of them are awfully inconsistent. Drinan would like to impeach Nixon, but he insists that Agnew face the courts. The President has indicated that he wants his case settled in the courts, while Agnew wants a hearing by the House. Personally, most Members are glad that they are not going to be put in the position of having to make a decision on the Vice President.

Wednesday, October 3, 1973

At the Wednesday Group meeting in Garner Shriver's office I learned that there are now serious moves afoot by the Republicans on the Judiciary Committee to get a hearing on the Vice President's request. There are several courses of action that can be taken, one a preferential motion by Paul Findley. Ham Fish, who conveyed this news to us, asked us to keep it quiet for the next few days so as not to alert the Democrats. It sparked some discussion about the wisdom of taking up the Agnew request. Pete McCloskey and some of the others said that we ought to do it, that the Vice President was either innocent or a fool. "Or clever," someone added. The best argument in favor of having a hearing was that the House would at least be trying to clear the air and remove the uncertainty that now exists around the Vice President. Some said that we had no guarantee that the Democrats would give Agnew a fair hearing, but this was generally discounted. Larry Coughlin raised the question of what this would do for the Republican Party. He doubted that we could come out of it without being bloodied further.

Most of the fellows indicated by their reports that their committees have just about finished their work for the year. Ways and Means has the Trade Bill, but that's about ready for floor action. Bill Stanton told us about his trip to Nairobi, Kenya, to attend the World Bank annual meeting. He was ragged about how many went on the trip. It turned out to be twenty-four. Someone quipped that last year, when the meeting was held here in Washington, only two went to the session. Bill said that wasn't so, that he went last year when it was held here. He said that George Shultz had made an excellent impression on him and did a fine job in representing American interests at the conference. The trip home lasted thirteen hours, and Bill said that he played bridge the whole time with Mrs. Patman, who had gone along with a number of the wives. "She must be a great bridge player," I said to Bill. His reply was gallant: "She's a great person."

Tuesday, October 9, 1973

The renewed war between the Arabs and Israelis has provoked less excitement than I expected. I was reading the news briefs from the wire service in the cloakroom today when someone came up and asked who was winning. Somebody else said, "Haven't you heard? They both are!" Congressman Bill Lehman of Florida has called for immediate delivery of all planes ordered by Israel, even if it means taking them out of the United States' inventory. That would be decidedly unneutral, and although the House is obviously sympathetic to Israel, such a move would produce not only deep resentment in the Arab world, where our standing is already low, but might even be counterproductive in the United States. I was interviewed by the local press when I was home and also got a call from a young lady reporting for a Jewish publication circulated among Tidewater Jews. I told all of them that I felt we should remain completely neutral and leave the fighting to the belligerents. I added that as far as Israel was concerned, the best thing that we could do would be to counterbalance any Soviet threat, and the Russians appear to be staying out of it, too. To the young Jewish reporter, I recalled the words of Golda Meir in 1970, when I was there: she told us that Israel wanted no United States forces, only the arms that we could make available to them.

It is clear that the Arabs secured the initiative in this conflict, but I'm still betting that the Israelis will pull off another win.

This has surely been a day of ironies. It began this morning with a breakfast at the Capitol Hill Club of about eighty Members, known as the "Good Guys." Sam Devine and some of the other more conservative Members put the group together several years ago. It's bipartisan, including Democrats as well as Republicans. I got an invitation to attend two weeks ago, but couldn't go. Yesterday I got another one from Sam, telling me that Senator Barry Goldwater would be the speaker. It sounded interesting, and besides, I was curious to find out who the "Good Guys" were.

I sat at a table with Clark Fisher, Sonny Montgomery, Jack Brinkley, and Jack Flynt, all Southern Democrats, plus some of my Republican colleagues, including Marjorie Holt, who is probably classified as a "Good Girl." Rog Morton was there, along with John Niedecker from the White House staff.

Senator Goldwater spoke for about thirty minutes, combining some remarks of his own with answers to questions from the floor. Almost all of his dialogue centered on the Agnew case, and he urged us to speak out for the Vice President. He stated that he was convinced that certain people high in the government were "out to get the Vice President." And then he mentioned some of the harassment that had gone on. He noted that a couple of weeks ago, Agnew had been a guest in his home in Arizona and had admired some Western art that the Goldwaters have. He expressed a desire to buy a painting for Frank Sinatra, and asked Mrs. Goldwater if she would make a purchase for him, saying that he did not want to spend over $1,000. The next week, Mrs. Goldwater went to a gallery and bought a painting for about $750, and, according to Barry, the Justice Department issued a subpoena to the lady who had sold her the painting. From there he went on to say that he knew where the leaks were coming from in the White House, and mentioned specifically the offices of Bryce Harlow and Mel Laird, although he hastened to say that he didn't think they personally had authorized them. But he said that he resented the efforts being made by the White House to get Members not to go out on a limb for the Vice President. Then he made his pitch for some vocal support for Agnew. Finally, he said that, contrary to the denials, he was positive that the Vice President had been asked to resign.

The pep talk, and that's the way it appeared to affect everyone, went over well. Barry Goldwater exudes strength and confidence, and he certainly communicated his belief in Agnew's innocence to the audience. In response to a question raised about the Nixon tapes, he reiterated his conviction that the President should release the information, but he surmised that it's probably too late now, and that the majority of the American people just don't seem to care any more. He said that he thought that the President had made a serious mistake and had lost a measure of confidence that he could never recover.

When 9:00 came, the meeting adjourned, the Members streamed out, generally pleased with what they had heard and some speaking of the shabby way that Agnew had been treated. So what happened this afternoon? The only possible news that could chase the Arab-Israeli war off the front page: the Vice President pleaded no contest to a charge of income tax evasion and resigned.

The news swept the House like wildfire. Reporters jammed into the Speaker's Lobby, jostling one another to get interviews with various Members. Les Arends was surrounded by a group of them, and Jerry Ford had a knot of Members around him at his desk on the Floor of the House.

Tomorrow the Republicans will hold a press conference in the House at 9:30. Discussion will center on the possibility of a successor, and there is talk on the floor of Jerry's getting the nod—Jerry Ford, the Minority Leader. Herman Badillo walked back to the office with me this afternoon, and he said that he had heard that Jerry had "a boomlet" going for him. He added that Jerry would certainly be acceptable to the Democrats.

Thursday, October 11, 1973

We added another chapter in the continuing drama of the Vice President this morning at the Republican conference in the House. Jerry Ford commented before we began that it was a milestone—not the topic, but the fact that we had a larger attendance than we've ever had before. After John Anderson opened the meeting, Jerry took the floor to tell us what had transpired yesterday. He said that after getting the news about Agnew's resignation, he got a call to be at the White House at 4:00. He and Les joined Senators Hugh Scott and Bob Griffin, the Minority Leader and Whip of the Senate, in the President's office to discuss the matter of a successor. The President told them he had not made up his mind about a successor and wanted the opinions of the Members of Congress. He said that he wanted to avoid the appearance of a mini-Republican Convention, preferring that there not be an organized effort behind one or two candidates, and that instead each Member should write to him immediately, giving up to three choices for the office. If more than one was named, then they should be listed in order of preference. The President told them that he was asking the same from the nineteen Republican governors and had also asked George Bush to get a sampling from selected leaders in the Republican Party.

Then the President listed the criteria for our choices in order of importance. First, we should choose a person most qualified to be President. Second, that individual should have a high degree of identity with the President's foreign policy. While his support of the domestic program was important, the foreign policy agreement was paramount. Third, it should be someone who has a fair chance of being approved by the House and Senate.

The President told them that the letters could be signed or unsigned, but he wanted them in his office by late this afternoon. Jerry put a time limit of 4:00 today, saying that he expected to have them in the hands of Rose Mary Woods, the President's personal secretary, by 5:00. He emphasized that the letters were going to her to be read by the President himself rather than to the office of Bryce Harlow or Mel Laird. The discussion that followed was interesting. Dr. Tim Carter and Sil Conte both declared that their choice was Jerry himself, and Sil read a copy of a letter that he had sent to the White House last night. Both statements drew applause from the Members. Peter Peyser and Howard Robison both spoke up for Governor Rockefeller. Peter said that he had spoken with the Governor at 8:30 this morning to get his consent and that he could say frankly that Rockefeller would accept.

One or two still thought that it would be a good idea for us to put forth a consensus candidate, and someone said that he had heard a report on the radio this morning to the effect that the President had already made up his mind. Sil Conte declared that under no circumstances would he support John Connally.

I spoke to Joel Broyhill about John Anderson and Jerry, and he reacted sharply to Anderson's name. "He's on the left. He would never do," he said, and added that he had never voted for John to be chairman of the Republican Conference. He expected to go with Jerry. Ken Robinson said that he was inclined towards Mel Laird, who I think would be a good choice. I didn't indicate my own preference and really wasn't certain. I walked slowly back to the office, mulling the thing over, recognizing that my input into the final decision would be minimal but still conscious of the fact that I had a voice in it, even if a small one. I thought of the men I've met who have impressed me since I've been here, men who I feel have what it takes to be President. There aren't many. I thought about the political aspects of it, whether or not such a person would have a chance to be considered a serious candidate in 1976. Certainly the political angle has to be considered.

I like John Anderson and believe that he is the kind of person who can inspire. The nation would respond to his kind of leadership, I think. And yet I knew that John is opposed by over a third of his colleagues in the House. Jerry would be a popular choice, but I don't think he would be the ideal candidate to succeed Nixon in 1976. As a team leader, Jerry is superb. He is so good that it is hard to imagine who could fill his shoes if he were tapped to become Vice President. But as the single individual with the mystique to lead a nation, I have my doubts. Still, he has the character and the trust of his colleagues that would restore a measure of confidence in this Administration.

I rejected the idea of jumping on a bandwagon for Rockefeller or Reagan or Connally. It had to be someone I knew personally. When I got back to my office, I called the staff together to tell them what had transpired at the conference. I felt it would be an interesting experience for them and that they ought to have a chance to share it with me. During the conversation, Janie mentioned my past statements about George Bush. It struck a responsive chord in me, and I recall recording earlier in this diary my conviction that George is Presidential timber. When everyone had gone back to their desks, I asked Janie to come back with her stenographic pad, and then I dictated a letter to the President, naming George as my first choice and Jerry as my second. A copy of it follows. It isn't likely that the President will pick George, but as Janie said, I was making a recommendation to the President rather than trying to guess who he was going to nominate.

October 11, 1973

The President
The White House
Washington, D.C. 20500

Dear Mr. President:

At our conference this morning, the Minority Leader advised us of his meeting with you yesterday afternoon and your request that we make available to you our suggestions for candidates for the office of Vice President. I appreciate this opportunity to share my views with you and therefore place before you for your consideration the following names:

My first choice is George Bush. I worked with him during my first term in the House of Representatives, and as a result of that relationship came to the conclusion that he is one of the few men who I feel is worthy to succeed you. His service as Ambassador to the United Nations has enabled him to appear in a world forum as a spokesman for our nation. I know that he is loyal to you and has endeavored to execute your policies. Finally, Mr. President, George Bush would have little difficulty in being confirmed by Congress.

My second choice is our Minority Leader, Gerald R. Ford. A number of my colleagues, I am sure, will put his name forward. Jerry inspires confidence by his leadership, and you have no finer spokesman in the House than he. My only reservation about Jerry is that he has been such a successful leader in the House that I can think of no one else who would fight for your programs here as effectively as he, and he would be hard to replace if he became Vice President.

There are other men, of course, whom I could support,

and I want you to know that I will support whomever you choose. In these critical times, you have our prayers and my pledge of absolute loyalty.

Sincerely,

G. WILLIAM WHITEHURST

Friday, October 12, 1973

In three hours, I'll be at the White House, where the President will make his announcement of his choice for Vice President at 9:00 tonight. There haven't been as many rumors about a successor to somebody since the last Pope was elected. It's a wonder Nixon didn't burn wet straw in the White House chimney, too. He flew to Camp David last night and returned early this morning with the word that he had decided on a successor. That's the closest thing to a mountaintop for contemplation within fifty miles. I suppose I shouldn't make light of this whole business. The entire thing, after all, was born of tragedy. But the rumors that flew through the House today finally became absurd. Someone noted that former Secretary of State Bill Rogers and his wife will be the special guests of the Nixons at a White House dinner on Monday night, and so it had to be he. Someone else said that it was John Volpe, and Peggy Heckler was elated about that. Then word came out that the mayor of Indianapolis was to be tapped. The latest rumor centers on Lin Holton, our Governor, who I almost listed as a third choice in my letter to the President. About 4:00 this afternoon, a UPI man called for me in the Speaker's Lobby to ask me what I knew about a rumor that Secret Service men had been sent to fetch the Governor in Richmond. I replied that until he told me, I had heard no such rumor. I dismissed it at once.

Subsequently, I saw Joel Broyhill, and he asked me if I was going to the White House tonight. I said that I had not been invited. He told me that the formula used for the invitations, since the entire Congress and Diplomatic Corps could not fit into the East Room, was to choose those Members who had been here for more than four terms, plus several other selected Members, including some freshmen. "That lets me out," I said, but when I returned to the office later I got a call from the White House inviting me to be present, and I accepted. Almost simultaneously there was a call from Wayne Woodlief, who told me that he had definitive word that Lin Holton had been at Washington and Lee this afternoon for a ceremony which several of us had been invited to attend, but couldn't, and Secret Service men had shown up to take him to Washington. If that's true, then it's the most substantive rumor I've heard all day. Lin would be a great choice, and I've no doubt that he would easily win confirmation by the Congress.

This morning I heard an interesting briefing on the Mideast war by Dr. Colby of the CIA. He told the members of the Armed Services Committee that both sides had suffered heavily in the fighting, but that the Israelis now had the upper hand on the Syrian front, and while they had not destroyed the Syrian army, they had mauled it badly and might finish it off in a few days. The Egyptians were being held on the Suez front, having penetrated for about twenty kilometers. He said that the original intention of the Egyptians did not appear to be to try to knock out Israel. They probably didn't expect to be able to do that. But they did believe that they could make some gains and win back some of the land lost in the 1967 war and then hope for Big Power intervention that would hasten a settlement. He discounted direct Russian involvement, but said that if things went really badly for the Arabs, the Russians would surely send advisors in to help. He also thought Jordan might lend a hand, even if they did not try to invade Israel directly. King Hussein, he noted, was under heavy pressure from his officers as well as from his people.

Saturday, October 13, 1973— Monday, October 15, 1973

A ll of the rumors that abounded on Friday afternoon faded in the lights of the East Room at 9:00 that night when the President announced that Jerry Ford was his choice to succeed Spiro Agnew as Vice President of the United States. As a matter of fact, the rumor favorites had begun to disappear even before the announcement. ABC declared flatly on their regular news broadcast early that evening that Ford was the President's choice. All of the talk about Holton dissipated when I saw him in the reception area on the ground floor of the White House about 8:30. "Congratulations," I said. "It ain't me!" he laughed. His precipitate trip from Lexington had come about because of the President's invitation to him as chairman of the Republican Governors' Conference.

There was quite a crowd waiting to go upstairs to the East Room when I got there. I spoke to Senator Barry Goldwater, all the while thinking of his plea to the "Good Guys" on Wednesday morning. I felt sorry for him, to have been left out on a limb like that. Besides the various Members of Congress, the Joint Chiefs were present, as well as a few of the Diplomatic Corps, including the Soviet ambassador, Dobrynin. About quarter of nine, we went upstairs to the East Room, which was brightly lit for the network television cameras mounted on a platform behind us. About 200 chairs were arranged on three sides facing the wall on which hang the portraits of George and Martha Washington. I found a seat in the middle between Louis Wyman of New

Hampshire and Jim Broyhill of North Carolina. Since everyone around me appeared to have put Jerry's name forward, it was obvious that the President had invited only those Republicans who had nominated Ford. It was a shrewd move, because it meant that there would be enthusiastic applause when Jerry's name was announced. The Democrats present were mostly conservative, so one could say that it was Jerry's crowd.

The whole business was not protracted, taking no more than about fifteen minutes. Jerry's eyes were red-rimmed, and it was clear that it was the highest point of his career. I cannot fault the President for his choice, although the *Wall Street Journal* today was sour about the President's selection and interpreted the move as catering to the "clubbiness" of the politicians here. I have already made my own analysis of Jerry's strengths and weaknesses. The wisdom of such an appointment is vested in the political persuasiveness that the President can secure for himself in having Jerry work for his programs on the Hill. Except for a few on the left, most Members predict that confirmation will be forthcoming.

In the meantime, a contest is shaping up over his successor as Minority Leader. The two principal contenders are John Rhodes of Arizona and John Anderson of Illinois. Other possible candidates are Sam Devine of Ohio and Les Arends, the Whip. And if a real deadlock developed, Barber Conable of New York could emerge as a dark horse. My own choice is Rhodes, and I have so informed him, although John Anderson has made a call to solicit my support.

Although I have previously backed John Anderson in his successful bids for election as chairman of the Republican Conference, and admire his eloquence and his effectiveness as a debater, and even feel he would make an excellent Presidential candidate, I don't feel that he is the best choice to succeed Jerry as Minority Leader. The post calls for someone who will unite the Republican Members behind him in support of Administration policies. John will achieve the opposite. He has often gone his own way, even though he is a part of the Leadership. This has caused the conservative Members to become angry with him on occasion, and they resent this sometimes-liberal streak of independence. The White House would also not be too happy with John as Minority Leader because of his past actions. He would not be easy to deal with.

I don't believe that John Anderson can get the majority he wants and perhaps not even a plurality if the race widens to three or more candidates. John Rhodes, on the other hand, is what can be best described as a "pragmatic conservative." He is innovative and intelligent, but he is not dynamic and lacks the visible strength that Jerry seemed to bring to the Floor in debate. He is relatively soft-spoken, and this could hurt his effectiveness. But he most nearly fits the mold for the ideal successor, and if he is successful in winning the post he may acquire the other characteristics that will enhance his ability to lead the House Republicans. Until Jerry actually resigns as Minority Leader, there will be only behind-the-scenes maneuvering, but there will be plenty of that.

As a postscript, Spiro Agnew goes on national television tonight to tell his story. Advance notice tells us that he will claim innocence of any wrongdoing. I don't think that will wash after his plea and the statements made by Richardson at his press conference last Thursday.

Wednesday, October 17, 1973— Monday, October 22, 1973

Richard Nixon seems to be exceeding any known limits in the game of "Can You Top This?" The events of the past few days have left the nation stunned, and if impeachment becomes a reality, we will have a crisis on our hands that will make the Dreyfus Case in France pale by comparison. On Saturday morning I learned that the President had decided not to pursue his tug-of-war over the release of the Watergate tapes all the way to the Supreme Court, but had offered instead a compromise that would send a summary of them to the Ervin Committee and grand jury while permitting Senator John Stennis to listen to the tapes themselves and serve as a kind of arbiter to ensure that what was released was what is on the tapes. It was the sort of thing that the President should have done three months ago. It would have spared him and the nation a lot of grief. Cox, the special prosecutor, refused to accept this proffered solution without even waiting for Judge Sirica's decision, and on Saturday night he was fired in a wild windup that saw the departure of the Attorney General, Elliot Richardson, as well as Bill Ruckelshaus, from the Justice Department. Neither of them would countenance the firing of Cox.

We were away for the weekend, but when we returned to Virginia Beach on Sunday afternoon, television reporters were waiting for me, to get a statement. I realized that I had to be circumspect. The crisis has certain ramifications. Nevertheless, I made it clear that I was deeply disturbed by the President's action. He had broken his word to the nation, and specifically to Richardson. Cox had been promised a free hand. When he attempted to exercise it, he was fired. The President's strategy might appear to be the one that would help him avoid both impeachment and a constitutional confrontation with the courts, although he still may face both. A number of senators and congressmen are calling for his impeachment now, but a careful examination of Nixon's action shows that he has not broken the law, only his word. The Justice Department is an Executive agency, and its employees are subject to the President. He can hire and fire at will, at least in those top levels, who are not Civil Service. I would not vote to impeach him on the basis of his firing Cox, and I told the reporters so. I did say that I had carried the President's flag for five years, and it was getting heavy, but I stopped short of outright repudiation of him. I also stated that I thought that the delay of Ford's nomination was reprehensible on the part of the

Democrats. The nation needs a Vice President as soon as possible. To delay is to engage in the most partisan politics. I heard a report today that Carl Albert will ask the Judiciary Committee on Tuesday to make an investigation to see whether or not the President has committed offenses for which he should be impeached. I am glad to see him make this move, because it will head off the hotheads in the Democratic Party who would force a showdown immediately and bring the business of the Congress, and thus the nation, to a halt.

Today, our phone at home never stopped ringing. I had a meeting with Admiral Anderson, Commandant of the Fifth Naval District, at 10:00, and when I got back home to pick up Janie for a medical appointment, she said that the calls had been incessant. Ironically, most of them were on the President's side, staunch conservatives who said that the liberals had "gotten" Agnew and now were out to "get" the President. One woman talked to me when I got home and said that if I voted to impeach the President, she and five others in her family would never vote for me again. I managed to keep calm and avoid what I was tempted to say, and simply stated that I would do that which my conscience and convictions guided me to do.

When we got back to Washington early in the evening, I opened eighteen telegrams and all of them asked for impeachment of the President. Half of them were out of my district, however. Also, a much larger stack, favoring the sending of jet aircraft and arms to Israel, was resting there, too, all of them from Jewish constituents. With the ceasefire agreed to today, however, the urgency has gone out of that problem.

At a meeting of the Wednesday Group on the seventeenth, the chief topic of dicussion was the choice of a Minority Leader to succeed Jerry. Both John Anderson and Sam Devine have dropped out of the running, and the candidacy of Les Arends is not taken seriously. What was interesting were the opinions offered on John Rhodes. They were mixed. At first, the judgments were critical. Several called him uninspiring and too willing to march in step with the White House. They declared that we ought to have a Leader who is more independent and willing to challenge the White House more often, coming up with ideas and programs of his own. The criticism of Jerry's leadership in this respect was implied. And then the trend turned the other way. Some others spoke up and said that John had more depth than he was given credit for, and would make a respectable leader for the House Republicans. There was some talk of getting John to come to the group and answer questions, but this was dismissed as being counterproductive. It was felt that better input would be achieved if each Member wrote John and asked him to give heed to some of the more moderate Members.

I was in the Republican lounge for lunch, and Jerry was there, too, eating his singular dish of cottage cheese with Worcestershire sauce. He told us that his complement of Secret Service guards were staked out in his driveway in a mobile van, because Jerry's house doesn't have room for them. Jerry added that he expected to convert his garage into living quarters, and Al Cederberg spoke up from one of the couches, "Sounds like San Clemente," a reference to the President's improvements which have caused so much of a flap. Jerry slapped his fork into the cottage cheese and retorted, "Cederberg, you son of a bit--," and bit off the word in deference to the two girls who serve lunch at the counter. He's not usually profane. He then laughed and said to everybody that the Secret Service would have to make some electronic additions, but that he had planned to make the alterations anyway. He must be having second thoughts about his prospective office.

Tuesday, October 23, 1973

The latest Presidential somersault has given substance to the prevailing view that in this town the unexpected can become the expected. Having fired his special prosecutor and accepted the resignation of his Attorney General, the President confounded his enemies and friends alike this afternoon by releasing the Watergate tapes to the grand jury.

I had a meeting this morning in Al Quie's office of the special committee that has been set up to study and make recommendations regarding the size of the Leadership and, in particular, who should be included among those who go to the White House for the weekly meetings (although after the events of the past few days, it may be hard to find volunteers). Present were Al, Howard Robison, Bill Dickinson, Les Arends, Charlie Gubser, myself, and Mel Laird, whom we invited some weeks ago to meet with us. Mel was late getting there, so the conversation turned at once to the news of the weekend. Everyone agreed that the President had dropped a bombshell, although all felt that he was unimpeachable on the narrow ground of firing Cox. The consensus was that if Judge Sirica held him in contempt, the impeachment resolution would be seriously considered, and we would face the wrenching question itself. The talk then turned to Nixon's possible successor. If Jerry were not confirmed as Vice President in the meantime, Carl Albert would be in line.

I went to a CIA-Defense Department briefing on the Middle East after my meeting in Al Quie's office and heard an especially clear and comprehensive analysis of the situation there. The ceasefire has broken down for the time being, but the consensus among the experts is that the Israelis have the upper hand on both fronts. The losses in men are about four to one against the Arabs, and the plane and tank losses of the Arabs have also been much heavier. Our witnesses were emphatic about the lack of involvement of United States forces. We have no advisors in Israel, and our only personnel there are either to observe or to help with the airlift. We have replaced about a third of the Israeli air losses, and our total resupply, either through our own airlift or in combination with the Israelis, just about equals what the Soviets have flown in. Plenty of questions remain unanswered about the ceasefire. Both sides have attached conditions to it which could make a peaceful solution difficult.

On the floor of the House today there was about an hour of one-minute speeches, most of them in denunciation of the President, with a few Republicans present to defend him. The Speaker wisely placed the issue in the hands of the Judiciary Committee, thus blunting the immediate attempt to impeach the President. The House then went on to the business of taking up a bill permitting the use of Health Maintenance Organizations in CHAMPUS. While that was under discussion, the wire services reported that the President had decided to release the Watergate tapes to the grand jury. It provoked the same kind of consternation that followed the news of Agnew's resignation. I saw a large group of Democrats huddling around the massive Tip O'Neill, his white head bent over as he talked rapidly to them. There were the usual jokes that are made at such a time. Charlie Vanik went up on the elevator with some Republicans, and one of them asked him what they were going to do now. "Impeach him for giving the tapes to Sirica," Vanik replied with a laugh. There's more truth than humor to that. Many of them would be pleased to get rid of the President, no matter what. Don Riegle got a Special Order this afternoon to demand that the President reinstate Cox so that the investigation could go forward. Don said that if the President did it and the evidence showed that he was innocent, Don would be "the first man in the Well of the House to congratulate him."

I came back to the office and gave several radio interviews to stations back home, giving my reaction to it all. I said that I was relieved that the President had sent the tapes over, because it meant that the possibility of impeachment proceedings was now diminished. I added that I had advocated release of the tapes months ago and that had the President done then what he has finally done now, all of the grief and anguish of the past few months, and particularly the last few days, would have never occurred.

It will be a few days before public opinion catches up. We have received well over 100 telegrams so far, probably closer to 200, and they are dated one, two, and even three days ago. One constituent wrote to say that she had tried to send a telegram and been told by Western Union that they were so far behind that she would have to be put on a waiting list. The sentiment is running about twenty to one in favor of impeachment. A professor at Old Dominion University said over the telephone and in a telegram, "Impeachment or bust!" Another telegram said that it was time I put down the President's flag and picked up the red, white, and blue, an obvious reference to my statement, which was carried in the news across the country, that the President's flag was getting heavy for me to carry.

I'm not sure that even the turning over of the tapes is going to affect the thinking of a great many people. They have made up their minds that they want the President impeached, and nothing could dissuade them, I'm afraid.

At 5:00 this afternoon I went over to a meeting at Happy Camp's office to talk with some of my fellow 91st-ers about the chances of Lou Frey's being elected as head of the Policy Committee of the Conference. Lou has spoken to a number of us to enlist our support. While we were there, the events of the past few days became a focal point of our conversation. Phil Crane told us that he had it on the best authority that, the Watergate business aside, the gravest danger to the President's position was in an IRS investigation now under way. According to Phil's source, the facts being dug up are "stomach-wrenching," and his man predicted that the President would be forced to resign and would then be given a $10,000 fine and a three-year suspended sentence. "That seems to be the going rate," I said. Someone mentioned the Riegle recommendation about rehiring Cox, and Phil said that the Democrats had better think twice about that. He said that Cox had run up a budget of over $2 million and was about to hire 500 investigators to begin a thorough investigation of the Members of Congress and their campaigns. There are allegedly 5,000 violations of the campaign law passed last year. I heard Sam Devine say that with his sixteen years in the House and five with the FBI, he just might call it quits and retire on his pension.

Then Lou came in to tell us about a meeting he attended with John Rhodes, Jerry's heir apparent, plus some other leading Republicans. John and Bob Michel said that the White House had completely miscalculated the reaction to last weekend's action. The President and his advisers had thought that the compromise they were offering would mollify everyone and didn't realize that the removal of Cox would trigger such an outburst. It was this that shocked them and prompted the change of heart and the decision to send the tapes to the grand jury. Lou added that they have learned that the tapes themselves do not implicate the President in a cover-up but do contain some rather salty language and comments that could be personally embarrassing.

Wednesday, October 24, 1973—
Monday, October 29, 1973

The curtain of the dramatic events which opened this week was lifted further on Wednesday night and Thursday morning. Wednesday morning began innocently enough. I had breakfast with a group of medical assistants up from home. Following that I spoke to a group of Navy wives at the Naval Observatory. I thought that I would be preaching to the choir, but I got some surprises. Several of the women, including two blacks, were after the President's scalp and rebutted me vigorously when I declined to go along with impeachment. I came back for a meeting with a former POW whose bracelet I wore when he was in Hanoi. His name is Captain Kenneth Coskey. He wanted some help with his application for disability compensation for the years he was a prisoner, but we also chatted about his imprisonment and the readjustment he has gone through since returning.

The afternoon brought the unveiling of a portrait of the late Phil Philbin in the Armed Services Committee room. Former Speaker John McCormack was on hand to say a few words, as well as Dewey Short, the last Republican chairman of the Committee. Dewey couldn't speak less than thirty minutes if his life depended on it. He went on and on with a style of oratory which had reached its peak seventy-five years ago in Chautauqua, New York. He recited part of Sir Walter Scott's "Lay of the Last Minstrel," as well as some verse from the Bible. One woman in the front was in tears, but a hell of a lot more were glancing at their wristwatches. Mel Price and Bill Bray were mercifully brief, and Carl Albert wound things up. It took exactly an hour. For the majority of those who had to stand throughout, it was an ordeal. Midway through it, Father Drinan came and stood in the corner until it was all over, then ducked out. Since it was Phil's seat he had won, it wasn't his crowd.

The principal event of the day was an evening get-together by about twenty of the Wednesday Groupers at John Dellenback's home in Glen Echo, Maryland. John had invited Elliot Richardson to come out to talk to us informally, and it was a remarkable two hours. Elliot's wife accompanied him, and we sat around the large comfortable living room, firing questions at the former Attorney General as he recounted the events of the past six months.

Although I had met him several times, I had never spent so much time with him nor heard him express himself so frankly. He is a bright fellow, very articulate, and extremely even-tempered. He reflects his Boston Brahmin background completely, and as he sat in an easy chair he puffed away at his pipe, pausing between sentences both for effect and sometimes to weigh his words carefully. It was quite a performance.

John began the questioning by saying that we had all been hearing a spate of rumors for the past two days. In light of these and in particular the warning that more surprises were in store for the nation, John wanted to know if "any more shoes are going to be dropped." The silence that ensued was unmatched the rest of the evening; that question was uppermost in everyone's mind. Elliot paused and then deliberately shook his head, saying that to the best of his knowledge nothing more ought to be expected that could be damaging to the President. He said that nothing Cox had said to him over the last few months indicated that Cox had information that caused him to believe that the President was guilty of a cover-up or was personally guilty of wrongdoing. He added that neither he nor Cox knew for certain what was on the Watergate tapes but that his personal feeling was that they would contain nothing that would compromise the President. Furthermore, in conversations with Haig and Buzhardt, the latter of whom claimed to know what is on the tapes, he has been led to believe that there is nothing to incriminate the President. There was visible relief in the room at this news.

As the discussion picked up, Richardson declared that if the President is to restore confidence in his office, he must appoint a new prosecutor, who will be unfettered in pursuit of his work, and the President must also make available whatever other tapes or information he has to the Justice Department for the government to prosecute those guilty of misdeeds.

In reviewing what had happened, Richardson said that the President had fired Cox for two reasons: first, he believed that to release the tapes would be to violate the Presidential prerogative of keeping inviolate information of a personal nature. To surrender them would be to set a dangerous precedent. Second, the President became convinced that Cox was out to get him, that he was a Kennedy Democrat who would stop at nothing short of a full-scale witchhunt leading to the indictment of a number of people who had committed no crime. Such charges, however, would be an acute embarrassment to the President. The President had been told that the people around Cox were of a similar vein, and the President saw them as a group of unprincipled vigilantes. These were not Richardson's exact words, but an impression that he believed the President held. He denied, however, that Cox possessed these feelings, and he honestly believed that Cox was not "out to get the President" as some have charged.

Richardson's attitude toward the President, now that he has resigned from the Administration, was one of moderation. He certainly manifested no bitterness or vindictiveness, and in answer to a question as to whether he would agree to return, he said that it was premature to consider that, but that he would not rule it out for the future. It was far different from the emphatic No that Ruckleshaus had given after being fired from the Justice Department.

Richardson told us that the last comprehensive discussion he had had with the President was at Camp David last April. At that time, he felt that he had gotten through to the President, and from what the President said, he felt that the President had nothing to hide and really wanted the kind of investigation which would bring wrongdoers to justice. But during the summer, the President's suspicions of Cox increased, especially under the influence of those around him in the White House who feared what Cox might do. More and more, the President became convinced that he must protect himself.

I then asked Elliot how he would analyze the President as a man. Nixon has been called paranoid, and his outburst against the press last Friday night has been cited as an example. Elliot reflected on my question for a moment and then said that the President has always been a man who has felt himself under attack, and that in the years before he became President he always seemed to be battling those on the inside. After Nixon took office, Elliot told us, he had a conversation with John

Ehrlichman, who he felt was one of the "broad gauge" individuals in the White House. He said that he told John that the President didn't seem to have lost his combativeness and couldn't accommodate himself to the idea that he was now inside and didn't have to maintain the old posture. At this, several spoke up to confirm the old trait. Al Bell said that he remembered back after World War II, when Nixon was a candidate for the first time, how sensitive he was to those around him. "If you're not for me, you're against me," was his feeling.

All of this seemed to confirm the apparent motive of the President in deciding to fire Cox when Cox refused to accept the compromise offer made at the end of the previous week. As he warmed to the analysis of the President, he recalled the first time that he had met him, all the way back in 1956, when Nixon was vice president. Elliot said that he had written a speech for Christian Herter to give on behalf of the Vice President. He worked on the speech pretty hard; he then brought it to Washington and went to Nixon's office to give it to him to read. He said that Nixon took the speech and read through it so rapidly that Elliot couldn't believe that he had absorbed it. Nixon gave it back to him, saying that it was pretty good and that it seemed to cover all the main points. Not believing that Nixon had really read it fully, Elliot then asked him if he could suggest any additions. At that, the then Vice President took the draft back and immediately cited three or four places where additional points might be made. It convinced him then of how quickly the President thinks. He said that over the years he has also seen other sides to him, in particular the President's sensitiveness and basic shyness and, of course, his defensiveness.

One of the most telling criticisms that Richardson made of the President's handling of the entire business was the lack of imagination shown by the President and his advisers. From the beginning, they hadn't tried to see the consequences of a particular course of action. They couldn't imagine what the firing of Cox would do, or what effect not releasing the tapes would have. On this point I was in complete agreement. In retrospect, the error is so fundamental that it seems incredible.

Asked whether or not he would consider a Presidential boomlet's being started for him, Richardson declared that it was too early, and he wasn't sure that he could sustain himself for such an objective.

I regarded him as calm and relieved to have the crisis behind him. It had obviously been a difficult experience, and it left him with some strong convictions about the nation itself. Not only must we maintain personal integrity in our conduct, but he emphasized that we must cease trying to con the people. They must be told the truth, and he harked back to his days at the Department of Health, Education, and Welfare, and to the unconscionable over-promising that has gone on for a decade. The moral he put forward would apply not only to those in the Executive Branch who have withheld information because it was unfavorable or incriminating, but those on the left who try to perpetuate the myth that Utopia can be legislated by the government.

On Thursday morning we got the White House side of it all. Simultaneously, we experienced a mini-military crisis with the Soviet Union. As a result of certain information the President had received regarding Soviet military activity, he ordered a partial alert of our military forces around the world. His critics accused him of manufacturing it because of the furor over the firing of Cox, but the information I have gotten from the CIA supports the President in this instance. Unfortunately, it can't be disseminated to the nation.

The Republican Members met in a conference in the Caucus Room of the Cannon Building. Present from the White House were Bryce Harlow, Len Garment, and Professor Wright, the President's lawyer on Watergate. Wright opened the meeting by reviewing the events that had led to the firing of Cox the previous Saturday. He emphasized that all along the President has only wanted to protect the confidentiality of his office and that the Stennis compromise, as it has come to be called, whereby the Senator would serve as an impartial monitor of the tapes, insuring that what was released was the substance of what was on them, was believed to be the answer to a vexing problem. According to Wright, the White House believed, after getting approval from Senator Ervin and Senator Baker, that the proposal would be acceptable to Cox, too. Cox, he said, "wanted total capitulation."

The Cox press conference of Saturday afternoon convinced the President that he had no choice but to fire Cox for his insubordination. In the eyes of the President and his advisers, the American people misunderstood what had happened. The White House believed in the beginning that the compromise was so fair that the people would accept it as the ideal solution. The President, in Wright's view, had to fire Cox, or else he would not have had control of one of his own employees. But he had obviously not foreseen the outburst that such a move would cause. Thus, on Tuesday, the President directed Wright to tell Judge Sirica that the tapes would be given up. The President sacrificed his constitutional conviction because of "the trauma" in the United States on Sunday and Monday.

Bryce Harlow acknowledged pretty much the same thing, again admitting that they had miscalculated but at the same time trying to persuade the Members that the White House position had been the correct one. The questions got rather tough, and the message that they conveyed was that the White House had better see things as they really are. The point was made that if the compromise, or Stennis proposal, had been offered some months ago, all of this might have been avoided.

The House adjourned without business today. There was no business scheduled, but even had there been any, it would have been postponed because of the death yesterday of John Saylor, who died following heart surgery in Houston. Strange to say, I talked last week with Clark Fisher, who has had the same operaton, a cardiac bypass involving the transfer of veins from the legs to the heart in place of clogged arteries. Clark told me that his operation had been a complete success, and that John was down in Houston for the same thing. John could be a bit pompous at times, but he was a decent fellow all the same. I talked with him about two months ago about his future and asked him why in the world he bothered to stay on, taking all of the flak we get, when he had twenty-five years under his belt and a sweet retirement for the asking. He said that he intended to remain until 1976, the 200th birthday of the nation, and then he would call it quits. Now he doesn't even have the memories.

Tuesday, October 30, 1973

W e got to the office shortly after 9:00 this morning, and I spent most of the morning answering mail and clearing my desk of business. Legislation in the House was light, and no business is scheduled on either Thursday or Friday, the first time that has happened for some months.

The principal event of the day was a meeting of Al Quie's committee in the Whip's office off the Floor to discuss further possible changes in the structure of the Leadership. That was also pretty routine, but there was some interesting discussion beforehand. Ed Hutchinson, the ranking Republican on the Judiciary Committee, was present and told us about developments affecting the impeachment activity on his committee. Rodino, the chairman, will issue subpoenas as he sees fit, but will inform Ed when he does. Ed said that he couldn't predict what course the whole thing will take. He told us that the Committee won't get around to Jerry Ford's confirmation hearings until next week, if then. Rodino said that he would wait until next week to decide when they would begin. Meanwhile, the Senate is going forward, and there is some jockeying back and forth as to who should start first. Meanwhile, the country waits for a Vice President.

John Anderson asked me to go on a letter with him and some others to the President urging him to "voluntarily and unilaterally waive any further claims to executive privilege over any Presidential papers sought by the new Special Prosecutor upon conclusive showing by him that they are essential to his investigation." It was a pretty good letter, although it was somewhat argumentative in tone. I agree with the recommendation, but I hesitate to sign it just now. I've gotten about all the publicity that I want or need over Watergate. The mail continues to run against the President, although not as high as it did initially. The ratio is about four to one at the present time.

Coincidentally, our annual questionnaire has gone out, and the answers are starting to come back in. This afternoon Helen came in to cheer me with some complimentary remarks that various constituents had written at the bottom of the returned forms. At the end, she said that there was one more she wanted to read just to keep me from getting a swelled head. It was in reply to the question, "What do you consider the most important issue facing the nation today?" This chap had written, "Dumb Congressmen." I wouldn't entirely disagree.

Wednesday, October 31, 1973—
Monday, November 5, 1973

The House adjourned early Wednesday afternoon, and there was no business today (Monday), so we had an extra long weekend at home. If the House isn't providing any activity, the same cannot be said of the White House. The Watergate business has taken another bizarre turn with the revelation that two of the crucial tapes do not exist. When I heard that, I thought that it might be the last straw, but the nation is still numbed by the previous events, and this just has the people shaking their heads even more. The ground swell of voices calling for the President's resignation continues to grow, with a number of his former supporters in the media now urging him to step down. In spite of that trend, I have found some strong sentiment still remaining in his behalf. Over the weekend, a number of people spontaneously urged me to stick by him. He has broken his word and bungled beyond measure the entire Watergate episode from the beginning, yet there are probably about 30 percent of the people whose loyalty is unshakable. Those who believe that his resignation will put an end to the division in the country have failed to take these people into account. These supporters will charge the President's enemies with having hounded him from office, and they will not be soon mollified.

Jerry's confirmation hearings seem to be moving ahead easily, and I doubt from what I've heard that there will be any serious obstacle thrown in the way. The sooner he's confirmed, the better.

Tuesday, November 13, 1973

On Thursday morning I will join a group of my Republican colleagues at the White House for breakfast to hear the President state his case in the Watergate affair as well as answer questions. He announced over the weekend that he would have all of the Republican Members in this week for that purpose. It was probably done at the insistence of the House Republican Leadership. I will be curious to see what develops from it, although I am not optimistic that it will turn things around for him. There is simply too much skepticism prevalent right now. The confusing and implausible story of the lost tapes and the nonexistent record of the conversation with Dean have cost the President the kind of credibility that cannot be recovered by a breakfast session. I think, however, that the sentiment for impeachment or pressure for resignation is less than it was, and my mail on the subject has just about ended. All in all, we will have sent out over 500 replies to letters and telegrams that we have received on the subject. The final tally is about four to one against the President.

Wednesday, November 14, 1973

This was a busy day and something less than fruitful. I got to the office this morning and promptly received a call from Roy Markon of the Navy Department telling me that my amendment to the Milcon Bill, authorizing $3.4 million for acquiring the leaseholds outside the Naval Station at Norfolk was in dire jeopardy. He read me a portion of the Military Construction Appropriations Subcommittee report, knocking it out of the budget and in strong language denying the validity of the Navy request for the project, and further, ordering the Navy to present arguments justifying it the next time it is brought up, which won't be before next year. Roy suggested that I call Harry Byrd over in the Senate to see if I could get it included in the Senate version and then try to have it saved at the House-Senate conference. It upset and angered me, because I had received assurances from Bob Sikes as late as Wednesday night that he was "looking after me." So I received another lesson up here in the college of hard knocks. I called Harry, and he promised to help. His aide called the Senate counsel for the Appropriations Subcommittee there and was told that it ought to be possible but that no final decision was to be made until next week. In the meantime, I went over to see Bob Sikes, and he had a distinctly apologetic air about him. He told me that he had wanted to help me but the Subcommittee had voted it out. I didn't remind him that I had supported his own projects before my Subcommittee nor press him about "looking after me." That wouldn't be the most effective strategy with the chairman of so powerful a subcommittee. I continued to play the role of supplicant. He assured me that he would support it in conference with the Senate. I thanked him, but felt considerably less gratitude than I had for the same assurance he gave me last week. He advised me to do some "missionary work" among my colleagues, and gave me a list of them, four Democrats and three Republicans.

This afternoon I saw Bob McEwen, one of the Republican Members of the Subcommittee, and he said that he would try to help but that I really ought to lay it on Burt Talcott. I saw Burt later on and reminded him that we had restored a barracks project in California that he wanted. He nodded and then said that he didn't know that this item was in my district, and that arguments had been brought up that the Navy was going to get "snookered" by some of the leaseholders who have long leases binding on the N&W Railroad, who had sold the land to the Navy. I declared this to be false and asked why they hadn't asked me to be a witness if they had any doubts. He asked me to send him some additional supportive information, and he would do what he could at the conference. So tomorrow, before going away on my trip, I've got to see what I can roust up from Admiral Walton in Norfolk and get it out to the Members to try to reverse what is a severe setback to my pet project.

I suppose that some would regard this episode as politics at its worst. Heaven knows, it hasn't given me but so much pleasure to "wheel and deal," and much less when I saw all of my horsetrading go for naught. Maybe it serves me right for being so smug about being able to manage a thing like this so far, but I feel genuinely badly about the leaseholders, who have been hurt by the transfer of the N&W property to the Navy and the consequent fall in real estate values. Several will face bankruptcy if this thing falls through, and the Navy will find itself an unenthusiastic landlord to some taverns, go-go girls, and a couple of porno shops, as well as the clothing merchants and restaurant owners who operate the leaseholds.

Thursday, November 15, 1973

I joined about seventy of my Republican colleagues from the House at a White House breakfast this morning. In talking briefly with the President beforehand, he once again asked me how things were in Norfolk. I told him he had the most remarkable memory of anybody I knew. He said that he could never forget the great receptions he's had there.

The President's preliminary remarks touched on the Middle East and on the energy problem. He said he felt that the foundation had been laid for permanent peace but that much remained to be done. On the energy question he was insistent that the United States be independent of any foreign government for oil and that by 1980 we be self-sufficient in energy. He was convinced that this could be done.

Despite these successes, he saw that Watergate has cast a shadow over all of it. "If I could not stand before my colleagues in the House and Senate knowing in the end that the Presidency will come through with integrity and unblemished, I would not invite you here this morning." He then went on to say that he would answer any questions on Watergate, ITT, the milk business, or anything else.

Louis Wyman raised the first question, asking the President if he had made a decision on a format for answering questions. The President replied that he hadn't quite decided yet on a specific plan, but these were some possibilities: going to Congress to speak, going before the Ervin Committee to answer questions, or perhaps a press conference. He said he wanted to reach the largest possible audience. He wanted to get all the facts out, and particularly through the medium of television so that as many people as possible would have a chance to hear him. He doubted the wisdom of a formal appearance before the Ervin Committee, so it is still unresolved who the questioners would be and where the questioning would occur.

Frank Horton then raised the question of the Agnew case, where the Vice President had professed his innocence and indicated that he would fight, only to end up capitulating by pleading no contest in federal court to the charge of income tax evasion. Frank asked the President if in spite of his continuous statements that he would not resign he might do the same thing. The President then reviewed his own relationship to the Agnew case, which he called "a tragedy." He said that we ought to have compassion and that he "would not pour any coals on Agnew's head." He added that he had just sent a handwritten note to Judy Agnew to express his condolences on the loss of her mother, and he said that if anybody says anything, "I'll say to hell with them."

He then went into a detailed explanation of the tapes. It was rather hard to follow because of the dates involved, but he emphasized that what he had said on May 22 and August 15 was still true, that he didn't know about Watergate, did not offer clemency, and did not know of the payment of hush money until March 21, when he started his own investigation. He said the tapes that are available would bear him out.

He also denied the contentions of his critics in the ITT case. He said that he felt then and feels now that no U.S. company can compete with all the other foreign industries. He does not oppose big companies abroad, and the rules are going to have to be changed in order to ensure their ability to compete overseas. At a Cabinet meeting, he declared that he would not attack a company just because it was big. On that basis, when the anti-trust division of the Justice Department lost its case, he ordered Kleindienst not to appeal it. Following this, John Mitchell told him that the appeal was already prepared, and the President then said that it could go forward. The government won its appeal, and following that the settlement was agreed upon. He said that his role in the case had absolutely nothing to do with contributions, and he repeated that we would not impair companies that compete abroad.

He went on to the milk fund and declared that the pressure on the Administration to increase parity came from Wilbur Mills and Carl Albert, both of whom urged the Administration to increase the support.

He then got into his own personal worth and the questions raised about his personal accumulation of wealth. The President told us that when he left office in 1961 his net worth was $47,000, and yet he has suffered attacks over the years that he has made money in office. He asked us to bear in mind that prior to 1961 he had served four years in the House, two years in the Senate, and then eight years as Vice President, and yet when he left Washington the $47,000 was all that he had amassed. At the present time his principal assets are in his properties at San Clemente and Key Biscayne. What people forget is that he had eight years of practicing law, from which he received a substantial income, and he also had written a book. He sold an apartment for $327,000, stock for $300,000, and a lot for $200,000, and those proceeds went to pay for his property.

As regards his avoidance of taxes, he said that LBJ had told him about being able to get tax credit for giving his personal papers to the government, so he donated his vice presidential papers for this purpose. He added that in 1970 the IRS made a full field audit and made no change in his tax return.

And to answer Frank's question, he said, "There is no other shoe to drop." He said that he has the facts, and he won't step aside. He was elected to do a job, and he feels that he is doing it well. He added that he had acquired a lot of knowledge about world leaders. He feels he knows how to deal with Brezhnev, Mao Tse-tung, and Chou En-lai, and then these words: "I am not going to walk away from this job. If shoes fall, I'll be ready to catch them."

Orval Hansen raised the point of impeachment, saying he questioned whether or not we should pursue that direction in order to get the air cleared. The President replied that the last seven months have been "straight, pure hell" and mentioned the various foreign and domestic problems which he had been trying to deal with in the face of the Watergate controversy. He said that impeachment proceedings could be dragged out over a long period of time and would have the most harmful effects abroad. The constant attention would weaken his credibility with people like Mao and Golda Meir, both of whom still have confidence in him.

He said that if the United States was lifted out of the world, the rest of the world would be living "in complete terror." He reviewed our role in saving Israel in the recent conflict. He pointed out that the United States plays a key role as a counter-balance between China and the USSR, helping to preserve the peace. An impeachment would therefore create "an impossible situation." If the President were weakened, miscalculation could result and the peace of the world be threatened.

He then talked about the appointment of Jaworski as the successor to Cox. He said that he had never met Jaworski, but believes that he has good credentials as an independent investigator. The man is a lifelong Democrat, was a close adviser to LBJ, and supported McGovern in Texas, although not too enthusiastically. The President said that in hiring Jaworski it was agreed that he could not be removed without the consent of key Members of Congress, including the Speaker, Tip O'Neill, and Rodino in the House, and Mansfield and the Majority Whip in the Senate. It was therefore clear that Jaworski would be protected, and the President concluded rather succinctly, "Let's get on and stop screwing around."

As a postscript he noted that Petersen had told him in April that the case was 90 percent ready to go to the grand jury, but Cox kept delaying, and he made this comment, that he wants the case wrapped up, while his opponents "don't want a decision, they want an issue."

Bill Harsha raised the key question of why it took so long to disclose about the missing tapes. The President answered simply that they didn't find out because they weren't looking for them. He recalled that his first decision was not to hand them over to the courts in order to protect the confidentiality of the Presidency. By the end of September he knew he had to find a solution for the courts, for which the Stennis proposal seemed to be the answer. The President then said to get the tapes in, and the search turned up seven of them. There was no tape of the April 15 discussion with Dean or of the alleged key phone conversation with Mitchell.

The President told us he listened to the tapes of September and December, which he says will clear him. Not until October 27 did he learn from Buzhardt that the April 15 tape was missing because of technical reasons, and he explained why. April 15 was a Sunday. On Friday the Secret Service filled the tape machine for six hours to cover the weekend. On Saturday he had a four-hour conference with Dr. Kissinger and on Sunday another long conversation with Kleindienst. The simple fact is that the tapes ran out. By Sunday night, when he talked to Dean, the box was full. He said that he has notes of his conversation with Dean which clear him. He added that on Monday he had another conversation with Dean, which is on tape, in which reference was made to the Sunday conversation but nothing that would confirm that what Dean said happened actually had.

He also mentioned the "plumbers," and noted that LBJ had everything wired when he came to the White House. Kennedy also had conversations recorded. But when Nixon took office he had all of that pulled out, and there are no tape recordings for his first two years. His aides persuaded him to start recording for historical purposes. He told us that the FBI under Kennedy and Johnson did wiretaps on the press and others, all done for national security, and he defended his own "plumbers" saying that they had found a leak of high national interest and that Senator Ervin agreed it could not be disclosed.

He said that in the climate that existed during the war in the late '60s and early '70s there were so many leaks of sensitive information that it was necessary to employ this kind of surveillance for national security. It is no longer being done now.

Finally, he promised more meetings with Members, specifically breakfast meetings of this type, as a means of having better communication between Members of Congress and the White House.

Personally, the President was sure of himself, forceful, and in a tough mood. He manifested complete self-confidence and received applause numerous times. On one occasion I saw one of his toughest critics, Pete McCloskey, clapping his hands.

Thursday, November 15, 1973—
Saturday, November 24, 1973

Janie and I drove to the apartment at about 6:30, and I packed a suitcase for the trip to the Middle East. The military liaison people had arranged for a car and driver to come to the apartment at 9:00 to take me to Andrews Air Force Base. There were twenty-one of us from the Committee, plus Sid Yates from the Appropriations Committee, who went as far as Israel with us.

Friday morning we touched down to refuel at Torrejon, outside of Madrid. Then it was on to Athens, where we arrived after dark. Dinner was arranged on the top of the King George V Hotel, but I was so weary from jet lag that I did not appreciate the dishes and left the table early to return to my room at the Hotel Amalia.

What was intended to be a two-night rest stop in Athens turned into an abbreviated stay, punctuated by student disorders which prompted a call-out of security and Army forces and a declaration of martial law the day we arrived. We noticed the beginning of trouble on Friday night when groups of students ran past the Parliament building near our hotel.

Early on Saturday morning I heard shooting and the heavy rumble of tank engines in the streets. Yet the next morning the streets were thronged with people and traffic was as clogged as ever. It appeared that the disturbances had been quelled, although we saw evidence of rioting some blocks away when we drove out to the U.S. Navy's new port facilities to the west of Athens. Broken glass littered the streets.

I had the feeling that we might be leaving Athens sooner than scheduled, and I was not mistaken. We were advised that we would be leaving for the airport about 3:30 Saturday afternoon. Martial law had been declared and a curfew set for 4:00. Ostensibly, the trouble began in the universities, where the students rebelled against the archaic operation of the schools and the rigid curriculum and discipline imposed by university officials. But underlying and complementing it was anger and frustration directed at the Papadopoulos government. The students were joined by groups of workers, and banners were carried denouncing the U.S. military presence and NATO. The unrest appeared to be fairly narrow, but the government obviously wasn't going to give it a chance to grow, so it struck hard and fast.

We departed Athens about 4:00 and flew on to Tel Aviv, arriving there after dark. The Israelis had a bus to take us from Lod Airport to the Hilton in Tel Aviv. The entire thirteenth floor of the hotel was assigned to us, not so much for luxury as for security purposes. Armed guards remained outside the elevators on a twenty-four hour basis.

On Sunday morning we went to the U.S. Embassy to get a briefing from Ambassador Keating and some members of his staff. Ken Keating could pass for a U.S. Senator and an ambassador, both of which he has been. He appears to be in his late sixties and has a stately mane of white hair, which ennobles his appearance. His blue eyes are lively, and he gestures and laughs easily. Physically, he fits his role perfectly, and in our brief encounter I found him articulate and knowledgeable.

He told us that he found his tenure in Israel more pleasant than India, where he had to deal with Indira Gandhi. Golda Meir, he said with a chuckle, appreciated him far more. He told us that the mood in Israel is one of deep gratitude for American military aid, and that he had received many spontaneous expressions of friendship from ordinary citizens as well as the prime minister. In spite of this, he told us that the Israelis are nervous. The visits of Dr. Kissinger in the Arab countries disturb them, as does the U.S. detente with the USSR. While there are mixed feelings, the prevailing view in the country is for a firm and lasting peace settlement. The militant minority are disappointed that the Egyptian Third Army was not destroyed. They want to give the Arabs a "real drubbing," he said, but he emphasized that they are a minority.

The Ambassador gave an assessment of the Arabs. He felt that the Egyptians had suffered "a pretty bad defeat" with the encirclement of the Third Army, but their papers have withheld the extent of this from their people. He pointed out that they would not permit their prisoners to be brought back in one group, preferring instead for them to be flown back in bunches so that their numbers would not create such an impact. Over 8,000 were held by the Israelis as against less than 300 Israeli POWs held by the Egyptians. And while the Egyptians treated the Israeli POWs fairly, there are disturbing reports of the shooting of Israeli prisoners by the Syrians. The same emotional scenes of returning POWs that we experienced early this year when our men came back from North Vietnam have been repeated in Israel. Every day the *Jerusalem Post* had accounts similar to our own homecomings.

Keating talked about the day the war began, Yom Kippur, October 6. To many Jews it was a blasphemy that the attack should be launched on the high holy day of Judaism. But it turned out to be a blessing in disguise, because everyone was either at home or at the synagogue that morning. The rabbis announced at the services that reservists should report to their units, and those at home were reached by phone. Since 90 percent of the Israeli Army is composed of reserves, including all of the enlisted personnel, mobilization is a critical factor in the nation's defense. As Colonel Karni, the Israeli intelligence officer assigned to us, said, "The Israeli Army is one that does one month of active duty and is on eleven months leave."

On Sunday afternoon we drove out to Moshe Dayan's home in a suburb of Tel Aviv for a purely social gathering. It was the prelude to a long session that evening at a VIP headquarters with the Israeli military leaders. I had heard about Dayan's home from news accounts, and particularly the garden filled with archaeological finds of which Dayan is so proud, and which occupies his free time.

The home was on a shady street, set back behind a low wall. Only the presence of soldiers and a sandbagged post beside the front gate distinguished the house from others in the neighborhood. We filed through the front hall, the fairly spacious living and dining rooms, to the stone terrace and yard at the back of the house. Mrs. Dayan stood at the head of a receiving line and her famous husband at the end. She is a handsome blond woman, with an easy grace. I did not have a chance to exchange more than a few words with her, in view of the size of the crowd, but a trace of her charm was enough.

The Minister of Defense was shorter than I expected, not an unnatural reaction since we tend to mentally match the size of military heroes with their reputations. Dayan wore his trademark, the black patch over his missing left eye. Otherwise, he was dressed in slacks and sports jacket, and his hands were those of a farmer, rough and gnarled. While he was at ease among his throng of visitors, congressmen, his own generals and officials, plus a gaggle of newsmen with television cameras, he would not allow himself to be boxed in and kept roving around his garden, letting his guests tag along behind him. Then he would pause in front of one of his archaeological treasures, discuss its significance with whoever cared to listen, and then wander off again when the crowd became too dense. In time the majority wearied of monument-hopping and began to turn their attention to the other Israelis present, in particular Generals Yariv and Elazar, the former special assistant to the chief of staff and the latter the chief of the general staff himself. I spoke to Yariv, reminding him that we had met in 1970 when I last visited Israel. Now he is in the limelight as the Israeli representative in the talks at Kilometer 101 with Egyptian representatives, endeavoring to resolve the ceasefire agreement and set the stage for a peace conference.

Early in the evening we left General Dayan's reception for a four-hour session with the chief Israeli military leaders at their headquarters. There was heavy security around it, and indeed the bus was barely able to squeeze through the gates.

The first speaker was Major General Eliahu Zeira, director of military intelligence. He spoke of Egypt and Syria as "Russian satellites, with all of the privileges but no obligations." He said they received more military assistance than North Vietnam had in the long war with the United States, and better quality aid to boot. In this regard, he mentioned the SAM-6 and SAM-3. Furthermore, he stated that the Russians indoctrinated the Syrians and Egyptians thoroughly. Soviet military literature in copious quantities was found. Over 1,000 Russian advisors were present in Egypt before the war, and more than 2,000 in Syria. He claimed that in return the Russians were permitted to station bombers in these countries, armed with missiles that could home in on U.S. aircraft carriers. In addition, Soviet intelligence-gathering aircraft operated from Syrian and Egyptian fields.

General Zeira contended that the Russians played a significant part in planning the Egyptian and Syrian campaign, all the way down to the brigade level. They provided advisers in engineering and mine fields, even handwriting instructions, which were captured by the Israelis.

According to Zeira, Russian officers held key positions at the SAM-3 and SAM-6 batteries, as well as the control centers of the enemy air forces, advising when planes should be sent up or missiles fired.

During the recent war, Arab plane losses were all replaced, and

General Zeira said that Russian test pilots flew with them to forward zones in Syria where Syrian pilots got them in flying condition. I might add that the U.S. did the same thing for the Israelis.

General Yariv spoke next and talked about the ceasefire arrangement arranged by Dr. Kissinger. He described it as one that was "wide enough for agreement and unclear enough for both sides to interpret as they see fit." Unlike other agreements, this one was "signed first by each side and then discussed afterward."

General Yariv manifested some concern about the POWs. They thought that about 400 were prisoners, but Egypt claims only 238. This disturbs the Israelis, because some of those missing appeared on the Cairo radio and were seen in the camps. Where they are is a mystery, and it is suspected that they have been killed. He repeated the story about the return in stages of the Egyptian prisoners that we had heard at the U.S. Embassy.

General Elazar followed General Yariv and described the war itself. He classified it as the most difficult of all of Israel's wars, even though from a military point of view he felt it was a success. The principal difficulty had been Israel's state of preparedness. They had begun the war without 75 percent of their forces on duty. He declared that at 4:00 a.m. on Saturday, October 6, he received word that Egypt and Syria would attack at 6:00 p.m. on that day. The actual attack came at about 2:00 p.m. General Elazar wanted to make a preemptive strike with his Air Force. Such a move would have spared them substantial losses and disrupted their enemies, but he was overruled by the government.

He said that when hostilities began they were outnumbered nine to one, and even when the Israelis were on the offensive with their forces mobilized, the odds against them were four and three to one. He added that when the Israelis began their offensive, the enemy began to behave more like they did in 1967. The Arabs, he declared, react poorly to new situations. When the war began, the Arabs used Soviet tactics and made a creditable showing, but they are slow to exploit a new situation and are not innovative.

General Peled of their Air Force filled us in on the vaunted SAM-6. He said that it did not stop the Israeli Air Force, but it did create a problem that could not be countered sufficiently. What carried the day, he reflected, was "sheer guts." Unfortunately, an entire SAM-6 complex was not captured. Orders had been given by the Russians to move them quickly if there was a risk of capture. So only part of a missile was taken.

General Peled was unimpressed by the helicopter as a battle weapon. On the occasions when it was used for daylight attack, it was easily shot down. But at night, below an altitude of fifty feet it could do a job. Otherwise, he said, it doesn't have, "as you say, 'a snowball's chance in hell.'" For him, a stand-off weapon with a range of forty miles would be an optimum weapon to deal with the anti-air missiles.

The cost of the war to Israel was one-third of her pilots and over a hundred planes, but by the end of the war the Israelis had driven the Syrian and Egyptian air forces to cover. He confirmed the presence of North Korean and Pakistani aviators flying Syrian jets, but said they avoided a fight.

They have developed their own concept of a navy, preferring small but modern boats developed in Israel. They have their own surface-to-surface missile, the Gabriel. Although this missile has a shorter range than the Russian Styx missile, it is more accurate. The Israelis used it with devastating effectiveness against the Syrians and Egyptians. In fact, they shut them out, sinking five Syrian boats off Latakia and losing none of their own, and sinking three Egyptian boats, also without loss to themselves. Most of the engagements were fought at night. Their tactic was to permit the enemy to fire his missiles first from a long range outside their own, then, by electronic countermeasures and evasive tactics they avoided being hit. Once the enemy had expended his missiles, they closed fast and fired their own.

Toward the end of the war the Syrians and Egyptians stayed in port and would not come out. They not only kept their own coast clear, they bottled up the enemy's and pinned down two Syrian brigades on the Syrian coast. There were 200 sailings to and from Israel during the war, all unhindered. Soviet ships, of course, were able to enter and leave Arab ports.

In summary, they told us that they were enormously impressed by our airlift and marveled at the C-5A. The plane has come out of the doghouse where critics like Senator Proxmire put it several years ago. I would not be surprised to see the Russians develop a similar aircraft. They *always* learn from *us*. They practically pleaded for additional arms, citing the need for more tanks. They mentioned the 200 we have promised them but declared that 800 more M-60s were vital. They mentioned more Phantoms, few of which were lost to SAM-6s, and Skyhawks, and they added another word about stand-off weapons. Acknowledging that there is an availability problem for us, they emphasized that they are hard-pressed, especially in view of the Russian build-up on the other side.

Early on Monday morning we flew by helicopter to the Sinai. Much of it is flat, with scrub vegetation, but there are also extensive dunes. The arid picture from the helicopter was relieved only by low mountains which erupted from the desert itself. That two nations should shed so much blood and treasure over such a barren piece of real estate is almost incomprehensible. We flew directly to Israeli headquarters on the west bank of the Suez, and there we received a briefing by General Miron, a short, jaunty, armored-unit type, complete with a black beret. He reviewed the counterattack north of the Great Bitter Lake across the Suez Canal, the fanning out of the Israeli armored columns and their subsequent penetration to Suez City and the cutting off of the Egyptian Third Army on the east bank.

We then began a drive which took us to the UN checkpoint in Suez and a tour of the city, much of which was destroyed or heavily damaged by the fighting. The refinery, which had produced oil for Egypt, was silent, although the damage to it appeared to be superficial. This was followed by a drive to the meeting place of Egyptian and Israeli military representatives at Kilometer 101, its only landmarks a few tents and UN personnel on duty.

From there we traveled to an Egyptian strong point on the west bank which had been captured when the Israelis crosssed the Canal. Evidence of fierce fighting was all around us—burned out tanks and trucks and the refuse of armies that is the flotsam of war. The crash of shellfire had shattered many trees, and the scene was not unlike the photographs taken of broken French forests after the artillery barrages of the First World War.

On the crest of one of the captured Egyptian redoubts flew the Star of David, while beyond the Canal on the east bank stretched the scorched and twisted tanks of a fierce battle fought less than six weeks before. The Israeli soldiers showed only mild interest in us, reflecting the boredom of inaction that is the hallmark of soldiers on duty in an outpost from time immemorial.

From here we drove back to an encampment for a mid-afternoon lunch with Generals Dayan and Yariv. Dayan repeated what came to be a refrain from all of the Israeli officials we talked to. He called for a pull-back by both sides from the Canal so that it could be opened. From this first step a final settlement could be worked out. Dayan declared that Israel wanted a peace settlement and, while admitting that Egypt had rejected the Israeli formula, he said that he did not regard it as a final word. "We shall not make any arrangement that would result in an attack on our forces," he said. "As a soldier, I like our position much better. If it's going to be war, let's have it on their soil."

When Yariv spoke, he noted that the talks are currently on the military level only, and not on a political one. Personally, he said that he sympathized with Sadat, since he had a volatile population at home and unstable allies abroad.

On Tuesday morning, our last day in Israel, we began by driving to an Israeli military base to view a display of captured Soviet and Warsaw Pact equipment. One entire yard was filled with tanks, trucks, bridging vehicles, armored personnel carriers, artillery, and a wide assortment of anti-tank and small arms weapons. All of it was sturdy and durable. It drove home the Russian penchant for developing a relatively unsophisticated weapon to do a job and then mass-producing it like Ford automobiles.

From this event, our bus took us to Jerusalem for a meeting with Israeli economic and political officials, including the Prime Minister, followed by lunch at the Knesset (Parliament) with some of their members. On the way there, several of us engaged in conversation with Colonel Karni, the Israeli intelligence officer who was our escort throughout our stay in Israel. He was a remarkable host, well-informed and with a fund of anecdotes and stories, perfect for a group of this kind, dispensing information when necessary, giving guidance where asked, and willing to make small talk as the occasion arose. I noticed when I first met him that his right arm was missing. Its place was taken by an artificial hand encased in a leather glove. Subsequently I learned that he had lost the arm from a burst of Arab machine-gun fire in the war for independence in 1948.

Colonel Karni told the most amusing story I heard on the trip. He said that he had captured the same Egyptian officer three times, in 1948, in 1956, and again in 1967. The first time, both of them were company commanders with the rank of captain. In 1956, the second time the Egyptian was taken prisoner, Karni saw him and they recognized each other. By this time, both were lieutenant colonels. Colonel Karni said that he took a liking to the man and treated him as a guest, taking him to his mother's home for dinner and also to his own home, where he introduced him to his family. In 1967, the Egyptian, now a brigadier general, was captured again, and Colonel Karni renewed the friendship once more. The Egyptian wanted to know why Karni had not kept pace in rank with him, and Karni told him that he didn't know, that maybe the Egyptian should speak to his superior. But the funniest thing was when Karni took the man back to his home. "I have a daughter named Yasmin," he said. "She was eleven years old when I brought the Egyptian officer to my home in 1956, and when he came back in 1967 she remembered him. She asked me, 'Why doesn't he come more often?' and I told her, 'He comes often enough.'" Then he added, "I've been looking for him this time."

As we drove north to Jerusalem, Colonel Karni talked about the war of independence and how close they had come to extinction. Then there were only 640,000 Jews, and the Arabs nearly defeated them. His company had both men and women in it, and his casualties ran to 50 percent, including two women killed. Subsequent to the war he took an M.A. at Columbia University, but his career has been in the army.

In Jerusalem we met with the director general of the Ministry of Finance. He impressed upon us the heavy financial burden that the war had imposed upon his country and the high cost of defense in general. For example, the nation imported $712 million in arms in 1972. The figure rose to $1.8 billion in 1973, and that amount is eleven times more than was spent in 1966. Turned another way, he said that 12 percent of their total imports were arms in 1966 and 30 percent in 1973. On the scale of Israel's GNP, in 1966 they spent 11 percent for defense, in 1972 25 percent, and in 1973 the amount will be 40 percent. "In your country," he said, "that would amount to $450 billion." The defense budget in the United States this year is $80 billion. $450 billion would be a Pentagon pipe-dream.

The impact of this terrific burden on the individual Israeli is almost mind-boggling. A man who earns $500 a month pays $200 in taxes to the central government. Property and other local taxes are on top of that. Anyone earning $1,000 a month takes home $450, and one earning $2,000 nets $600.

The Director General told us that he grosses $650 a month and pays $350 in taxes to the state. A fraction of it is in a compulsory war loan which pays 3 percent interest. His extras as a high government official include a car and a telephone. Compared to a United States Congressman, he's on welfare. He jokingly said that he brings honor home while his wife brings home the salary. She works, too.

The meeting with Prime Minister Golda Meir was lively. She looked as I remembered her from 1970, a short little woman, carrying too much weight, but with her energy and sparkle seemingly undiminished. She continued to smoke constantly from a package of Chesterfields, her fingers perpetually nicotine-stained.

She began by saying, "The relationship with the U.S. is the greatest we've ever had. We are always conscious of what American friendship means to us." She then commented on our visit and said that while it was good that we could talk to the leaders, she hoped that we would have a chance to see the people. "The source of Israel's strength is in the people," she declared.

Sam Stratton asked her what her reaction was to Dr. Kissinger's suggestion that there might have to be an American guarantee of Israel's security. She said that when anyone says that Israel must have a guarantee, they are implying that Israel's borders are not defensible, and they are right. She said that for a guarantee to mean anything, soldiers must be stationed on the frontiers to hold them. "Who will do this? We've never asked for soldiers in the past. It is our fate. We have to do it." And then she added, "The greatest tragedy would be if the time came when we were attacked and could not defend ourselves." She cited the Golan Heights, which were supposed to have been demilitarized before. "The President of Syria must learn a lesson," she said.

Agreements by themselves mean little, she added, and she noted that King Abdullah had signed a peace treaty with Israel in 1948 only to be assassinated later. The same thing could happen again, so although Israel wants to sign as firm a peace agreement as possible, she wants defensible frontiers to go along with it.

Mention was then made of the Arab oil embargo to the West. She told us that she had talked to the presidents and prime ministers of most of the European countries and knows that they are in a tough situation. But the Dutch prime minister told her that his people would not give up Israel for this. She said that she warned the European leaders that this was only the first step by the Arabs, that they would end up not only dictating to the Europeans on their relationship with Israel, but also with each other. And then she uttered these words: "With blackmail you only know where you begin, not where you end."

In discussing the truce lines, she repeated what Dayan had said, that for the truce to be effective, the Egyptians and Israelis ought to return to the pre-October 6 line. From this they could retire for a dozen kilometers and create a buffer zone. Then the Canal could be reopened. As things stand now, there are too many risks of incidents. She defended the decision not to order a preemptive strike on the morning of October 6. To have done that would have cost Israel her friendships in the West, and this she couldn't risk. She admitted that an investigation was going to be made into the war and the failures that had occurred.

She concluded by reviewing the defensible areas that Israel insists upon as conditions for a final peace, including control of all of Jerusalem. It was identical with what she had said in 1970. On this there appears to be unanimity among all Israeli leaders.

After a quick side trip to Bethlehem, we drove back to Tel Aviv and a buffet dinner at Ambassador Keating's residence. There I renewed an acquaintance with a member of the Knesset, whom I had met on my last visit. None of us lingered after supper, knowing that we had to be up early on Wednesday to go to Egypt.

The weather in Egypt was cool, much to my surprise, because in the Sinai we had found it rather warm. Our Ambassador-designate, Hermann Eilts, greeted us and then spoke of the situation as he saw it. He said that although the Egyptians have agreed in principle to exchange ambassadors, they are delaying until the peace shows some substance. In particular, they are looking for the United States to put pressure on Israel to withdraw from Arab lands. To take such a step now would risk an adverse impact on the other Arab states as well as the Egyptian people.

Eilts told us, however, that he had been received by the Egyptian foreign minister three hours after arriving in Cairo. Such courtesy is most unusual and indicated that the Egyptians are very serious about doing business with us.

He went on to say that the Egyptians are torn by conflicting emotions. First, they feel much pride. After years of a lot of talk and no action, they went to war and believe that they made a good showing. This they could not do before from a position which they regarded as abject surrender. Second, they feel that now that they have shown Israel that they can fight, the Israelis ought to realize that peace is in their best interest. The fact that the Israelis have not moved more quickly puzzles them. Third, a sense of Arab unity is prevalent. Eilts doubted that it is as real as the press makes it out to be, but the oil embargo has proved to the Arabs that they have found an effective weapon on which they can unite. For his part, Eilts believes that the Arabs are overplaying their hand with the oil embargo, and that if they carry it too far, it will provoke a backlash in the West which could be counterproductive. He urged us to impress this fact upon our Egyptian hosts, because he doesn't feel that they are getting the message from him.

The Ambassador-designate continued his statement by saying that he felt that the Egyptians themselves honestly want to improve their relations with the United States and don't want to become dependent solely upon the Soviets. They remember with a certain nostalgia their long period of friendship with the United States.

Feeling that the right is on their side, they bitterly resent American aid to Israel, a fact which was made all too clear to us by the Egyptians themselves in the ensuing two days. Eilts said that their willingness to receive us reflects an attempt to come to terms with us. At first they decided to receive us just through the People's Assembly and then through the Ministry of Defense. This, he felt, was a broadening of thinking.

In conclusion, he cautioned us against mentioning to our hosts the visit we had made to the west bank of the Suez Canal. There was some resentment about this. Second, he advised us not to inquire about Egyptian losses, since this might be looked upon as an attempt to elicit information of use to the Israelis. On this note we departed somewhat uncertainly for the People's Assembly to meet and talk with the Speaker of that body and some of his associates. It was clear that we had considerable inhibition and none of the sense of ease that we had felt among the Israelis. In time, these inhibitions diminished somewhat, although to the end there was still a sense of being "on the other side."

The People's Assembly Building to which we went was not particularly distinguished in its architecture. We met in a high-ceilinged room adorned by portraits of Nasser and Sadat at one end. The usual rectangle of tables was set up, and we faced our Egyptian hosts around it. Soft drinks were served, and this custom followed us at every meeting we had with Egyptian officials. The choice was orangeade or limeade in most cases. Sometimes hot, sweet Arab tea, served in glasses, was substituted.

The Speaker, Hafez Badawi, made a toast, declaring that, "Whoever drinks from the Nile should come back to drink from it again." We returned his courtesy, and Sam Stratton thanked him for the hospitality which we had received.

Following this our Egyptian host came to what was really on his mind. He said that Egyptians were peace-loving and wanted to live in peace, that they wanted peace in order to develop and build their nation. "Peace," he said, "brings a happy life." He recalled the 7,000-year history of his country, which he said was a history of peace. "We are not aggressors and want only to build a better world." And then he added, "The peace we are asking for should be based on truth and a fair peace. We want peace, but we will not surrender. . . . The UN Charter states that it is illegal to occupy land by force. We are always willing to accept UN resolutions, but Israel is not."

He went on in this vein for a while and then turned the theme toward us. "The Egyptian people have always been friendly to the American people, and some at this table have studied at American universities. We want to establish a closer relationship with the American people, but unfortunately this is not possible. The American government has taken a stand in favor of our enemy. This is not fair, and you know it. I need not tell you the facts that you know, but will repeat them. Israel has occupied our land, she has destroyed schools and mosques and killed our children—all with U.S. weapons! This is hard for us to understand, because we have never provided weapons to hurt the American people. We know who is supporting Israel, as does every man in the street. He knows that our people are being killed by American weapons. We want to be friendly. Why aren't you giving us the chance?"

Badawi repeated over and over that all they wanted was the return of their own land. "Tomorrow," he said, "you will meet with our President, Anwar Sadat, and he has the full support of all our people and you will hear the voice of all our people. When you visit the front, you will meet the Egyptian soldier and you will see his sincerity and his desire to get his own land back."

Sam replied, thanking him for his candor, and told him that he was glad that he spoke from his heart. Sam noted that this was a historic occasion; it had been over six years since a congressional delegation had visited Egypt. He added that is was important for representatives of both our people to meet.

Sam acknowledged that we have supported Israel, but the basis for that support is the belief by the American people that peace is best maintained by a balance of military strength. Then he said that it didn't help much to review the past. We preferred to look ahead to the future, and that was the reason that we support Dr. Kissinger's efforts. "The conflict," he said, "is a source of tragedy on both sides, but it has opened up an opportunity for a breakthrough that has not occurred before." Sam concluded by telling our hosts that our chairman, Mr. Hébert, had appointed this committee to come here and follow an even-handed policy by talking to both sides. We would not talk to the press but would return and deliberate to see what is the best way to reach a peaceful solution.

The Speaker would not be put off. Apparently he sensed some sensitivity on our part, because he bored in. "What have we done that the American people would send money to a government that hurts us? Have we ever done this to you?" He said that the papers had a report that a group of American congressmen went to Israel to ask, "What do you need?" Sam hastily replied that none of our party had said such a thing. John Ford whispered to me that it was probably Bella Abzug and Ed Koch, who were in Israel at the same time that we were. I remembered that Bella wanted to fly down to the Sinai with us, but Sam turned her down, saying that the Chairman hadn't authorized her.

The Speaker continued, "We like you, and you are advanced. We want to cooperate, but on a basis of mutual understanding and respect. This is what we feel deep in our hearts. While you are settling items in your budget, settling the war will be done by preventing the aggressors from keeping up their aggression."

From there we drove to the Tahrir Club for a dinner with various members of the People's Assembly, hosted by Speaker Badawi. Lucien Nedzi, Bob Daniel, and I sat at a table with about six Egyptians. All spoke excellent English, and their conversation was practically a repetition of the Speaker's earlier. They asked us how we could support a country that was on their soil. "We want our land back," they chorused. I ventured to give them the benefit of Golda Meir's thinking, and they fell silent when I told them that we had talked to her the day before. But they were unimpressed by her arguments. The only question that bothered them was when I mentioned the erratic Libyan leader, Qaddafi. "You declare that you are willing to live side by side with Israel, yet Colonel Qaddafi announced this week that Israel must be destroyed. Who does he speak for?" I asked. They looked at each other and one said softly, "There are many voices in the Arab world. Qaddafi speaks for only a few." I smiled and nodded. At least there was one point of agreement.

On Thursday morning, November 22, we drove out to the summer residence of President Anwar Sadat in the suburbs of Cairo. Sadat's residence is a sand-colored building set amid grounds of trees and shrubs. The structure looked to be exactly what it was, an official residence, built in the Arab style with pointed arches and grillwork. A crenellated tower adorned one corner. The entire compound was surrounded by a fence and high hedge, which gave both privacy and a certain amount of security.

We were ushered into a large room, red-carpeted, with white columns between French windows. A picture of Sadat was hung over the door at one end. The scene reminded me a little of the room in which we had met President Thieu in the Presidential Palace in Saigon in June 1970.

The usual soft drinks were served, and after about five minutes Sadat strode into the room. He stands about six feet tall and was dressed in a well-tailored khaki tunic. He shook hands firmly, gazing each person steadily in the eye, and then moved on. A faint trace of sweet cologne followed him. Clutched in his left hand was a gnarled walking or swagger stick. It seemed to be too short for the one purpose and too long for the other.

Once seated, Sadat took out a pipe, which he lit and allowed to go out periodically. He said that he had no opening statement, but preferred for us to begin with our questions. He projected a strong will and the mood of one who is used to being in charge. His pictures do not project the strength of his predecessor, Nasser, but in person he exudes self-confidence and authority.

Sam began by defining our mission as he had done the evening before. "We hope we can find a formula for the future," he said.

"Let us hope," replied Sadat. Sam then said that there was a feeling in the United States that the Arabs wanted to eliminate Israel and asked what the position of the UAR was in this regard. Sadat, whose English is excellent, replied that he had made a peace initiative in February 1971, and said at that time he was willing to conclude a treaty with Israel. He said it was the first by any Arab leader in twenty-two years. He called then, as now, for the implementation of Resolution 242 of the UN. I remembered that the people at our table the night before had cited the same resolution. When Secretary of State Rogers was in Cairo later, Sadat asked him what else he should do, and he said that Rogers told him nothing. He waited then in vain for Israel to act. At this point, his voice grew louder, and he said, "We will not cede an inch of our land. Let Israel withdraw and we will sit down to peace."

Like his Speaker of the People's Assembly, he took us to task for backing Israel while she occupied Egyptian land, and then he made a statement which surprised me. He said, "You cannot compare the arms that the U.S. gave Israel with what the Soviets gave the Arabs." Remembering the effectiveness of the SAM-6, I was skeptical of this remark.

He went on to tell us that the Soviets did not dominate his country, and he reminded us that he had expelled them at one time because he disagreed with them.

"Nothing stands between the U.S. and Egypt but Israel," he declared. "When the U.S. always says that it will maintain a balance of power, we see it as a move to give Israel a dominant position among the Arabs. We ask to be friends with America. We need friendship with everyone.

"Where are your interests here? You want guarantees of Israeli land, but we ask you not to back the acquisition of others' land by force. Give them a tank and a plane for every Israeli, but not to occupy our country." He seemed to be speaking in slogans, but it was forceful, and he occasionally emphasized his point by striking the table with his hand, his voice rising as he did so.

Sadat categorically denied Israel's contention that she wanted only land for her security, and he suddenly betrayed a hatred which was reminiscent of Nazi Germany forty years ago. He spoke of how the Jews controlled Egypt before 1952. "Everything was in their hands," he exclaimed. "They are trying to tell you that they need security, but it is we who need security."

Someone raised the question of the Palestinians. On this Sadat was vague, saying that they should be permitted to come to the peace conference where "we can all work together to solve it." On Jerusalem, he was just as adamant in his position as Golda Meir was in hers. The holy places in the Arab portion of the city must be returned.

And then he returned to the familiar theme: "All I ask is that you stop backing them. We want to live in peace with you. They are still living in the dream of 1967, but they have been humbled. They have only a pocket on the west bank." It occurred to me that with 20,000 men of the Third Army cut off, it might be Sadat who was living in a dream.

When Bill Armstrong asked him if the Russians were sending in nuclear arms, Sadat denied it, and he repeated that the Russians had supplied only "primitive" weapons, the SAM-6 being one of the earliest types, whereas the U.S. had sent the Israelis weapons from its inventory that it hadn't even used yet. His anger broke through at this. "I am ready for disengagement, and a peace conference can follow, but they must leave my lands."

The session had lasted for well over an hour. In retrospect, I think that Sadat wanted not so much to have a dialogue with us as to give us the benefit of his views and have us take that message back to America. A number of the Egyptians told us that they realize that they have not been effective in getting their message to the American people. In this they concede that the Israelis have had our eyes and ears almost exclusively to themselves. They keenly feel wronged in this conflict, and their manner of arguing is one of outrage and frustration. Their pride, which is a sensitive characteristic among Arabs, has been badly damaged. Now that they have scored some slight military success, they have inflated the results and demand that their terms be met. They sense that time is on their side and feel that they can remain mobilized far longer than the Israelis. Therefore, the Americans must be persuaded not to give military aid. That will deny them the prize that they feel is within their grasp. The oil embargo has already brought much of the West to heel, an event that they also find new and heady; so it is only the Americans who stand in the way. Without us Israel will fold.

This same set of facts is also known to the Israelis, and as we learned, they fear that we will put pressure on them to compromise on key issues. Peace is closer than it has been before, but only because the Arabs believe they are in a position to gain their objectives. For the same reason, it may be further away, because if the Israelis will not yield and the Arabs not compromise, both then will fully realize that only force of arms will settle the long-standing dispute.

On Friday, our last day in Egypt, we spent the day in the Suez Canal area, leaving by bus early in the morning for Kantara, the headquarters of the Egyptian First Army. Here there had been bitter fighting on the east bank of the Canal. We drove up to a tent, where we met with the Egyptian generals in command. The evening before we had met with General Ismail, the Egyptian defense minister. He had spoken confidently of the Egyptian successes in the war and dismissed the Israeli penetration on the west bank of the Canal.

It appeared to me throughout these talks that the Egyptians, who had been so starved for military success over the past twenty-five years, have built in their minds a victory which doesn't approach the magnitude that they project. They showed courage and determination in crossing the Canal, and they took some heavily fortified positions, but the fact is that the Bar Lev Line was a series of fortified positions rather than a single line manned in depth.

As we approached the tent, we saw a military band drawn up. It was playing a stirring march, with part of the band members playing and the rest of them singing. Inside the tent we found chairs while the music continued outside., It was the damnedest potpourri I've ever heard, a combination of marches, selections from "Mary Poppins," and the Grand March from "Aida." The Egyptian commander gave us a brief outline of the Canal crossing and then took us outside to see the Israeli redoubt which had been successfully assaulted. I had to admit that it was impressive, a massive hill with connecting trenches heavily bulwarked by stone and sandbags. Barbed wire covered the approaches. Severe fighting had marked the attack. The Egyptian commander swelled with pride as he reviewed the taking of the redoubt.

Later in the day we drove north near Port Said and stopped at another Egyptian fortified position, this time on the west bank. Again we got out and trudged up to the crest to hear another presentation. Here occurred some unexpected comic relief. The Egyptian commander had a microphone and spoke earnestly about the events of six weeks before while we crowded around him, both to keep warm and to hear him. The day was cold and windy, and it was decidedly uncomfortable standing on the top of a hill with the wind blowing off the Canal. With our hands in our pockets, straining to hear the general's words, the spell was broken by Bill Bray. Flatulence is the bane of old age, and the wind that broke from him could have been mistaken for a violation of the ceasefire. Bill instinctively glanced to the left and right, endeavoring to convey the impression that the guilt for his intestinal intrusion lay with someone else. The Egyptian general blinked a few times but continued his monologue without further interruption. Afterward, poor Bill caught it. On the bus, he got a ribbing that lasted until the next morning. Considering that he is the ranking Republican, I thought that he bore up rather well.

We got back to Cairo early in the evening, in time to attend a reception given by the Ambassador-designate at the Sheraton. Since we were leaving at 7:00 the next morning, none of us had a desire to make it a late evening.

Our departure on Saturday was on schedule, a number of our Egyptian escorts coming to the airport to see us off. The flight home was without incident. We stopped again at Torrejon for refueling, and then it was on to Andrews, where we arrived at 4:00 p.m. Eastern Standard Time, but 11:00 p.m. Cairo time. I had a plane waiting for me which had been provided by the Navy to take me to Norfolk, where I landed just as the sun was setting. It had been a very long day and the end of a remarkable week.

Tuesday, November 27, 1973

My efforts to save the leaseholds in Norfolk have paid some slight dividends. We have been able to get the project preserved in the Senate version of the bill, and this morning I called on several of the Appropriations Committee members who will be House conferees, including the ranking Republican, Glenn Davis. Glenn didn't commit himself, but he promised to look into it carefully. I did get a commitment out of Bob McEwen and Burt Talcott on the Republican side. I also went back and bent Bob Sikes' ear, and he said that he was sympathetic but would be guided by the conferees in the House. I said that I was doing my best to bring them around, and he encouraged me to continue to do so. Clarence Long, one of the Democrats, called me back this afternoon on the matter and said that he would try to help me. He suggested that I get one of the Senators to give it a nudge when they got to conference, and that would help the House conferees to accede. I told him that I would do so. They will go to conference on Thursday, so the issue should be resolved by the end of the week. In the meantime, I got a couple of calls from the affected parties down home, and I told them that I had done everything that I could and just to sit tight. I surely hope that I can pull this one out of the fire. It's been one whale of a fight.

Wednesday, November 28, 1973—
Thursday, November 29, 1973

I began Wednesday morning by making a run over to the Senate to see if I could get some help on my leasehold project from Harry Byrd. He suggested that I see John Tower, who is on the Appropriations Committee of the Senate and would be a conferee. I dropped down to John's office and made my plea. He agreed to speak for it at the conference. That was the last effort I could possibly make. This afternoon (Thursday) I saw Clarence Long, and he told me that they had gutted the proposal, leaving in about $700,000 for those lease-holders immediately affected by proposed Navy construction and leaving the others until the land was actually needed. I asked what effort Bob Sikes had made, since he had promised to be "guided by the Subcommittee." "Not a damned thing," he replied. I smiled wryly and told him what Bob had said to me. He said that he experienced the same thing from Sikes in the past, that Sikes was big on promises and solemn assurances but often reacted in just the opposite way when the time came for a decision. I had to confess a certain amount of disillusionment. So much for my own attempt at politicking a pet project. Looking back objectively, I suppose that I have no reason to harbor resentment at failing. I was perfectly willing to cut a California project to balance my own request in the budget but my clout didn't extend all the way to the

Appropriations Committee. It would be futile to try to retaliate against Sikes in the future by denying him authorization of his numerous add-ons which he requests of us. That would only lay us open to having our own projects cut down at the appropriations level. He surely has the best of all worlds, which his seniority has gained him, but it is certainly tough on the rest of us.

1974

Wednesday, January 23, 1974

This afternoon I stayed in the House to hear most of the debate on the bill authorizing about $1.5 billion for the International Development Association. H. R. Gross, who seems to be unusually conscious of the fact that he won't be in the lists next year to do battle against the foreign give-aways, got positively emotional over this one. He got some help from some of the others on both sides of the aisle, including, of all people, Clarence Long, who declared he was for helping the poor people of the world but that the money from this bill would end up in the pockets of the wealthy and the bureaucrats rather than the needy. He's probably right. Wayne Hays also took to the Well of the House to oppose it but took the opportunity to lecture the Republicans on the increased spending of the Nixon Administration and warned us sarcastically not to vote for this, or we would suffer additional resentment at the polls. He is one caustic individual. When he finished, he got some faint applause from a couple of people on his side of the aisle. Even a majority of his own people don't like him.

This is no year to come up with a bill to commit additional billions abroad, not with the beating we are taking from the increase in oil prices and the general competition we're having in the world at large. The bill went down, as I knew it would, so·decisively, in fact, that the Asian Development Bank, which was scheduled for tomorrow, has been pulled off the calendar, giving us the rest of the week off.

The Wednesday Group meeting today was a seance of gloom. Stu McKinney, who seldom peddles any optimism, reached a new low, telling us that the Fourth District of Connecticut, which he represents, is now unique in that it doesn't have a single gasoline station open. Mark Andrews, who can also draw a pretty dark picture, was not to be outdone, telling Stu that the problems in Connecticut paled beside his forty-below weather he had left in North Dakota. His kick was about the high price of propane gas, which is heavily used by farmers in the West. Garner Shriver of Kansas confirmed the same thing. The anti-Nixon feeling in Connecticut was shared in varying degrees by others in the room, although some said that many people still shy away from impeachment.

Joel Pritchard said that he had met with the Senate Wednesday Group today at lunch, and the sentiment there was for the House not to send over an impeachment to them. All of them have been telling their constituents that it's up to the House to take the first step, but they're saying privately that they hope the House doesn't take it.

Just what progress is being made in the Judiciary Committee is hard to tell. Ham Fish, who is a member of that Committee, told us that he resents the secrecy of Rodino in not making all the information available to the rest of the Committee. Furthermore, he said that they haven't even had a meeting. We asked him what Drinan, Conyers, and the other liberals were saying about that, and he said that they were apparently content to let Rodino run the show. He added that there was some question of whether or not they were going to be able to get the information that the special Watergate prosecutor had compiled. If it was not forthcoming, he didn't see how in the world they could put it all together before the summer. If the public knew half of this, I can imagine the outcry that would come.

Frank Horton told us that he had been down at the White House with part of the Leadership to hear the President's plea for cooperation on the energy measures which he has proposed. Frank said that Nixon looked drawn and spent, which isn't surprising considering what he's been going through. He said that Nixon repeated himself several times and just didn't seem to be in charge of the situation as he had in the past. We were tipped off that O'Neill will have a major statement in *Time* in its issue next week, calling for the President's resignation. If that isn't enough, there was a report by Ed Morgan in *The Wall Street Journal* that Egil Krogh is going to "spill his guts" and implicate the President in the White House "plumbers" operation. Morgan used to be a Treasury Secretary but resigned this past weekend. He may be in trouble as a result of his role in the President's tax break when he donated his vice-presidential papers to his library. Nobody would look the picture of health with all that grief around.

Monday, January 28, 1974

Well, Krogh didn't "spill his guts" after all. In fact, he declared that the President didn't know about the extent of the "plumbers" operation, nor was John Dean telling the truth about the President's knowledge of the coverup of Watergate. The press could scarcely conceal their disappointment. Like vultures, they were waiting expectantly for the death blow to be dealt by Krogh, whose credibility as a sinner-returned-to-the-fold seemed high. The pendulum does seem to be swinging back a bit for the President, but it sure makes for a dizzying ride trying to hang on to it. Today I received a proposed letter to the President from the Republican Leadership. It stated that recent statements by two of the leaders in the House calling for the President's resignation were not representative of the entire House and were inappropriate. It repeated the thesis that the Members of the House ought to reserve all judgment until the work of the Judiciary Committee is completed and its findings reported to the House. While it doesn't give the President a clean bill of health, it at least assures him that there are some fair-minded people left to consider his case. I had mixed feelings about signing it. I don't want the President or anyone else to get the idea that I'm in favor of a whitewash, but after reading over the letter three times, I decided that it reflected my personal feelings, and I therefore shouldn't have any reservations about putting my name on it.

Thursday, January 31, 1974— Monday, February 4, 1974

The President's State of the Union Address on Wednesday night was a two-part affair; the first part was a traditional message covering the major items in the President's budget for this year. He placed a lot of emphasis on his health care plan, energy measures, education, a changed welfare program, and mass transit. He spoke of an enlarged defense budget and the need for flexibility in the forthcoming trade negotiations. In addition, he added something new: a recommendation on legislation to protect personal privacy. It got a good hand from both sides of the aisle.

The House was packed, as expected. I'm sure that the question in the minds of many of us was what kind of reception the President would get. His last appearance there with Jerry Ford had placed him in a decidedly secondary position, and the applause then had been for Jerry. Yet on Wednesday night the President got a good hand as he entered the chamber. Some Democrats were missing, but several of his bitterest critics were there. Many of them refused to applaud. John Brademas said afterward that he stood when the President came in and when he left out of respect for the office, but he couldn't applaud for the politician who held it. I couldn't fault him for his convictions. The most amusing reaction was Rodino's. He stood toward the front with the Democratic Leadership and didn't seem to know what to do with his hands. He would clap and hold them, almost as if he were clasping them and unclasping them. Presiding over the committee that will determine whether or not a bill of impeachment should be brought forward, he didn't want to appear to be approving of Nixon, but at the same time he didn't want to let any bias show. He probably wished that the President had sent the message over as he did last year.

The President didn't seem to look particularly weary, as some have said, but I thought that he betrayed either weariness or tension, or both, in his voice, physical symptoms that I have noticed in myself when I have addressed an audience under pressure. The President betrayed one other sign of nervousness in his speaking: his delivery was too fast at first, although he slowed down as he progressed.

The speech progressed without any unusual commentary or reaction until toward the end. The President then made reference to his desire for peace, that it was his first priority in the "eight years of his Presidency." It brought prolonged applause from the Republican side, and then John Rhodes stood, followed by most of the other Republicans. There were a few sitting on the Democratic side, including Barry Goldwater, Jr., John Myers, and Peggy Heckler. Barry and John stood, but not Peggy. It was the first of several partisan demonstrations of the night.

When the President finished his prepared address, some of the Senators thought that it was the end and prepared to leave, but Nixon indicated that he was not finished, and the applause subsided. Then the President began some extemporaneous remarks about Watergate. He said that "one year of Watergate is enough." He would have done well to have omitted that phrase, because it appeared to urge that the investigation be swept under the rug. When he declared that he was "not going to walk away from the Presidency," he got another standing ovation from the Republicans. It was the most partisan manifestation that I've seen in the House since we chose the Speaker, and that lacked the emotion of this occasion. Somebody quipped that while we were standing clapping our hands, Rodino was making a quick count to see how many would go for impeachment. The President got a few boos and catcalls when he said that he intended to cooperate with the Watergate investigation, but then added that it would be within the limits of preserving Presidential privilege.

In retrospect, I don't think it was a wise move to have added that P.S. to the State of the Union Address. It contained nothing that Nixon has not already uttered, and it served only to anger those who would have to regard it as a gauntlet thrown at their feet. It was, however, a gutsy thing to have done. After all, it will be in the House Chamber that the first step will be taken to remove him from office. Richard Nixon was telling his foes that he's not intimidated one bit and is going to fight them every inch of the way. I am still prepared to vote either way, depending on the substance of the information provided by the Judiciary Committee, but the thought occurred to me that if he is guilty of participating in a cover-up of Watergate, he has certainly taken advantage of a great well of good will that still exists for him in the House and in the country at large. Over the weekend, I heard again and again the refrain to stand by the President—at a Lions Club banquet of about 200 people, and from two postal employees when I stopped in a branch office at Virginia Beach this morning to pick up a parcel. It reminds me over and over of the Dreyfus Affair in France in the last century. Not that the two events are similar in themselves, but in the division they have produced in a people they are parallel. The scar from the Dreyfus Affair is still visible in France today, faintly so, but more than three generations have passed, and that is a long time.

Ironically, the President's remarks at the Prayer Breakfast on Thursday morning were never more appropriate or meaningful. Several times in the past, he said nothing of import, or something so trivial that it was worthless. But on this occasion he spoke with deep feeling, mentioning some personal things from his youth that were reflective and meaningful. It was by far the best Prayer Breakfast that Janie and I have ever attended, and it was actually worth getting up at the unholy hour of 6:30.

Monday, March 18, 1974

Although the Arab oil embargo was lifted this afternoon, all is not well in this town. The White House is feeling the heat more than ever from the Watergate investigation. This afternoon I got a call from Max Friedersdorf of the White House staff. He asked me confidentially how I would react to a motion to censure the President if he refused to turn over the forty tapes in question. I replied that I didn't know, and, not being a lawyer, I would probably rely on the judgment of several of my colleagues like Caldwell Butler and Ed Hutchinson, fellow Republicans on the Judiciary Committee. Max said that he understood, and his next question was what I would do if such a motion was passed— would I then regard it as grounds for impeachment. I said again that I wasn't sure, that I would want to hear some legal arguments. I said that I was not out to impeach the President, and, indeed, wanted to see him cleared if possible. Max sounded worried, and the White House must be if they are counting noses.

Tuesday, March 19, 1974

My Committee met at 10:00 to consider a Defense Supplemental Bill. Normally, these things don't encounter much trouble, and sail through with a minimum of opposition. Not so this one. It's headed for some stiff opposition in the House, and the Chairman admitted it to me this afternoon when we were coming back from a vote in the House. Deputy Secretary of Defense Bill Clements was present, along with Admiral Tom Moorer and a host of other military witnesses. One of the criticisms was the fact that the Defense Department makes available out of its inventory, on its own, from time to time, arms to, say, Vietnam, without so much as a by-your-leave to Congress. Then, with its inventory down, it comes back and asks for a supplemental authorization and appropriation to get it back up again. Bill Dickinson leaned on them particularly hard about this. Jim Jones asked Clements if he had any comment to make on the President's statement last week about possibly cutting our forces in Europe if our allies there didn't act more cooperatively. Clements paused a moment and then said no. It caught Jim by surprise and brought a few laughs. I guess everybody thought that Clements would say something more. A few minutes later, John Ford came over to me and said that we shouldn't let the record look so terse, that we ought to get the Defense Department on the record in favor of sustaining our NATO commitment. I agreed and said that I would raise the question. I went over to the Chairman and whispered to Eddie that I wanted five minutes for that purpose and he agreed. When the time came, I told Clements that I was also a member of the Special Subcommittee on NATO that had been in Europe, and that I was convinced after talking with our people there that we ought to maintain our current level of strength pending the outcome of the MBFR talks in Vienna. I said that I viewed with dismay the President's remarks of Friday, and I thought that we ought to have a statement as to whether or not the Defense Department had changed its policy on NATO. At this Clements protested that he had not meant to imply any change in his answer to Congressman Jones, and that our policy was the same. At that point, Sam Stratton asked me to yield so that he could say that he had written to the White House to express his concern, but that he felt that the President's remarks were directed primarily against the French and had had a salutary effect, judging from the remarks made by French Foreign Minister Jobert. The truth is that much of the European press was taken aback by the President's words, and I know that our people in Brussels, Stuttgart, and Vienna must have been thunderstruck by Nixon's remarks. When I left the committee room, Bill Randall stopped me to thank me for my comments, as did John Ford. Charlie Wilson, who cordially dislikes Nixon anyhow, leaned over to add his view, which was rather earthily put: "Anybody knows you don't make foreign policy in a ***** question and answer session." So much for the verdict on the President's "Operation Candor" appearance last week.

The afternoon session heated up over the issue of Diego Garcia, a small island in the Indian Ocean owned by the British, where we've had a weather station for some time and which is now the object of a $75 million port improvement and runway extension by the U.S. It's in the Supplemental Bill. With the increased Soviet naval activity in the Indian Ocean, and more to come when the Suez Canal opens, the U.S. needs a permanent base it can count on in that body of water. All the other ports bordering on the Indian Ocean have to be used on a special-case category, although the Soviets enjoy a developed port in Iraq, into which they've poured $100 million. Both Clements and Moorer told us in the morning that the only objections to the project were coming from

India and some leftists in Britain. This afternoon, Otis Pike declared that we had been lied to, and he took out a piece of copy taken from the AP wire service in the House cloakroom, in which Whitlam, the Australian Prime Minister, criticized the U.S. action in building a naval base in Diego Garcia. He was quoted as having said that it threatened the objective of keeping the Indian Ocean a peaceful sea or zone. I think that Otis believed that he had caught the Defense Department in an outright lie or gross ignorance, and he said as much, but Dennis Doolin, a sharp Defense official, stood up and stated flatly that he had been in Australia two weeks ago, and Whitlam had just said the contrary, that he hated to see Diego Garcia become a major naval base but that he could see the necessity for it. He added that the New Zealanders shared this view. Otis offered an amendment to cut all the funds for the project, but Doolin's statement stood up, and Otis lost his amendment by a substantial majority. The only cuts made were on an amendment by Mel Price, out of research and development money. I voted with the majority, feeling that getting the bill through is going to be difficult at any price, and we might as well cut it some now. The bill passed with about seven or eight dissenting votes. The House fight will make it close, very close, and I wouldn't be completely surprised at all to see the money for Vietnam cut out entirely.

I saw Dave Dennis this afternoon and told him about my conversation with Max Friedersdorf yesterday. He said that he felt that I had given Max the best possible answers. I then asked him whether or not he thought that Nixon would be censured if he didn't turn over the forty-plus tapes the Judiciary Committee has asked for. Dave said that he wouldn't have much trouble voting to censure on that issue, but what worried him was the rest of the Judiciary Committee's demand that they have access to all of the cross-filing and record on Haldeman and Ehrlichman. That part he regarded as a fishing expedition. He added that he and the other Republicans are disappointed in Jenner, the Republican counsel for the Committee. Apparently Jenner is weak and Doar calls the signals. The Republicans can't fire Jenner because of the adverse publicity it would create—a kind of mini-Saturday Night Massacre—so they find themselves dragged along. As Dave put it, the commentators always say, "Even the Republican counsel agreed to etc., etc. . . . ." I asked Dave when he thought we would get a vote on impeachment. He said that with everything falling into place, he didn't think we would see one before June, and it would probably come later than that. I was glad to hear him say one thing: like me, he feels that if the President lied in denying any knowledge of the cover-up, he ought to be impeached, but not on some of the other, spurious charges that Nixon's enemies have made. To top it all off, Senator Jim Buckley called for the President's resignation today. Tonight the President was on the air again. I didn't hear him, because we were out, but a clergyman in Norfolk called me in a rage at Dan Rather, who had editorialized afterward. I suggested that he write to the head of CBS and express his view. Still, he had to tell me that he wanted the President's friends to stand up for him, and said that he wasn't going to vote for anybody this fall unless they did. I suppose that includes me, although he didn't say so exactly. I have a feeling that by this fall I'll have made a lot of people mad by my vote on impeachment, no matter which way I go.

Tuesday, April 30, 1974—Monday, May 6, 1974

Another week behind us, and suddenly it's May. The time seems to slip by even more quickly than when I was teaching, and those years are a brief panorama now. The weather has turned generally good here in Washington, with most of the days being warm and the nights cool. It is a pleasant time of the year, although the climate of politics shows only gathering clouds and a distant rumble of thunder. Watergate overshadows everything. It will not go away, and for the first time I believe that the President's impeachment is a probable thing. I would not have thought this as recently as several weeks ago.

Nixon's speech on Monday night was damaging, and I wonder who suggested that the release of the transcripts would be in the President's favor. Their release has instead lowered the President's standing even further. His vulgar language in the Oval Office has exposed him as a hypocrite. The people generally knew that Lyndon Johnson used that kind of language. He never attempted to hide the earthy side of his personality, but Nixon's posture of piety manifested in the religious services at the White House are now regarded as a sham. None of this would warrant his impeachment, but the President should have realized that it would shock a substantial portion of his strongest supporters who believe the Presidency is a temple of decency. Worse are the transcripts of conversations in which he demonstrated not a determination to "throw the rascals out," but a desire to protect them. That he would have even considered paying Hunt a bribe came as a shock to me.

The press, most of which has been hostile to him, is turning almost completely against him. Reporters have plied me with questions, both here and at home. In many cases they have endeavored to get me to commit myself, but I have steadfastly declined to take a position which might reflect a bias prior to our hearing the matter in the House. The editors of the *Virginian-Pilot* at home have been on my back for not becoming more vocal, but I am determined to wait for the report of the Judiciary Committee and listen to the debate on the evidence.

Although many people at home have talked to me personally about the issue, we have not received an extraordinary amount of mail on the transcripts. In fact, fewer than two dozen have come in at this point. The situation is so fluid that I am reluctant to get too far out in front. The whole business has taken a course that I would never have predicted, and with this pattern in back of us, it would appear best at this point to act with caution. I will continue to reply with as much candor as I can to inquiries from the press and individuals, but I just have a gut feeling that nothing more is necessary at this time.

Tuesday, May 7, 1974

We drove in at the usual time this morning, and I attended a meeting of the full Committee before going off to a meeting of my Energy Subcommittee. We had a technical vote on the Defense Authorization Bill, to report out what is known as a "clean bill" to the House. In this case, it simply means that all of the changes that have been made are drafted as a fresh bill. The vote on it reflected the same views expressed last week. There were three nays today and thirty-six yeas.

The Watergate transcripts occupied some of the conversation before we got started. Sonny Montgomery said that the President's language had offended some of the Bible Belt people in his district in Mississippi. Carleton King showed the same outrage as many of us over the cover-up mentality displayed by the President and his advisers. Last week, some of us were in the Republican lounge off the Floor discussing it, and Gene Snyder of Kentucky was particularly outspoken, saying that the President ought to resign. At this point Les Arends came in and in a mild way chastised Gene for saying that. Gene snapped back at him, "You aren't running for reelection this year!" It's true, of course. Les is retiring at the end of the year.

I went to the Bull Elephants luncheon today. This is an organized group of Republican aides, both administrative and legislative, who meet periodically to hear from various leaders in the government or party. Today Jerry Ford was the speaker. After giving a pep talk on reelecting Republicans this fall, he answered questions. Not surprisingly, many were about Watergate. He said nothing new, declaring that he believed that while the transcripts "did not confer sainthood on anyone," they did indicate that the President was innocent of any wrongdoing. I suppose that one could say he was loyal without being enthusiastic. He said again that he was not a candidate for President in 1976 and would not attempt to win any delegates, but he said nothing about refusing a draft.

Wednesday, May 8, 1974—Wednesday, May 15, 1974

Another week has gone by without a chance to get to this journal, but tonight we have an evening at home again. Janie and I have both felt tired, and she has nagged me gently to have us block off some time for ourselves. What we need are several free weekends to do nothing.

We went to the Thai Embassy on Wednesday night. The Panyarachuns honored Under Secretary of State Kenneth Rush. Senator Hiram Fong and his wife were there, along with Janie and me from the House. Among the others were the New Zealand ambassador, a former official at State, and a Thai minister, whose name and exact title escape me now. It was a pleasurable evening, although the conversation was strictly the dinner party variety. I think that all of us were glad to leave our problems back on the Hill or at the office.

The following day I attended a luncheon of generally conservative Republicans and Democrats, at which the economist Milton Friedman spoke. At the table with me were Ed Derwinski, Phil Crane, and Stan Parris, plus several other Members. Naturally, the talk turned to the President. Derwinski and Crane were outspoken in their defense of him, but Stan quipped that his solution was "a heart attack with honor." Derwinski, ever the clown, told us that Bill Harsha had come up to him on the Floor the other day, angry at one of the Democrats on his committee named Mezvinsky. Ed said that Harsha told him, "Mezvinsky has set back the Polack cause by a hundred years!" Ed then replied, "You dumb SOB, he's not a Polack, he's Jewish!"

I was busy in the office this morning and went to a luncheon sponsored by the directors of the Bank of Virginia. Dan Daniel sat next to me and said that he had seen the President yesterday. He said that the President reaffirmed to him that he was not going to resign. He also said that the President told him why he had released the transcripts. My ears really perked on that one. "Why?" I asked. "Because he said that the conversations would have been leaked out by the Judiciary Committee, and he wanted to beat them to it," he replied. "He would have been better off to have had them leaked," I answered. I thought that it was just one more manifestation of paranoia. Carl Madden, an economist with the National Chamber of Commerce, was at the table with us and joined in the discussion, saying that the release of the transcripts has had a profound effect upon the business community, which had been formerly standing by the President. "They've gotten out of his bed," he said. Still, the wave of demands for the President's resignation has subsided, and the general reaction of most of my colleagues now is to push ahead with the work of the Judiciary Committee and bring the matter to House according to constitutional procedure.

Thursday, May 16, 1974—Tuesday, May 21, 1974

We had some unusual visitors on Thursday morning, the sixteenth. A group of boys who are members of a choir, plus their director and several parents, came to Washington to give a concert on the Capitol steps. This sort of thing has become increasingly popular, although the performing groups are usually bands. Every spring we have classes of students for visits, and it has gotten so that the House is sometimes filled with several groups from all over the United States, with House Members giving a spiel on the House, its traditions, and their duties. I sometimes think that any of us could easily substitute for the professional guides who take parties of tourists through the Capitol. Since the first of the year, I have had close to twenty groups from home.

The day was warm, and I had experienced some discomfort in my chest the day before which had persisted. I reflected on the fact that having felt well all year, I was having all kinds of complaints since having my annual physical examination a few weeks ago. Nevertheless, I thought I would be better off if I went to see the physician in the Capitol to get checked over. Besides examining me with his stethoscope, he ran a cardiogram on me, which was unchanged from my previous one. My heart appeared sound. I felt foolish and asked the doctor if many of my colleagues often came in on false alarms as I had. "Oh, yes," he replied. "I just wish they'd send me some Democrats to look at for a change." It broke me up and gave me a good yarn to tell at home over the weekend. When I told Tom Downing about it, he said, "He should have been over there two years ago when McGovern was running. The Democrats were going in in droves."

Wednesday, May 22, 1974—Tuesday, May 28, 1974

Most of this period was spent on the Memorial Day recess, which gave us Friday and Monday at home. Although I stayed pretty busy back in my district, I found some time to relax on Sunday and Monday and came back refreshed today (Tuesday).

I began last Wednesday morning by meeting a group of elementary school children outside my office and giving them the usual tour and group picture on the House steps. At 10:00 I went to a meeting of my Standing Subcommittee to hear from the three services on some real estate acquisitions and disposals. That afternoon I was on the floor for the debate on the amendments to the Defense Authorization Bill. It was an interesting afternoon, and surprisingly none of the amendments carried. I thought that Les Aspin's amendment to cut the budget by over $700 million would go over as it did last year, but it went down by about twenty or so votes. Les hurt his own cause by pointing out that the Appropriations Committee would cut the authorization amount, and so many Members just reasoned that if that were so, we ought to leave it alone.

For me, the most engrossing part of the debate centered on the two amendments offered by Ron Dellums and Tip O'Neill to cut U.S. forces abroad. Dellums' motion would have cut the U.S. forces by almost 200,000, while O'Neill's would have reduced them by 100,000. O'Neill's was in the form of a substitute to the Dellums Amendment, so the real fight was on the substitute. Obviously, if we defeated that one, the other would lose, too.

Tip is a good debater, but he got himself in trouble early by declaring that he didn't want to recommend specifically where the troop cuts should be taken. At this point, John Ford leaned over to me and said that someone ought to bring up the statement that Tip had made when he was in South Korea back over Easter. The papers quoted him as promising that there would be no reduction of the 48,000 U.S. forces in South Korea this year. If Tip didn't want to take any of those, then where would he want them to come from? Clark Fisher took the floor and proceeded to flail away at the amendment, and it was only a few minutes before he mentioned Tip's promise to the South Koreans. Tip asked him to yield and protested that it was unfair to bring this up, that his amendment called for the reduction to be made by the middle of 1975 anyway. He intimated that something was in the works to cut part of the U.S. troops in South Korea next year, but not now, which protected his pledge to the South Koreans. Some of the Members began to smell a secret deal and asked out loud if this were so. Tip looked miserable and went back to his seat. What clinched it against him was a brief statement by the Speaker, who declared that a cut of this kind and in this way disturbed him. It was a definite signal to any Democrats who may have been on the fence. Most of us made the point that a cut would obviously affect our NATO forces, and that it would be foolish to reduce unilaterally while the MBFR talks were in progress, and the Jackson-Nunn Amendment has a year to go. I took the occasion to speak briefly, using the five minutes allotted to me to cite the direct U.S. investment of some $30 billion in Europe, the upcoming aircraft replacement for the F-104, which could go to us or the French, and the beefing up of our combat forces in Europe by cutting down on the headquarters and logistical forces. I closed with a history lesson, recalling the debate nearly forty years ago over whether to fortify Guam and the defeat of the move to do so. Then I mentioned the words of Bruce Barton, who gloated over it and cried, "Guam, Guam with the wind!" I declared that it might have made good copy at home, but that it was surely poor vision. The House grew quiet at the end, for everyone likes a good story, and I knew that I had their attention. I don't often take the floor and prefer to speak only when I have something that I really want to say.

I was amused by the Chairman. Bella offered one amendment that would have cut much of the research and development for missile technology. She was beaten on a voice vote, but somebody told Eddie that there was a contingent of Russians in the Gallery. So that they would get the message in spite of Bella's verbiage and that of a few of her supporters the House was overwhelmingly opposed to any such amendment, Eddie called for a record vote. It was decisive, but the Russians had departed by the time the vote was taken. The debate ended and the final vote was taken by about 8:30. It was a good victory.

The only retreat that Eddie made was in the portion of the bill relating to aid to South Vietnam. To head off a large cut, Eddie offered a Committee amendment to reduce it to the level of the current year. The next morning the *Post* played this up, and a reading of the headline would have the reader believe that the Committee had taken a licking on the Floor.

We raised the debt limit on Thursday, but it took a vote by the Speaker to break a 190 to 190 tie. Tom Downing, Caldwell, Joel, and I voted to raise it, while the others in the delegation voted no. That kind of vote strikes me as a charade. The way to hold spending down is not by refusing to raise the debt ceiling but by restraining spending in the first place. Some of the liberals aggravate me. They vote to bust spending bills wide open, and then vote against raising the debt limit.

After a weekend in Virginia Beach, Janie and I drove back to Washington on Monday morning in time for me to make the first quorum call in the House. There wasn't much business, just the general debate on the Community Services Act. That was completed by early afternoon, and the House adjourned. The day was noteworthy, all the same. I asked Caldwell Butler if he would meet with the delegation in my office about 4:30 to discuss the work of the Judiciary Committee to date, and he agreed to come. I called the others, and all but Joel, Dave, and Stan showed up. Caldwell told us that he is still undecided about the President insofar as Watergate is concerned. It is still not completely clear to him whether or not the President ordered a payoff to Hunt. Tomorrow the Committee takes up the President's tax problems, which may be more substantive, and some time later the milk contributions will be explored.

We got into the subject of the Committee's requests for additional tapes and the President's refusal to deliver them. Caldwell said that he believes that the Committee will refrain from either going to court to get them or asking the House to hold the President in contempt of Congress. Rather, he feels that the Committee will advise the President that his refusal will be noted in the proceedings and weighted as part of the decision to impeach him. Caldwell agrees with this position, because he feels there is a need now to press forward and get a decision as quickly as possible. There shouldn't be further delay in bouts with the White House over the release of tapes. He told us that he had listened to some of the tapes which Jaworski had provided and found it hard to follow the conversations along with the transcripts because of pauses, changes in some of the words, and the like. Contrary to the impression the transcripts give of the President being led by his advisers in the White House, Caldwell said that the conversations clearly indicate that the President was in charge and carrying the conversation.

We asked Caldwell what sort of time frame he thought the Committee would operate within for the remainder of the hearings. He said that it depended on whether or not the Committee held open hearings. Rodino, who has shown consummate skill so far, and has risen in my book, doesn't want to go public, because he knows that the ensuing demagoguery will delay a decision by another month. However, the "crazies" on the Committee, as Caldwell calls them, are pressing for public hearings, and Rodino is wavering. As if this weren't enough, Ed Hutchinson, the ranking Republican, has been out for the past week following a hemorrhoid operation, which probably made the whole business more than just a symbolic pain in the ass for him.

Caldwell said that the President's lawyer, St. Clair, has been present taking copious notes the past two weeks, and he could make some unexpected moves before the hearings are concluded.

Before we adjourned, I asked Caldwell how he would vote if it came up now. He said that he didn't know. He is obviously unhappy about the President's refusal to hand over the evidence the Committee needs to fill in some of the gaps and unanswered questions. He seemed to indicate that, constitutionally, the grounds are there to send the President to the Senate for trial, but the enormity of it gives him cause for pause, as it does nearly all of us. At this point, Dan and Bob Daniel both spoke up to say that the people in their district were heavily opposed to impeachment, and Bob stated that his people would never regard his vote as a grand jury type of action. Dan concurred in this. Dan said that he had received over 200 letters today telling him to get off the President's back, although he really hasn't been on it.

Had we had a vote this afternoon, we would probably have had a split in the delegation, which is one thing that all of us want to avoid. In truth, none of us should be swayed by polls or letters or constituency feeling on this matter, but so far it appears that we are going to be denied the kind of hard evidence which would make a decision obvious one way or another. We have agreed to have more meetings, and I will be interested to hear what the missing three have to say, but it may well be that no consensus will be forthcoming, and for some of us the decision will not be made until the very end. As much as I like and respect Caldwell, I wish that Dick Poff were here. His splendid legal mind and his uncompromising integrity might have peeled away some of the layers of vagueness and indistinctness that could lead some of us astray. His guidance and experience are surely missed, although I know that he must be counting his lucky stars that he left the Congress when he did.

Wednesday, May 29, 1974

The most interesting thing today was the Wednesday Group meeting this afternoon. Ham Fish and Bill Cohen talked about the Judiciary Committee's activity. They mentioned the moves that Caldwell alluded to yesterday as to whether or not the Committee would send another letter to the President telling him that he was in noncompliance. They are also waiting to see what success Jaworski will have with the Supreme Court in getting the tapes he wants. Both Bill and Ham sense a change coming over the Republicans on the Committee. There seems to be less militancy in defense of the President than there was even a few days ago, and some rising feeling that the President ought to hand over the tapes. Ham said that Charlie Wiggins is emerging as a bellwether on the Republican side. Charlie has been very tough so far, questioning the staff closely much as a defense attorney would. Charlie, in fact, has cited his work as a defense lawyer before he came to Congress. But Ham said he feels that when it comes down to the wire, Charlie will vote on the impeachment of the President as he sees the evidence, that he will call it honestly. Other Republicans on the Committee have been impressed by Charlie's work and are watching to see what he will do.

One of the Members mentioned a quotation from Tip O'Neill about legislation "maturing in committee." He pointed out that a decision in the Judiciary Committee appears to be following this pattern. This sounds logical to me, because I believe that most people seek and take refuge in a consensus.

At that point, Stu McKinney called attention to something that those of us in the Virginia delegation have brought up to Caldwell. He said that the press had noticed that many Members on the Republican side were looking at the Republicans on the Committee and in all likelihood would lean toward the position of their colleagues there. Stu said that in his mind, when it was all over, most of the Republicans in the House would not rely half so much on how John Rhodes voted as they would upon Ham, Bill, Charlie, and the others on the Committee. And to think that Caldwell didn't want to be appointed to the Judiciary Committee because it would be too dull; I wonder how he feels about that now.

Tonight Dan Daniel is out aboard the *Sequoia* with the President. Dan told us at lunch that he had been invited. The President appears to be making a pitch to some of his strongest supporters in this way. About ten days ago, he had about a dozen Democrats and Republicans on the *Sequoia* and informally let it be known that he was going to see it through. It may also be a way of getting some feedback from his base of strength. Dan asked us what to ask the President. We told him that he ought to tell the President that the House is very uncertain about the possibility that the President ordered Hunt to be paid off. I'll be curious to hear Dan's account of what happened.

Wednesday, June 19, 1974

The Wednesday Group was hosted by Mark Andrews in the afternoon. John Anderson, who is one of our new members, spoke out against the campaign by Republican right-wingers, who are trying to intimidate Republican Members into voting against impeachment no matter what. John, who can be fiery and dramatic as the occasion requires, and it seems to more often than not with him, denounced these efforts and warned us that the Republican Party would be forever condemned to be a minority party if we allowed ourselves to be armtwisted by this element. At a Republican conference this morning, Bob Michel had pointed out that we could be in jeopardy if we didn't heed these voices, and he pointed to a stack of letters he had received from supporters of the President. John replied that he had an even bigger stack from conservatives in his district, but he wasn't going to be intimidated by them. All of us are getting some of this to greater or lesser degrees, but I'm doing my best to discount it as a factor in my decision on what to do about impeachment.

There is considerable anger over the continuous leaks emanating from members of the Judiciary Committee hostile to the President. Not only members, but some of their staff members, are letting confidential information out to the press. It is a disgusting business and has infuriated many of the Republicans both on and off the Committee. I feel sorry for Rodino in this instance, because he had deplored the leaks and begged the members to honor the rule of secrecy imposed on the committee. What he ought to do is to put some of them under oath. That would button them up in a hurry. Ironically, the leaks are bolstering the President's cause by arousing more sympathy for him. The Virginia delegation will meet with Caldwell again on Monday in my office to discuss developments.

Monday, July 1, 1974

Today the Watergate-impeachment affair reached the House Floor temporarily. Rodino offered an amendment, which had passed the Judiciary Committee, to authorize suspension of the five-minute rule for the impeachment inquiry. By way of explanation, when witnesses appear before a committee of the House, each member has five minutes to question each witness. There are thirty-eight members of the Judiciary Committee, and there will probably be about eight witnesses. Obviously, if every member took his five minutes with each witness, it would prolong the hearings. Nevertheless, to suspend the rule would be to deny members of the committee a fundamental right and place interrogation in the hands of the committee staff, even though members would be permitted to submit questions in writing for the staff to ask. Although Ed Hutchinson and Bob McClory, the senior Republicans on the Committee, went along with Rodino, several of the conservative Members, led by Dave Dennis, did not. Dave did a whale of a job attacking the move. When the vote was taken, it was soon apparent that the necessary two-thirds majority could not be had, and the measure ultimately lost. I voted not to suspend the rule, despite my desire to get on with the thing and get it over with. In the words of one of my colleagues, the hearing must not only be fair, it must also have the appearance of fairness. I overhead Bob Michel tell another Republican that suspending the rule in this case would be a mistake because "that's how we've gotten our tit in the wringer before, letting staff run hearings." He was particularly critical of the Senate in this regard. What amused me was that Caldwell, the only Member from Virginia on the Committee, voted to suspend the rule while all the rest of us voted not to. Caldwell said that it was "no big deal" as far as he was concerned, but he felt that it would produce a lot of delay. "We've got a bunch of Clarence Darrows over there," he said, "and you can be sure that every one of them will take five minutes, and more if he can get it." That may be true, but the matter is too important to worry about an extra week or so being lost. When it is all over, it should not be said that the President was not given a fair shake by permitting a modified gag rule to prevail.

Dan Daniel told some of us later that he thought that Rodino might then go to the Rules Committee and seek a rule from them which would let him have the five-minute rule suspended, and so he asked Jim O'Hara about it. O'Hara said that Rodino would stick with the House decision, and at that point John Conyers, one of the blacks on the Committee, spoke up to say that he had actually been glad when the resolution failed, yet he had voted for it. Obviously all of the hypocrisy isn't in the White House.

Caldwell met with some of us in the Virginia delegation late in the afternoon to discuss further developments in the Judiciary Committee. Without actually saying so, he indicated that they have nothing impeachable yet. Doar is supposed to provide a broad statement for the Committee which would give a kind of umbrella to all of the charges and hold the President guilty of failing to prevent wrongdoing by his subordinates. I said that this seemed risky to me, since it would set a dangerous precedent for similar action to be taken against future presidents. Caldwell mentioned a column by Scotty Reston in the *New York Times* yesterday which underlined the Committee's failure to mount a convincing impeachment wave, one that was persuasive and reflected a foundation of arguments and evidence. Instead, Reston said that he felt the Committee had fallen into the rut of nit-picking. Caldwell agreed with this analysis. He said that he didn't expect a great deal new to emerge from the questioning of Butterfield, Dean, and the other witnesses.

The one big hurdle that remains for the President is the Supreme Court ruling on Jaworski's demand for additional tapes. Caldwell declared that, should the President defy the court, he felt certain that even Charlie Wiggins would vote for impeachment. The others in the room, including Tom Downing, Ken Robinson, and Joel Broyhill, nodded their assent, but Dan Daniel raised the question of the separation of powers. Caldwell replied that it would not apply in this case, since the President himself had already made some of the tapes available and had been named an "unindicted co-conspirator" by the Watergate grand jury. He could not then, in effect, be above the law. Finally,

Caldwell mentioned the precedent of Harry Truman's attempted seizure of the steel mills during the Korean War and his bowing to the court when it ruled against him. I had forgotten about that episode and can't remember whether it was the coal mines or the steel mills.

At the end of the meeting, Caldwell mentioned the fact that Waldie, one of the leading Democrats on the Committee, had made the motion to keep the hearings secret. Caldwell then noted that Waldie had done much of the leaking to the press, and that if they went to open sessions Waldie wouldn't be the prima donna he is now. The best story was told by Tom Downing. He said that he heard Kika de la Garza say that he wasn't taking his confessions to Father Drinan because "he leaks." Both Drinan and Waldie have been the most flagrant in betraying the confidence of the Committee, but Rodino does nothing but bewail it, Caldwell said.

My freshman neighbor down the corridor from me, John Conlan, has had what has to be one of the most embarrassing experiences on the Hill. John is a staunch conservative and has found, like so many of his fellow conservatives, that HEW and OEO make tempting targets. About ten days ago, he dug out a choice item against the OEO. He found that OEO had established a condom stamp program for teenage boys in Philadelphia and Cleveland. The initial grant amounted to $47,000 and provided for the mailing of thousands of coupons, each worth a dollar, toward the purchase of a dozen condoms at participating drugstores. According to a GAO report, almost 32,000 letters were sent out with a coupon, along with free sex training and counseling on how to select the best contraceptives. Only 183 teenagers responded and bought 2,640 condoms, which, John pointed out, came to $17.06 for each condom. That made them 136 times more expensive than the price through commercial outlets. John then lit into the agency for engaging in this kind of enterprise at the expense of the taxpayers. It made for a choice press release and was picked up by the wire services from coast to coast at once.

However, the response has been something that John didn't anticipate. Besides drawing upon himself the wrath of the Planned Parenthood people, John got an unexpected windfall, a deluge of condoms in assorted shapes and sizes that defy description. The poor girl who opens the mail apparently lives in daily mortification.

Tuesday, July 2, 1974—Wednesday, July 10, 1974

I met with my Subcommittee on Military Construction this morning for the purpose of marking up the Navy budget. As we began, Otis brought up the matter of permitting the mark-up to be done in open rather than closed session. His reasoning was that unless the business related to national security, which military construction does not, it ought to be open to the public. Carleton King disagreed with him and said that there was a difference between "clout" and argument in some projects which some Members would be hesitant to bring up. Otis replied that that was exactly why he wanted open sessions. I made the point that I thought that little would be served by having the discussions open, that it seemed to me we would encourage subterfuge, with Members working out private deals with their colleagues in offices ahead of time and that we would simply foster inhibition by going to open sessions. Carleton's motion to go into executive session carried by four to three. Robin Beard cast the deciding vote, and Otis ragged him a little about it.

We went through the Navy budget rapidly and cut a substantial number of items, including over $5 million worth in my district. Still, I came out pretty well. We'll be spending close to $40 million there this year. Bob Sikes of Florida had sent over some requests for additions in his district, but they weren't acted on. Charlie Bennett, who usually is the advance man for Bob, said that Bob hadn't asked him to present them, and Otis, who is peeved at Bob's record for getting additions to the budget every year, indicated that he wasn't going to bring them up. After last year's episode involving my efforts to get the leaseholds funded, Sikes hasn't been exactly one of my heroes, but I need his help if we are to get any money this year. Roy Markon suggested to me that there was a way for me to pick up about $700,000. It seems there was a project near Jacksonville which was approved and funded last year, but the money wasn't needed because other arrangements were made. Sikes has an addition calling for the purchase of some land outside the Pensacola Naval Air Station. If he can get it authorized, he can take part of the money that wasn't used for the Jacksonville project and pay for the Pensacola property with it. The remaining money could then be earmarked for some more of the leaseholds on the recently acquired railroad property in Norfolk.

Seeing that no one else was going to propose Sikes' requests, I called him this afternoon to apprise him. I must confess that it gave me a little satisfaction not to have to go as a supplicant. He was surprised that Charlie hadn't made a pitch for him. I said that Charlie appeared to be under the impression that he hadn't been asked. Sikes then asked me if it was too late. I replied that I didn't think so, and that I would be pleased to help him out on one of his projects, but I wanted to make a deal with him. I then explained it to him. "You've got yourself a bargain," he said. I'm still not sure that we can get it through, and doing Sikes' work for him isn't a role I especially like, but there's just no way I'll ever get the remaining money out of the Appropriations Committee for those lease-holds unless I do it. So what does all of the foregoing prove? That we have to resort to subterfuge whether we have open sessions or not.

The Virginia Republicans and Dan Daniel held their monthly meeting with Bill Scott at 12:30. The chief topic of conversation was the release of the Watergate transcripts by the House Judiciary Committee. The *Washington Post* gave most of its front page over to them this morning and made a point of quoting the President's language when he declared that he "didn't give a shit. . . ." They emphasized the difference between Nixon's version of the conversations and that of the Committee. There's no doubt that the President emerges with less credibility and a diminished reputation for veracity.

Both the *Post* and the *Star* note that the President wanted the scandal contained by his subordinates. As we sat around the table, Stan Parris was the most vocal in his criticism of Nixon, and he wondered out loud how we could avoid impeaching him. Even Dan Daniel, who is certainly the strongest supporter the President has in the delegation, admitted that the revelations had put serious doubts in his mind for the first time. When Caldwell arrived, he put a damper on it and understandably showed no shock, since he had already been privy to the information as a member of the Judiciary Committee. He said that we ought to remember that the *Post* gives emphasis only to the information which is most damaging to the President, and he added that the information coming from the witnesses so far has been generally favorable to Nixon. He said that he still hasn't made up his mind on how he will vote. He told us that he had asked Doar about the charge that has been promised, and Doar replied that the charge would be based on a strong case of circumstantial evidence and actively worked at not being informed.

Discounting anything that the Supreme Court might do, Caldwell said that he had still not made up his own mind, and he reverted to his view of a week ago, that the whole thing could hinge on some key votes in the Committee. He felt that Jim Mann of South Carolina had gone over to the pro-impeachment group but that Walter Flowers was uncommitted, as was possibly Ray Thornton. On our side, he thought that Ham Fish and Bill Cohen would vote to impeach. Dan Daniel observed that he had heard that a "lot of pressure" had been put on Mann, and he added that if the Republicans in the House were fractured in their vote, many of the Southern Democrats would go their own way and not bite the bullet for the President.

Stan came back to the *Post*. He hates the newspaper with a passion and laments the fact that it's the only paper the people in the Eighth District read. He has gotten a heavy bunch of anti-Nixon mail and is clearly bothered by it. The others talked about the sentiment in their districts, and Joel Broyhill said that he isn't bothered too much by it. "Let's face it," he said, "most of the people writing to us against Nixon won't be voting for us in the first place. On the other hand, if we vote to impeach the President, we're going to lose the support of a lot of people who work for us." There is certainly much truth in that, and in spite of our desire to cast a vote uninfluenced by such considerations, it will cast a shadow over all of us when the time comes closer for us to weigh the President's fate. We'll be weighing our own right along with his.

We received a letter last week which tops any request I've gotten since my election nearly six years ago. A woman wrote to me that her breasts are mismatched and one has grown larger than the other. She wants to have plastic surgery and needs money for hospitalization. What is causing her so much grief is the fact that her husband wants a divorce because of her physical condition, although he stuck around long enough to father two children. Unfortunately, there isn't a thing we can do for her, although I think we could justify spending money to pump silicones into the smaller of her two breasts sooner than we could with the damned condom program on which OEO squandered $47,000.

Thursday, July 11, 1974—Monday, July 15, 1974

Before I left the House for the weekend, Les Arends came over to me and voiced some concern over my position on impeachment. I told him that I hadn't made up my mind and didn't expect to until we had heard the evidence from the Judiciary Committee. He said that he had heard that I was leaning towards voting against the President. I said that I was unhappy about the way the President had handled the whole business, and I took particular note of the contrast between Nixon's behavior and Dwight Eisenhower's. I mentioned the conversation on the tapes in which Nixon himself declared that he was going to back his people and not react as Ike had in the case of Sherman Adams, as well as in his own case. Les agreed that Eisenhower would have shown better judgment. I also mentioned that a lot of us were going to rely on Caldwell to show good judgment. "Don't tell me that he's flaky on this," Les exclaimed. "He's not flaky at all," I replied. "He's holding judgment until all of the evidence is in." When it was over, I wandered into the Speaker's Lounge, where the wire service machines are located, and read the print-outs. There I discovered that the Republican Leadership had been down at the White House that morning, and John Rhodes was asked afterward if impeachment had been discussed, and he replied that it had, at the end of the conference. I may be wrong, but it wouldn't surprise me if they were counting noses this morning to see how many votes the President can count on. If that is true, then he is still approaching this thing all wrong, by treating it like a vote to override a veto rather than as the momentous event it is. It would also mean that his outlook is purely political. It makes me wonder if he has learned anything from all of this.

We had some bills on the Suspension Calendar today, one of which would have appropriated a million dollars to print up the Judiciary Committee's transcripts to date. I voted No, and we amassed enough votes so that the necessary two-thirds could not be attained, and the measure was lost. As Caldwell said, why should we spend that kind of money to print 50,000 copies, when private printers could print the same thing in paperback and sell it for $1.50?

We're home tonight, and I suspect we'll be in bed early. These have been a busy few days.

Were it not for impeachment drawing ever closer, this would have been one of those weeks that typify the summer here. The legislation in the House, albeit highlighted by the Strip-mining Bill, hasn't been overpowering, and few of us have been swamped by committee work. But impeachment is no longer a moot question before the Judiciary Commitee; it is now an imminent question for every Member to ponder. We realize that in less than a month, the proceedings will be under way in the House. I am no closer to a decision on how I will vote than I was six months ago, nor should I be. If integrity means anything, it requires me to reserve judgment until the presentation of evidence is made to the House.

In another entry, I noted that this whole business more and more takes on the cast of the Dreyfus Case of three generations ago in France. It is provoking a deep division, emotional and unreasoning. On Friday night, I spoke at a banquet at a Methodist church in Virginia Beach. A retired minister present pulled me aside to declare his unswerving loyalty to the President, and he tried to extract a similar commitment from me. On Sunday, at an outdoor art show in Norfolk, a young man approached me to ask why I had not included a question on impeachment in my most recent questionnaire which I sent to everyone in my district. I replied that it was a matter that did not call for a poll of my constituents, that I felt that it would violate the appearance of justice if I tried to get a reading from my constituents. "In other words, you don't care what your constituents think; you're going to do as you please," he said. I bristled at this and told him that there were plenty of instances where the opinion of my people was important, but in this case neither he nor anyone else in the community would have access to as much information as I would sitting in the House and hearing the evidence, and therefore it would be improper for me to seek anyone else's opinion. When he persisted, I quoted to him the words of Edmund Burke, "Your representative owes you, not his industry only, but his judgment; and he betrays instead of serving you if he sacrifices it to your opinion." He wanted to argue further, but I cut him off. I was seething inside, although I calmed down soon enough. Bob Daniel told me this afternoon (Monday) that one of his supporters told him over the weekend that although he approved of everything that Bob had done, if he didn't vote to impeach the President, Bob would forfeit his support. And so it goes.

Caldwell and the others are now the objects of much speculation by the media, both nationally and locally, but most of our people on the Committee are keeping their judgment to themselves. While I am deeply disturbed by the evidence against the President and would vote for a motion to censure him in a minute, I am equally bothered by the prospect of what impeachment means to the heart of the government.

Richard Nixon's fate is secondary by many degrees to the strength and independence of the office itself. I am worried that unless we see the "smoking gun" evidence, and vote to impeach on circumstantial evidence alone, we will have taken a grave step, one whose consequences will be far-reaching and more injurious than leaving a weakened and ineffective leader to serve out the remainder of his term. Which, then, is the lesser of two evils? That is what I think will become the fundamental question.

Meanwhile, the routine of making laws goes on. My Subcommittee on Military Construction has just about completed its work of marking up the bill. This coming week should see it completed.

Tuesday, July 23, 1974

We must have slept over nine hours last night, the kind of solid sleep that comes only after being on the go as much as we have. I didn't realize that we were so tired.

I didn't have too much activity in the morning but managed to get my desk clear. I went over to the House shortly after noon and talked for a few minutes with Walter Flowers, Tom Downing, and Dan Daniel. It was the first time that I had talked to Walter about the impeachment proceedings in the Judiciary Committee. Without actually saying so, he indicated that he would vote to impeach the President. He said that not to do so would make a mockery of justice. What disturbed him in particular was the record of the President's conversations with Henry Petersen, who was the acting attorney general after Dick Kleindienst bowed out. Walter said that for a month the President carried on conversations with Petersen about the Watergate case and simultaneously fed the information to Haldeman and Ehrlichman to use as they saw fit.

At lunch with Tom and Dan afterward, I noted that it seemed to me that Walter was going to vote for impeachment, but Dan said he wasn't so sure, that he had talked to Walter last week and he seemed to be of a different opinion then. However, I think that Dan is mistaken, based on another conversation that I had with Caldwell Butler later on in the afternoon. Caldwell said that he and several of the others on the Judiciary Committee, including Jim Mann, Walter, Tom Railsback, and another Member whose name escapes me, were going to get up a statement. He added that he felt certain that Walter would vote to impeach, which indicates that all of them will. Tomorrow we have a Republican delegation luncheon, and Caldwell will probably tell us that none of us would feel bound by his decision. I replied that I was sure that we would not, but that he would probably have some company.

The big news in the afternoon was the press conference held by Larry Hogan, at which he announced that he was going to vote to impeach the President. Larry is an announced candidate for governor of Maryland, and his press conference today was universally interpreted as being politically motivated. Bill Bray and Dr. Tim Carter commented on it while reading the board with wire service news on it. Both of them declared that the move would be the end of Larry. I'm not so sure. Impeachment cuts both ways. A reporter asked me in the Speaker's Lobby whether I thought that Hogan's announcement was based on political considerations. I said that I was sure that it wasn't, that it was based on the same judgment that the rest of us would try to bring to the rest of the case, one of conscience and best wisdom. He nodded, but his face showed that he didn't believe a word of it. What else did he expect me to say?

Most of my afternoon was spent in my subcommittee, where we managed to pass several of Bob Sikes' amendments, including the one involving acquisition of land adjacent to the Pensacola Naval Air Station, which means that he will support funding the purchase of additional leaseholds in Norfolk. At least, that is what he said he would do. I'm going to do my best to see that he does.

Wednesday, July 24, 1974

The Supreme Court dropped the other shoe today, and the President's lawyer responded this evening by declaring that he would yield and begin the "time-consuming" task of compliance by compiling and turning over the subpoenaed tapes. So the President will not defy the Court, as few expected that he would. His strategy is as I expected, to spin the thing out as long as he can, at least to the point that the Judiciary Committee will be denied the opportunity to examine whatever evidence can be extracted from the tapes. I may be wrong on this, but I doubt that the tapes will be available prior to the Committee's reporting a bill of impeachment to us.

At the luncheon today of the Virginia Republicans (and near-Republican Dan Daniel), Caldwell laid out to us what he planned to do. It was largely a confirmation of what he said to me yesterday, with the addition of several more Members from the Judiciary Committee. He said that he and Ham Fish, Bill Cohen, Tom Railsback, and possibly Harold Froehlich on the Republican side, along with Ray Thornton, Walter Flowers, and Jim Mann on the Democratic side, were getting together to see if they could draw up a couple bills of impeachment of their own to submit to the Committee. The kind of charges they want to formulate would be more specific than those already presented by Doar to the Committee. These they regard as too broad and indefinite. We asked him what his charges would be based upon, and he replied that one would be based on the President's abuse of power by his use of the IRS against his enemies, and the other on obstruction of justice.

Caldwell claimed that they could document the charges, and that in fact they were going to be very careful to include only the evidence that bore directly upon the charges.

Caldwell reviewed some of the evidence that he felt was critical, in particular the President's conversations with Petersen, which were on an official basis. Petersen told him that he ought to fire both Haldeman and Ehrlichman because they were "up to their navels," as Caldwell put it, in the Watergate coverup. Instead, the President went to both men and endeavored to orchestrate a way out for them. He added that he is convinced that the conversation Nixon had with Haldeman a few days after the Watergate break-in, the one with the eighteen minutes erased from the tape, concerned the entire episode, and that Nixon knew then about the involvement of his Attorney General, Magruder, Hunt, Liddy, and the others. According to Caldwell, it is evident that from the beginning the President knew what had happened and sought to protect his people.

When he concluded his summation, he asked us to protect his confidence until they had presented their proposed bill of impeachment. He said that he did not want to try to influence our decisions, but that in his own mind the President was guilty of gross misconduct and ought to be impeached. "Either we preserve the Presidency as an office we can respect, or we just walk away from it," he said.

He asked me what my reaction was. I replied that I had said some time ago that I could not condone the President's lying to the American people, that I felt that no person who held public office should be permitted to lie deliberately. The President has stated publicly that he knew nothing of the coverup until his March 21 conversation with Dean. If the evidence were conclusive to me that he knew about it beforehand, and especially that he had been a party to the coverup, then I would vote to impeach him. The only other person to offer an opinion was Dan Daniel. Bob Daniel, Bill Wampler, and Stan Parris, who were also at the table, remained silent. But Dan stood up to leave and announced that he could not vote to impeach the President unless the evidence was absolute, and that he would not vote to impeach him on circumstantial evidence. Caldwell started to rebut him and tell him that the evidence was far from circumstantial, but he apparently thought better of it and let the matter drop.

The lines are beginning to form on this thing, and the divisions that have occurred in the nation are now being reflected in the House, first on the Judiciary Committee, then with state delegations, and finally within each party. Barring any other developments, my guess is that the Virginia delegation will split, at least in half but probably a shade against the President. I am still uncommitted and will remain so, but Caldwell's and Walter's statements of the past two days have made a profound impression on me. I don't want to jump on their bandwagon, but I respect the judgment of both of them and know that they would bend over backward to find the President innocent if they could. What the others on the Republican side of the Committee will do remains to be seen, but it would appear that the circle of the President's supporters is growing smaller. I think that the House will vote to impeach him.

The fracturing that is going on among House Republicans is a remarkable thing to watch. Today I overheard Bob McClory and Les Arends having a spirited discussion over the Supreme Court decision. Les was trying to defend the President from the Court, but McClory would have none of it and flatly told Les that if the President didn't comply, it would be all over. The spectacle of Les endeavoring to enlist support for the President among Republican Members is, and there is no other word for it, pathetic. Here is a man who has served forty years in the House and has always been a party stalwart. Now, in the last year of his long congressional career, he is making one final effort to keep his colleagues in line in what has become the greatest test of loyalty for everyone. But the boys aren't buying it. The refrain that I hear over and over is, "I'm hanging loose on this one." And for good reason. The way this thing is unraveling, no one can predict what might happen next. The person who makes a commitment before he has to could well find himself taken over by events. Finally, with the exception of a few of the die-hard conservatives, nobody feels any degree of loyalty to Richard Nixon. But for his mishandling of this whole business, many of us would be facing reelection with considerably less worry than we now have.

As if all of this weren't enough, poor John Rhodes has come under fire from a segment of the membership, primarily the conservatives, for not providing the proper leadership as Minority Leader. Their kick is that John isn't on the floor enough and that he doesn't speak out the way Jerry did nor give directions on voting. Some have complained that they have voted one way, expecting John to do the same, and he has ended up going in the other direction. It got so bad at a meeting of the "Good Guys" last night that at the Wednesday Group meeting today, Howard Robison urged everyone to drop John a note to tell him that he has their confidence. Frankly, I think that this is another impeachment side effect.

Thursday, July 25, 1974—Tuesday, July 30, 1974

The first impeachment articles have been drawn, and the predictions with regard to the members of the Judiciary Committee have largely been on target. In a few weeks, the attention will be on the rest of us, and the same sort of speculation is already going on. Today, the *Washington Post* and the Associated Press, among others, called Vic Powell, my press aide, to try to get a reading on how I'm going to be voting. He told them all that I intend to reserve judgment until I have heard the evidence presented on the floor of the House, and that I will then make up my mind on the basis of the facts. This is the same thing that I have repeatedly said publicly, as well as in letters to constituents who have urged me to state my intentions now. I believe that my constitutional duty requires me to wait until impeachment is actually under consideration in the House before reaching any conclusions.

Thursday was a big day around here. Caldwell delivered a scathing attack on the conduct in the White House and made it clear that the President ought to be impeached. We borrowed a television set from Dale Milford's office across the hall from us, and the staff gathered with me in the office to watch Caldwell when he spoke early in the afternoon. Afterward, I was called by several reporters and asked my reaction. I told them that it was a "powerful statement," but that I was, as I continue to say, holding my judgment until we had heard the evidence in the House. At home over the weekend, I had a large number of inquiries but continued to repeat my stand. One woman called me on Friday afternoon and was so angry that she actually bit off the ends of her sentences and practically spit them out. She was ticked off because the rest of us hadn't spoken out like Mr. Butler. I tried to explain that he had had access to the evidence while the rest of us had not, and that from a constitutional point of view we ought to wait till the evidence was brought to the House. Not surprisingly, she was unaffected by these arguments and hung up. I was buttonholed in the grocery store on Sunday and at several functions we have attended, I was pushed on the matter. The same thing appears to be happening to everyone else around here, because the chief question that one Member asks another is, "What are you hearing about impeachment in your district?"

We held a delegation luncheon on Monday (the 29th). Mills Godwin was in town for a meeting in Bill Scott's office with Secretary of Transportation Brinegar to discuss the extension of I-66 in Northern Virginia. It's a hot topic up here, and the fellows like Bill, Joel, and Stan wanted the rest of us to show up to manifest solidarity. Bill Wampler sat next to me at lunch and brought up the reaction in his district to Caldwell's statement. Bill said that he had gotten up early on Friday morning to shake hands with workers going into a plant in Southwest Virginia, and nine out of ten told Bill that it was Caldwell who ought to be impeached. Clearly, the hostile reaction to impeachment is going to be a factor for some of these men.

Joel Broyhill is anxious to get the delegation together before we vote on the matter. He said that it would be ideal if we could vote unanimously. That means at this point that we would all be joining Caldwell. It is Joel's thinking that we should at least discuss it thoroughly among ourselves. I declared that I was all for it, but I told him in a conversation today (Tuesday) that I didn't think anything would change Dan Daniel's mind short of a personal appearance and confession by the President in the House. Joel is leaning toward impeachment, although his public stance is the same as mine. He told me that he had talked to Bob Michel and told him that we ought to be thinking about how to save Nixon. "I don't want to be the last rat to leave the ship," Joel said, "but I sure as hell want a life preserver."

Our Leadership is making plans to poll the membership and even apply some persuasion. This afternoon I received an invitation from John Rhodes to meet "with a small group" in his office on the morning of August 20 to discuss the evidence presented to the House. I sent a confirmation.

Everything else that has happened pales beside all of this. Nevertheless, a lot of my time has been spent at other pursuits, which is probably a good thing.

The Armed Services Committee has had a couple of meetings, one last Thursday to take up some minor bills, and one today to approve the Military Construction Authorization Bill. The latter passed by a unanimous vote. We took care of the amendments that Bob Sikes wanted after a last-minute mixup over the exact amount, which was corrected in today's bill. I called on Bob yesterday and presented him with some proposed language for the Appropriations Committee which would release money for my leaseholds in Norfolk, and he promised faithfully to attend to it. I certainly hope he keeps his word. Heaven knows I have carried out my end of the bargain. I'll just have to wait and see.

Wednesday, July 31, 1974

In the House the conversation continues to be centered on impeachment. The rumors that are flying about are incredible, and the press corps has been swollen by an influx of reporters from out of town, all here to bleed this episode in American history like nothing else in this century. I have continued to talk to my colleagues in the Virginia delegation about it. Bill Wampler declared this afternoon that there was just so much hard-core sentiment in his district against impeachment that he didn't see how he could vote for it on the basis of evidence so far available. As much as I like Bill, I hate to see him allow political factors weigh so heavily in his thinking and eventual judgment. God knows that I don't want to alienate a segment of my supporters either, but I just don't see how we can permit politics to interfere with our constitutional duty. Bill talked about the hypocrisy of many of the President's enemies on the other side of the aisle. While that can make our task more frustrating, it's no argument of consequence to base a defense of the President upon.

For those fellows on the Judiciary Committee who have voted in favor of the articles of impeachment, it hasn't been easy. I learned today that some of the mail that Walter Flowers has received has been positively vicious. Caldwell told me that his mail for the first couple of days ran fifty-fifty, but now has changed to about four to one in his favor. As of this afternoon, I've gotten nineteen letters urging me not to impeach the President, thirteen urging me to impeach him, and seven assuring me that my judgment was good enough for them.

There was a news story on the wire services that Nixon was

113

considering the so-called Frey Plan, whereby the President would ask the House to impeach him at once so that he could have a swift trial in the Senate. Lou had made the suggestion some months ago but recently has disavowed it, saying that it is now too late. Since Senator Buckley has advocated it, Lou is telling everyone that it ought to be called the Buckley Plan. Mel Laird was at the Republican table in the House Dining Room today, and he said that there was no chance that the President would do such a thing. I don't think that the Leadership would accept the offer. There is a determination that the Committee should present its evidence. The consensus is that the President's position has eroded as a result of the open hearings of the Judiciary Committee for the past two weeks, and that if the House chooses to permit the televising of the impeachment debate, more damage will be done. My personal feeling is that this is probably true, although Charlie Sandman and Charlie Wiggins both scored with a segment of the public. Neither of them is among the star orators in the House, however. What can really hurt the President is a strong statement against him by someone like John Anderson, who is a powerful speaker and whose righteous indignation shines through like a beacon.

At the Wednesday Group meeting today, John told us that the Rules Committee, of which he is a member, will hold an informal meeting tomorrow afternoon to discuss the kind of rule to be granted the Judiciary Committee for presentation of the articles. He said that he thought a modified open rule would be agreed on, since a totally open rule would permit anyone to offer any kind of an amendment, and a circus would ensue. Rather, it is likely that changes in the provisions of each article will be permitted by amendment, and each of these will be voted upon. He did not mention how much time will be allowed, which will give us some idea of when we might expect the business to be concluded.

We learned that the 93rd Congress Class had a meeting with John Rhodes today. According to Jim Johnson, a freshman Member, some of those in the class who have been wearing their American flags in their lapels and exhorting one and all to stand firm are now wavering and looking for a way out. Apparently the Buckley-Frey Plan was discussed, and some suggested that the Republican Leadership might take this to the President. It caused a lot of laughter, some of it derisive. Mark Andrews said that he didn't think it was such a bad idea, but Stu McKinney spoke up quickly to say that after what the Judiciary Committee had gone through, the public would see it as a rank copout. This got agreement all around.

Ham Fish was present but offered little new. His work is largely done now, and the decision has passed from his hands. Both he and Caldwell, as well as Walter, appear to have a great weight now lifted from their shoulders.

The one piece of light news is good. The Republicans defeated the Democrats in the annual baseball game last night, 7-3. It was our eleventh straight victory, but Pete McCloskey quipped afterward that it might be the only thing we'll win this year.

Thursday, August 1, 1974—Friday, August 2, 1974

With impeachment pending, the House has pushed legislation as it hasn't in a long time. We ran through a succession of bills, beginning with insisting on the House amendments to S 425 regarding surface mining, then the USIA Authorization, District of Columbia Campaign Financing, Atomic Energy Omnibus Legislation, the National Forest System conference report, the conference report on Animal Health Research, Small Business Act Amendments, and finally, the Defense Production Act. All of this was yesterday, Thursday, and today we came in at 11:00 and are taking up the Federal Reclamation Projects and Programs plus the International Broadcasting Board Amendment. The Republic won't rise or fall on any of these items, but they are all part of the pattern of bills that comprise the work schedule in a given week. Only we are compressing more of them in. Next week looks even wilder, with a load of bills on the Suspension Calendar (nineteen, to be exact) on Monday.

My appointment to meet John Rhodes was changed suddenly yesterday afternoon from August 20 to this morning at 9:00. I went over to John's office and was joined there by Les Arends, Jim Cleveland, Marjorie Holt, Victor Veysey, Dave Martin, John Rousselot, and Henry Smith. It was certainly a mixed bag. John said that he wanted to discuss impeachment with us and took a line that indicated that if a way could be found to avoid impeaching the President, he would like to see the House take it. For himself, he said that he had to define what an impeachable offense was, and he clearly isn't happy with the articles drawn by the Judiciary Committee. John would like to see them more specific.

The question was raised about whether or not the Rules Committee would permit a motion to recommit to be offered which in turn would allow a motion of censure to be substituted in place of impeachment as a course of action. John said that when he mentioned this to O'Neill, "Tip just about went up the wall." Both he and Les then said that the parliamentary tactic to be followed would be to "defeat the previous question," which in layman's terms means to vote down the rule granted by the Rules Committee. I think that it will be awfully hard to muster enough votes to do that, although a number of Members on both sides would clearly rather vote to censure than impeach the President.

The rule that has been granted permits fifty-five hours of general debate to be followed by thirty-two hours more of arguments on motions offered from the floor. It will not be possible to offer any other articles, although it will be possible to alter the articles reported out by the Committee.

Although no one committed themselves outright, it appeared that only Marjorie and I had serious ideas about voting for impeachment on the basis of what we know now. The others seemed to be leaning the other way. Obviously, Henry Smith has already declared himself by virtue of his being on the Committee. Henry went over some of the charges, including ones that have so disturbed Caldwell and the other Republicans who voted for impeachment. In particular, he reviewed the charge that the President ordered the IRS to audit the McGovern campaign contributors. Henry said that George Shultz at Treasury and Walters at IRS wouldn't comply. Nothing came of it. Henry said that he would censure the President for this, but he didn't think it was impeachable. At this Les spoke up to say that the Democrats had done the same thing when they controlled the White House. He also downplayed the seriousness of Nixon's conversations with Petersen in April of last year, explaining that the President was told by Petersen that Dean was trying to gain immunity by giving information, but that he was dribbling it out. Petersen therefore wanted to keep Dean on the White House staff for a while longer to get more information out of him. The President replied, according to Henry, that he couldn't very well remove Haldeman and Ehrlichman and not fire Dean, too. This part of it appeared a little fuzzy to me, and I'll want to go over the evidence personally.

I asked Henry why someone like Caldwell should read things differently. Henry said that he respected Caldwell as he did the other dissenters on the Republican side, but that he simply did not see the evidence in the same light. The same thing was true of the President's statement to "get it," in reference to the money for Hunt. Henry didn't believe that there was a direct connection between the statement and what was finally done. He mentioned the rest of the conversation, and then John Rousselot, who declared that he had worked with Nixon many years in California, recalled that it was Nixon's manner to go around the room in a meeting and ask everyone to express an opinion, commenting occasionally on each before declaring what he would do. In this light, the President's words could be misinterpreted.

While I found Henry's remarks interesting and persuasive to a point, I am apprehensive about following such a line of thought. Clearly, Marjorie is, too. She said that she hadn't made up her mind, but was awfully unhappy about the conduct in the White House. She also took up for Larry Hogan, who has been the object of severe criticism from many of his colleagues. Apparently some of them have come down on him real hard. John said that he could not fault Larry for drawing his own conclusions, but he felt that the way he went about revealing them was a mistake. Les chimed in and said that everyone knew what his motives were. Marjorie disagreed. She felt that Larry had searched his soul and had every right to go with a press conference as he did.

What bothers John and Les is the delay the Democrats have forced on consideration of the impeachment articles by the House.

Originally, it was thought that the House would take them up by the 15th, but now the 19th has been set. John and Les speculated that either the Democrats hope to get some of the tapes that Sirica has turned over to Jaworski, or they need the extra time to get their own people in line. John said that he had asked Rodino yesterday why they were delaying, and Rodino didn't reply.

At the end of the session, John Rousselot asked John Rhodes what he planned to say on Monday, it having been rumored that John is going to announce that he will step down as Minority Leader if he finds that he must vote for impeachment. Rhodes quietly replied that he would leave that until Monday to answer. Then he told us that he would respect all of us no matter what our decision was, that after this is over we will still have a party to preserve, and that he personally would have no vindictiveness toward any Member, no matter which way he voted. On that note we adjourned.

On the way back to my office, I encountered Pete DuPont. He had just been to a meeting with Charlie Wiggins and had been hearing the anti-impeachment position from him. Pete said that Charlie is very persuasive and extremely knowledgeable about the entire case. I think that Pete defined the real difference that will emerge among the Members as this unfolds in the House and what was apparent to me this morning in comparing Henry's view with that of Caldwell—what is impeachable? For some, it is a broad question, and for others it is narrow. On this Richard Nixon may well stand or fall.

Saturday, August 3, 1974—Monday, August 5, 1974

I had thought that this would be only a perfunctory entry, with just a review of the weekend events and a summary of the nineteen bills on the Suspension Calendar today, but the bombshell statement released by the President this afternoon changes all that. He is finished. There is absolutely no way that he will avoid being impeached in the House, and I believe that he is in grave danger of being convicted in the Senate. If he has any rational thoughts left, he ought to consider resigning now.

There was speculation all morning that something was brewing at the White House, particularly after the news that his speech writers and close confidants were with him at Camp David this weekend. I'm not sure that any of us expected that the statement of this afternoon would be of the magnitude that it is. I need not repeat it in this journal. In effect, the President admitted that he had lied to the American people as well as to the Judiciary Committee in providing information on his knowledge of Watergate. In fact, he admitted that he had misdirected the FBI in its investigation, a clear admission of obstruction of justice.

When this reached the House, its effect was devastating. Charlie Sandman announced to a group in the Republican lounge that he would change his vote on the first impeachment article and now vote in favor of it. Charlie Wiggins, unquestionably the President's most able defender on the Judiciary Committee, gave a statement to the press calling for the President's resignation while declaring at the same time that if he did not, Charlie would vote to impeach him. Wiley Mayne and Carlos Moorhead, both anti-impeachers on the Committee, issued statements reversing their positions. I don't think that Nixon will have a single vote left.

There were huddles of Members all over the House. Manuel Lujan quipped that the way things were going now, it would be possible to dispense with all of the debate and bring the impeachment articles up on the Suspension Calendar, meaning that they could clear them with an hour's debate and a two-thirds vote. Jamie Whitten, who has long been a supporter of the President on the Democratic side, told Bill Dickinson that the President's trouble was that he hadn't had a country lawyer in the first place, that if he had, the lawyer would have gotten rid of the evidence in the first week. I heard someone tell Rodino, "Well, Peter, there goes seven months' work." Rodino smiled and shook his head.

It is curious how a thing of this magnitude, an event that is really tragic as well as historic, will provoke, not outrage or indignation, but wry humor. I think there is also a feeling of relief by an awful lot of Members, including this one. We now have the "smoking gun" we have been looking for. Those of us who were preparing ourselves for an awful lot of heat now have solid grounds for voting for impeachment.

We held a caucus of the Virginia delegation late in the afternoon, after the last vote on the Suspension bills. All of us except Tom Downing, who wasn't here, met in Les Arends' office just off the Floor. We agreed that it would be unwise to issue a joint statement. Joel had told a reporter that we were meeting, but it was agreed to tell the press that we had merely consulted together about the impact of the President's statement. It was Joel's feeling that the way events are breaking, none of us should get out on a limb by revealing our convictions, since the President might well end up resigning before the thing comes to a vote. Some of the others chimed in and noted that we still had a lot of people at home who are strong supporters of the President, and to denounce him now might unnecessarily provoke them.

I was amused by this political analysis, yet there is a certain wisdom in at least keeping up the appearance of impartiality. Ken Robinson said that he was going to say that he still didn't want to vote to impeach the President, but that the President's statement was very damaging and would have to be considered in light of the other evidence. The matter of the President's resignation was brought up, but there was strong feeling that we would be wise not to call for it, although I think Joel would have liked to see such a move.

When I got back to the office, I had a couple of calls from radio stations back home, and I did my best to convey the feeling that although I found the President's words unsettling, I still had to reserve final judgment until the House met formally to consider the evidence.

Off the record, I told the two reporters exactly how I felt, that the President had lied and didn't have a prayer of survival in the House. It is an uncomfortable position to be in. I really would have given anything to see evidence that would preserve Richard Nixon, and I am still keeping the door open, but I know that there isn't a chance now that we will get evidence that will clear him. He has convicted himself out of his own mouth.

Ironically, I spent the early part of the afternoon listening to some of the tapes which were made available to the Judiciary Committee, and from which transcripts have been made and published. They were set up in several rooms in the Rayburn and Cannon Buildings today. I listened to the tapes of conversations of June 30, 1972, September 15, 1972, and February 28, 1973. Since I had spent part of the weekend reading the transcripts of these conversations, I learned nothing new. The fact that the President led the conversations was evident, but I had been told this before. There was also a lot of background noise, but generally the conversations were audible. I had planned to listen to the other tapes, but it seems academic now. Dave Satterfield told me that he had spent the whole weekend reading the volumes printed by the Judiciary Committee and taking copious notes, and in view of what happened today, he regards it as all wasted. All of us wonder now what will happen in the next two weeks. Bob Griffin, the Republican Whip in the Senate, today called for the President's resignation. With the near-total evaporation of his strength in the House, the momentum might well force Nixon to throw in the towel. The repeated declarations that he will not resign are given little credence around here. Everybody remembers Agnew's statements right up to the end.

THE WHITE HOUSE

STATEMENT BY THE PRESIDENT

I have today instructed my attorneys to make available to the House Judiciary Committee, and I am making public, the transcripts of three conversations with H. R. Haldeman on June 23, 1972. I have also turned over the tapes of these conversations to Judge Sirica, as part of the process of my compliance with the Supreme Court ruling.

On April 29, in announcing my decision to make public the original set of White House transcripts, I stated that "as far as what the President personally knew and did with regard to Watergate and the cover-up is concerned, these materials—together with those already made available—will tell all."

Shortly after that, in May, I made a preliminary review of some of the 64 taped conversations subpoenaed by the Special Prosecutor.

Among the conversations I listened to at that time

were two of those of June 23. Although I recognized that these presented potential problems, I did not inform my staff or my Counsel of it, or those arguing my case, nor did I amend my submission to the Judiciary Committee in order to include and reflect it. At the time, I did not realize the extent of the implications which these conversations might now appear to have. As a result, those arguing my case, as well as those passing judgment on the case, did so with information that was incomplete and in some respects erroneous. This was a serious act of omission for which I take full responsibility and which I deeply regret.

Since the Supreme Court's decision twelve days ago, I have ordered by Counsel to analyze the 64 tapes, and I have listened to a number of them myself. This process made it clear that portions of the tapes of these June 23 conversations are at variance with certain of my previous statements. Therefore, I have ordered the transcripts made available immediately to the Judiciary Committee so that they can be included in the record to be considered by the House and Senate.

In a formal written statement on May 22 of last year, I said that shortly after the Watergate break-in I became concerned about the possibility that the FBI investigation might lead to the exposure either of unrelated covert activities of the CIA, or of sensitive national security matters that the so-called "plumbers" unit at the White House had been working on, because of the CIA and plumbers connections of some of those involved, I said that I therefore gave instructions that the FBI should be alerted to coordinate with the CIA, and to ensure that the investigation not expose these sensitive security matters.

That statement was based on my recollections at the time—some eleven months later—plus documentary materials and relevant public testimony of those involved.

The June 23 tapes clearly show, however, that at the time I gave those instructions I also discussed the political aspects of the situation, and that I was aware of the advantages this course of action would have with respect to limiting possible public exposure of involvement by persons connected with the re-election committee.

My review of the additional tapes has, so far, shown no other major inconsistencies with what I have previously submitted. While I have no way at this stage of being certain that there will not be others, I have no reason to believe that there will be. In any case, the tapes in their entirety are now in the process of being furnished to Judge Sirica. He has begun what may be a rather lengthy process of reviewing the tapes, passing on specific claims of executive privilege on portions of them, and forwarding to the Special Prosecutor those tapes or those portions that are relevant to the Watergate investigation.

It is highly unlikely that this review will be completed in time for the House debate. It appears at this stage, however, that a House vote of impeachment is, as a practical matter, virtually a foregone conclusion, and that the issue will therefore go to trial in the Senate. In order to ensure that no other significant relevant materials are withheld, I shall voluntarily furnish to the Senate everything from these tapes that Judge Sirica rules should go to the Special Prosecutor.

I recognize that this additional material I am now furnishing may further damage my case, especially because attention will be drawn separately to it rather than to the evidence in its entirety. In considering its implications, therefore, I urge that two points be borne in mind.

The first of these points is to remember what actually happened as a result of the instructions I gave on June 23. Acting Director Gray of the FBI did coordinate with Director Helms and Deputy Director Walters of the CIA. The CIA did undertake an extensive check to see whether any of its covert activities would be compromised by a full FBI investigation of Watergate, Deputy Director Walters then reported back to Mr. Gray that they would not be compromised. On July 6, when I called Mr. Gray, and when he expressed concern about improper attempts to limit his investigation, as the record shows, I told him to press ahead vigorously with his investigation—which he did.

The second point I would urge is that the evidence be looked at in its entirety, and the events be looked at in perspective. Whatever mistakes I made in the handling of Watergate, the basic truth remains that when all the facts were brought to my attention I insisted on a full investigation and prosecution of those guilty. I am firmly convinced that the record, in its entirety, does not justify the extreme step of impeachment and removal of a President. I trust that as the Constitutional process goes forward, this perspective will prevail.

STATEMENT BY HON. JOHN J. RHODES
HOUSE MINORITY LEADER

August 6, 1974
Washington, D.C.

For me, this is a sad day. I admire Richard Nixon, for the many great things he has done for the people of America and the people of the world. I have no doubt whatsoever that the final analysis of history will be that few American Presidents did more for the solid advancement of world peace than Richard Nixon.

But the most important aspect of our entire system of Government is equal justice under the law—the principle that no person—whether he be rich or poor, black or white, ordinary citizen or President—is above the law. Coverup of criminal activity and misuse of Federal agencies can neither be condoned nor tolerated. And as long as we adhere as a Nation to this principle, our Nation will remain great and strong.

I have considered the evidence to the best of my ability. When the role is called in the House of Representatives, I will vote "aye" on impeachment Article I. In addition, the new evidence made available yesterday has considerable bearing on my decision concerning Article II, a decision which I have not yet finalized.

I make my judgment as a lawyer, a person with some acquaintance with the Constitution, and as a Member of Congress from Arizona. Others may interpret the evidence differently. This requires a highly personal decision.

I still believe that impeachment is not a party matter. It is strictly a matter of conscience. Thus, I have no intention of imposing *my* interpretation of the evidence on any other Member of Congress. For a party Leader to attempt to dictate a matter of individual conscience would be entirely ill-advised.

The past year has been a difficult period for the American people. However, we have come through it with our fundamental belief in justice and the law intact. As was said by President Dwight David Eisenhower:

"America is great because America is good.
And if America ceases to be good, America will cease to be great."

I have every confidence that America will remain both good *and* great.

Tuesday, August 6, 1974—Wednesday, August 7, 1974

If any sands are left to run out for Richard Nixon, there can't be more than a couple of grains. The Judiciary Committee now stands unanimously for impeachment, and the only two Members of the House that I know of who are still standing by him are Otto Passman and Earl Landgrebe. Earl made a pledge of loyalty to the President on Tuesday afternoon, declaring that he would remain loyal to the point of their being taken from the Capitol and shot. Sonny Montgomery may still be leaning toward the President, but he isn't saying much, except to joke with Tip O'Neill and several others in the Well of the House that he was going to ask for twenty hours of time in the impeachment debate and give two hours to Otto. He said, "If I give him more than two hours, he'll wear his suit out on television." It brought Tip almost to tears, he laughed so hard. Everybody remembers Don Riegle's classic comment about Passman's gyrations when he speaks. Don said that he's the only Member who wears his suits out from the inside.

The succession of statements made by Tuesday night read like a list of Who's Who in Congress. They were all topped by that of John Rhodes, which I have attached to this diary. I went into the Republican lounge to watch it on television. Poor old Les Arends watched it and shook his head. He said very little and left immediately afterward. It's hard to believe that only last Friday I sat in Rhodes' office and heard him try to make a case for the President. Every person in that room except Les has now come out against the President.

Late Tuesday afternoon, I saw Dan Daniel and talked briefly with him. Although Dan has expressed deep disappointment with the President's admissions, he has withheld an opinion that might be construed as indicating that he was going to vote to impeach. He told me that he could vote either way and added that all day long he had been getting messages from people in the Fifth District to stand by the President. Tom Downing called for the President's resignation, but all the rest stopped short of calling for impeachment. This reaction, I think, has stemmed from Monday afternoon's meeting.

On Tuesday morning I was besieged by calls from the press, and I declared that the President's admissions were grave and damaging. I stopped short of saying that I would vote for impeachment, but I did say that anyone who had willfully lied to the public had betrayed his trust and ought to forfeit his office. When asked about the President's resigning, I demurred, saying that it was a decision that only the President himself could make, although it was one to which he should give serious consideration. I concluded by saying that I wanted to wait to make a final decision until the matter was before the House.

Late in the afternoon, I read a transcript of the June 23, 1972 conversation which the President had with Haldeman. It was published in the *Washington Star*. It was even more disturbing than the

President's words of Monday. I knew then that the evidence was incontrovertible. When Janie and I got home late last night (Tuesday), there was a letter waiting for me from Mike Rorer, who has been active in support of the President at home and led a meeting on his behalf in Norfolk last Saturday morning. Mike was unhappy about some press reports that he had heard over the weekend that I was preparing to vote to impeach the President. His letter had been written on Sunday, so the events of Monday had superseded it. When I came to the office this morning, I knew that I had to answer him, and I also knew that I could no longer refrain from stating forthrightly my conviction that the President ought to go. I dictated a letter to Mike and one to Virginia Murphy, one of my best workers, who is also a member of Mike's organization and has been a staunch and outspoken supporter of the President. I had, in effect, crossed over, but I wanted these people to know it first. The events of the day overtook me.

In mid-morning I got word that a news team from WTAR-TV was coming up to interview me. Janie said that I could not very well say one thing privately and anything less publicly. I knew that she was right and agreed to prepare a statement announcing that I would vote to impeach the President on the basis of the evidence I had read in the published transcript. I have slipped into this by degrees, restrained inside by the instinct to somehow avoid taking such a drastic step, moving only as I felt that I had to, and finally convinced by a Presidential dialogue that is simply indefensible. I have speculated in my mind as to what I might have done had that June 23, 1972 tape never come to light so that I would have had to make up my mind on the basis of the evidence brought forth by the Judiciary Committee. I found Caldwell's arguments very persuasive and the circumstantial evidence strong. I was terribly unhappy over the way that Nixon had handled this whole business, and might, in the final analysis, have voted for impeachment anyhow, but, thank heaven, that path is closed. Looking over the record as objectively as I know how, I believe that my reaction to it all was a human one, filled with self-doubts at times, an effort to accommodate my position at others, but a true inner resolve to vote my conscience and convictions at the end. I know that I never counted personal political consequences as a factor in my thinking. The very magnitude of the thing pushed any consideration of that aside.

This afternoon the wildest kinds of rumors swept the Capitol and the House offices. At one point it appeared that the President's resignation was imminent. The news teams from home are staying in town just in case it happens by tomorrow. Gwen told me yesterday that she has a source of information that is unimpeachable (a bad pun in this instance) who told her that the President would step down by Thursday. For awhile this afternoon I thought it might be true, and it is still possible that tomorrow will see the conclusion of this tragedy.

Following the breakfast, I attended a Republican conference in the House to review the Federal Election Campaign Act. Not surprisingly, the Democrats have brought forth a bill that will give them some advantages in future campaigning. We agreed that our best strategy would be to try to get a change in the rule by voting down the previous question when the bill came up today. We agreed that there was little chance to do this, and, not surprisingly, we lost this afternoon on almost a pure party vote. I'll probably vote for the bill on final passage, because there is such a demand for campaign reform.

We're home tonight, the House having adjourned without finishing the Campaign Reform Bill. It could be a long session tomorrow. Before coming home, I called the Virginia Beach chief of police to ask if he could have his men patrol my street the next few evenings. While I have not received any threats, I know that there are enough vindictive people about who might want to vandalize our home while we are away. It just seemed to be the prudent thing to do. He was in complete agreement and promised to have a team look out for us. What a sad business all of this is!

Thursday, August 8, 1974—Monday, August 12, 1974

Sitting here in the office this evening (Monday), with Jerry Ford scheduled to speak to the Congress in less than two hours as President of the United States, I find it hard to believe that one week could contain so many developments. Not only has there never been another week like it in my brief career in Congress, but I would venture to say that there has never been another week like it in American history. May there never be another.

It was only last Monday that Nixon's bombshell message fell on us. By Thursday it was clear that he was going to resign. It was announced on Thursday morning that the President would speak that night at 9:00 and declare then that he was going to resign. The only speculation was about how the President would announce his leaving and the specific time that he would step down.

The President's speech was about what I expected. I didn't think that he would make an act of contrition on national television. It wasn't in his character to do so. Actually, I thought that the President's words were well chosen, and he emphasized the things that I would have had I been in his place. His efforts for world peace are to his everlasting credit and he had a right to cite them. He should be remembered for his other accomplishments: bringing an end to the war in Vietnam on the only terms we could hope for, a return of the prisoners of war to their families; a pragmatic relationship with China and a concerted effort to achieve a reasonable relationship with Russia; and finally, his efforts to bring peace to the Middle East.

His remarks of farewell to his staff, which were broadcast on Friday morning, were also to be expected, but I found myself untouched by the sentimentality which the President sought to arouse and obviously achieved for millions of people. He successfully surrounded himself with a cloak of pathos, albeit sincere. He honestly feels that he has been driven from office, and he does not see his mistakes with the severity that his critics and former supporters in Congress saw them. But this is natural. Few of us see our sins as critically as others do. In Nixon's case, though, he has behaved like a schizophrenic. I could not help but compare his words of Friday morning with those I had heard on the tapes on Monday afternoon. They seemed to have been spoken by two different men. In a sense, they may well have been. Someone at home said to me over the weekend that the President must have been somewhat unbalanced. I replied that anyone who wants to be President has to be a little crazy.

Janie and I left for home in the middle of Friday afternoon. It rained hard on the way down, and a tractor-trailer overturned in the middle of I-95 just to add to the fun. For such an inauspicious start, the weekend didn't turn out too badly. Blanche had said that the calls on Friday were pretty terrible. She said that she had stopped counting after the number passed twenty-five. Some threatened me, saying that they were going to "punch Bill Whitehurst in the nose," when they saw me. One chap declared that he was going to hit me over the head. All of this was a reaction, an understandably emotional one, to the President's farewell speech of Friday morning. In light of that, I looked like a heartless villain. Nevertheless, we thought it prudent to switch the office appointments on Saturday to the Norfolk office in the Post Office, where a guard is on duty to screen everyone coming in, rather than keep them in Virginia Beach, where anyone can walk in from the outside. My personal feeling is that people will get over this in a few days. I remember the intense ill feeling against Harry Truman after General MacArthur made his famous farewell speech to a Joint Meeting back in 1951. In less than a month, it had all died down, and ultimately a majority of people recognized that Truman had been right in firing MacArthur.

We knew that things weren't all bad on Friday night, when, after having eaten dinner in a restaurant in Portsmouth, we drove toward the tunnel to Norfolk and were passed by a young man who gave us the thumbs up sign as he preceded us to the tunnel. We followed him to a toll booth, and as we pulled abreast of the toll collector, he told me that the driver ahead of me had paid our toll as well as his own. I was dumbfounded and said that I wanted to pay for my own car. "I can't collect twice, Mister," he replied. Fortunately, we got the license number of the young man's car and later tracked down the ownership so that I could convey my thanks.

At the office on Saturday, we had four letters waiting for us, all complimentary about my actions. No calls at the office that morning were hostile, and we received none that weekend at home, although I must confess that we didn't answer it every time it rang. Most people, it appears, are thankful the thing is over, and there seems to be a real desire to put it behind us and get on with trying to solve our problems in cooperation with the new President.

Both Janie and I found that we were not immune to the effects of the strain of the week. Both of us suffered from depression over the weekend, and she confided to me that she had wept while in bed on Saturday night. We had dinner guests last night, including Admiral Jerry Denton of POW fame and his wife Jane. They and the other two couples we had invited helped lift our spirits, and we've picked up some today.

Tuesday, August 13, 1974

If one sentence could sum up Jerry Ford's appearance at the Joint Session last night, it would be: "He spoke as if he were at home." Janie and I got to the House at 8:30, and it was already nearly filled. I found a seat at the back of the Chamber in a row with Don Rumsfeld; Bill Scranton, former Member and governor of Pennsylvania; Bill Springer, another former Member; Bill Wampler; Chuck Mosher; and Bill Avery, another former Member from Kansas. I saw quite a few former Members here, and there were former Cabinet members in the gallery, including George Romney and Mel Laird. I was surprised to see Don Rumsfeld, and said so. "Who's holding the fort in Brussels?" I asked. He replied that he had left those things in good hands. I understand that he's going to be helping President Ford put a new team together.

In the row across the aisle I saw George Bush, and I remembered at once that I had written to President Ford during the day to nominate George for Vice President. The President has followed the same procedure that Nixon used. He has asked every Republican Member of Congress to send him up to three names. Having sent the names of Ford and Bush to Nixon, I thought it appropriate to send George's name alone this time.

August 12, 1974

Dear Republican Colleague:

President Ford has indicated to me that he would very much appreciate receiving your suggestions for the office of Vice President.

If you have a candidate in mind, please forward your recommendation and comments to this office before three o'clock tomorrow afternoon in a sealed envelope addressed to the President of the United States. I will see that your recommendation is directed personally to the President.

Yours sincerely,

John J. Rhodes, M.C.
Minority Leader

August 12, 1974

The President
The White House
Washington, D.C. 20500

Dear Mr. President:

Having been advised that you were interested in suggestions for a Vice President, I would like to take this opportunity to recommend George Bush. Last year, when President Nixon asked us to forward the names of those people we felt would be proper choices for Vice President and who could step into the Presidency if necessary, I recommended you and George Bush.

It is natural now that I should resubmit the name of George Bush. Certainly I need not recount his virtues to you. I'm sure that you know George far better than I, but I remember how much George impressed me during my first term in the 91st Congress, and I thought then that he, like you, had those special characteristics that qualify a man for the highest office if fate so designates.

There are many other eminent men and women available, but none of them impresses me so much as George.

Let me also take this opportunity to pledge to you my absolute support, and I would add that I expect to make the principal theme of my reelection campaign the need to be sent to the 94th Congress in order to sustain your programs.

Janie joins me in very best wishes to you and Mrs. Ford.

Sincerely,

G. WILLIAM WHITEHURST

By the time everyone, including the Senate, the Cabinet, and the Diplomatic Corps had arrived, the House was more crammed than I have ever seen it. Quite a few didn't have seats, including some of the ambassadors, who stood with a mixture of late-arriving Members, doormen, and pages. Julie Eisenhower and David arrived to sit in the President's family area of the Gallery, and they received prolonged applause. When the Senate came in shortly afterward, someone commented that the senators got less applause than Julie and David. "They deserve less," someone else replied. I think everyone admired Julie's spirit in coming to the House to hear her father's successor speak just a few days after her father was forced to resign.

When Jerry was announced, the ovation was loud and prolonged. Carl Albert had a wide grin on his face, and for once the applause seemed to be as heavy on the Democratic side as on the Republican. There is little I can add to the many press accounts of the President's remarks, or say as well. He had some well-turned phrases in his statement, but while they were clever, they weren't sophisticated. His prose was solid and uncomplicated. It lacked the grandeur of other words spoken from that podium, but grandeur isn't the tonic that's needed now. Even Jerry's occasional stumbling over words seemed to fit. His lack of polish was an asset. At the end I was afraid that he might talk too long, a characteristic that I have noted in the past, but he concluded shortly after 9:30. I was glad that he came down hard on inflation and the need to exercise fiscal restraint. His appeal for cooperation was not only politically wise but publicly popular. The nation needs to hear such words and feel that this man is going to try to pull the government together.

The press reports this morning were unanimous in approval of both the tone and the substance of the President's speech. Some grumbling occurred on the Democratic side about the President's formula for fighting inflation, but the truth is that none of them has any better answer. We're in for some belt-tightening, but the President was right in calling for it.

A familiar sight to anyone traveling with Congressman Bill Whitehurst. Many a trans-oceanic flight passed quickly for me as I transcribed my notes from another foreign adventure.

November, 1973, meeting with Moshe Dayan at his home in Tel Aviv.

April, 1975, chatting with Admiral Hyman Rickover at Newport News prior to the launching of the USS Memphis.

July, 1975, with Rep. Sam Stratton (D—N.Y.) on our way to Somalia to verify the Soviet military presence there.

The controversial Soviet barracks ship at Berbera.

Congressman Sam Stratton confronts a Russian Marine in a futile attempt to board the Soviet barracks ship.

Saying farewell to Berbera, the hottest day of my life.

October, 1975. A remarkable Washington acquaintance, Oleg Yer-mishkin, Second Secretary of the Soviet Embassy.

Paying our annual Christmas visit to the Naval Supply Center in Norfolk, a chance to combine business with pleasure.

April, 1976. The most chilling experience of my China visit: school-children from an elementary school in Dairen, Manchuria demonstrate their discipline and marksmanship at a firing range beside the play-ground next to their school.

1975

This morning I was visited by four South Vietnamese, three of whom were from the legislature in Saigon and the other from the Embassy here. It was clear why they were on the Hill. They were making a last-minute effort to lobby on behalf of the aid that the President has requested. Their trip also may have been inspired by the visit of our House delegation to South Vietnam and Cambodia last month. One of the group today was a woman, attractively attired in the fashion of her country, slacks and a knee-length dress which was beautifully embroidered.

I told them that I had visited their country back in 1970, when U.S. forces had swept the communist sanctuaries, and I recalled the late General Tri, who had made such a favorable impression on us. I declared my admiration for those elements of the ARVN forces I had seen, but then said that I felt that I should speak frankly, for if they had traveled all of this distance and were given only platitudes by my people, we would be doing them a disservice.

As gently as I could, I told them that I had long supported our policy toward their nation, but that most of the mail that I now received ran heavily against further assistance being rendered. The American people, I said, have watched the events that have occurred since we withdrew our forces, and the record they have witnessed has been one of almost uninterrupted reverses. If Americans thought, I went on, that the money being sought now would save South Vietnam once and for all, there would surely be support for providing it, but the feeling of the majority of our people is that any money spent now would be wasted, and this is a time of economic distress for the United States.

"Before coming to Congress," I continued, "I taught American history, and I remember a battle which occurred in our war for independence. In 1777 we needed a victory badly, and in October of that year we defeated and captured a British army under General Burgoyne at Saratoga in New York. While the war continued for six more years, that battle insured our independence because it convinced the French that we could win and persuaded them to support our cause openly. What you need is a Saratoga. If you could win a great victory at this time, it might change opinion in the United States. Unfortunately, you have just suffered a severe defeat in the loss of the highland provinces in your country."

It was a strong dose, but I did not know how to put it more tactfully, and I felt that drawing upon a historical parallel might have some meaning. I went on to say that we were unhappy about the enormous expenditure of ammunition by South Vietnamese forces, much greater than that expended by the communists. At this, one of them noted that he had formerly been a Ranger in the ARVN and had been trained at Fort Benning. He made the point that the Americans had trained the ARVN to fire into an area with suppressive rounds first and then maneuver in toward enemy forces. Now, he said, they were having to change this pattern of fighting, and it took time. I smiled inwardly at this tactic of trying to force us to share the burden of their defeat. Still, the occasion was too far-reaching in import to treat it simply as a verbal tilt. These people were returning to their country in another week and were here making a plea for help that is desperately needed if they are to save themselves, both as a nation and quite literally as individuals; their own lives are at stake. I avoided making a personal commitment one way or another, but spoke in terms of "the Congress," thereby sparing myself or them embarrassment. On leaving, we exchanged gifts. They presented me with a handsome lacquered tray and a book with illustrations of South Vietnam. I gave the lady a silver replica of the House mace, and the men replicas of the Norfolk mace made into tie clasps. I felt badly about being so discouraging, but in the final analysis they must take back an accurate picture to their own government, so that it can be factored into whatever decision they can make that will determine their own fate. They told me that of all the Members they had visited so far, I was the only one to give them such an honest answer.

As they walked out, one of them turned to me and asked, "What did you say the name of the place was in New York where the battle occurred?" "Saratoga," I replied. "Isn't there a racetrack there now?" he asked. "Yes," I answered, somewhat nonplused. "A non sequitur if I ever I heard one," I thought.

Wednesday, April 9, 1975—Sunday, April 13, 1975

The main event that has absorbed the nation's attention for the past few weeks has been the near-collapse of the defense of Cambodia and South Vietnam. Cambodia is on the brink of complete defeat, and the Saigon government doesn't seem to be far behind. Here at home, be it in Tidewater or elsewhere, there has been an outpouring of concern for South Vietnamese orphan children, particularly those fathered by American soldiers. While I was gone, Rena and Janie were tied up with an effort to bring a group of orphans to the Norfolk area. A monumental foul-up occurred, largely as a result of one well-meaning woman who had neglected to insure that the departure of the children had been cleared through Saigon; she turned out to have been something less than truthful in her statements of what had been done along the line. Quite honestly, I believe that this national reaction is nothing but a pang of conscience. The nation is unwilling to send military forces to save South Vietnam again, being unconvinced that large amounts of military aid could reverse the tide but unwilling to stand aside and do nothing. Somehow, humanitarian aid strikes the right balance between aloofness and all-out help. We are surely a strange people. What angered me while I was in Europe was to read the European press and some government reaction, taking us to task for ignoring the deteriorating condition in South Vietnam, which somehow was still supposed to be our responsibility. Vague suggestions were made that Kissinger ought to be out working his magic again. Lord, but they do know how to strain an alliance! When we were mired down in Indochina, they were complaining that we weren't giving Europe enough attention and were expending our strength in Asia.

The President is still living in the world of make-believe. He addressed a Joint Session of the Congress on Thursday night and made a plea for military and economic-humanitarian aid. I wasn't there, having come home to attend another Repubican fund-raiser, this one in Virginia Beach. It really didn't make any difference. The speech would still have left me unconvinced, and I told the reporters who interviewed me the following day just that. My Virginia colleagues on both sides of the aisle, I noted, were saying nearly the same thing. Jerry might get some money for humanitarian assistance, provided that there are guarantees that it will be administered properly and will get to the right people, but he won't get a dime for military support. It's just as I told the South Vietnamese who came to see me three weeks ago: the American people don't think the South Vietnamese can win.

Ironically, before I left to come home on Thursday, Oleg Yermishkin, an acquaintance from the Soviet Embassy, came by my office to present me with an issue of the magazine Soviet Life, commemorating the thirtieth anniversary of the victory over fascism in 1945, the end of the "Great Patriotic War," as the Russians like to call it. We had a rather frank exchange. I commented on what was happening in Cambodia and South Vietnam and observed that it was the last bloody chapter there for everybody, and the final humiliation for the United States as well. "Oleg," I said, "it goes beyond Indochina. It is, I think, the last chapter in the American involvement on the Asian continent." And then I recited the events: the failure of our China policy, of which we have been reminded by the death last week of

Chiang Kai-shek; the deadlock and semi-victory in Korea; and now, over a decade of spent blood and treasure in Indochina. "But if it were really vital to your national interest, you would commit your forces," Yermishkin said. It was an important observation, I thought, and I said so. Some people have been saying that our unwillingness to save the situation in South Vietnam might be interpreted by the Russians as a sign that we would be unwilling to take a stand elsewhere, such as the Middle East or even Western Europe. Yermishkin wisely saw otherwise, and I said nothing that would disabuse him of this notion.

He said something else that I thought was cogent: "People say that Moscow controls this government or that, and that we pull strings everywhere. This is not true. We cannot control like people say we do."

"I agree with you, up to a point, at least," I replied; "Asia will develop from forces within and will be subject to only peripheral control from without." I went on to say that for his country the consequences of this would be far greater than for mine, since they had their feet planted on two continents. The Thais have already begun a reassessment of their policy toward us and China, and I expect that most of our forces will be withdrawn within a year or so. That will have little impact. Of more importance is what the Japanese may do. So long as we continue to maintain a military force of consequence in Korea, they will probably be content with their present relationship with us, but if the Congress votes to cut back that force this year or next, the Japanese will be bound to make a significant reassessment.

My Russian friend reads the picture just as I do, and while he may privately take some satisfaction in witnessing the triumph of the communist cause in a corner of Southeast Asia, he also knows that if it leads to a complete abdication of American power in the Far East, the balance that now exists will find a substitute in a yet-unknown formula, one perhaps less to the Russian liking than the present one. So much for pontificating. I am glad that I have met Yermishkin, and I think that he enjoys and even profits from these conversations.

Monday, April 14, 1975—Sunday, April 20, 1975

The Armed Services Committee met on Tuesday to hear Secretary of Defense Schlesinger and General Weyand, chief of staff of the Army. They were present to make a pitch for military aid to South Vietnam. It turned out to be little more than window dressing. Both made statements, but rather than a genuine question-and-answer session following, the last-ditchers on the Committee took the occasion to make speeches declaring their undying support for our South Vietnamese allies. These included Eddie Hébert, Bob Wilson, Sam Stratton, and one or two others. It was near noon at that point, and I saw it as a pointless exercise since the Committee had no intention of voting on the matter, preferring to let it die. I wasn't sure that more aid would be voted by the Committee, and it wouldn't have a chance in the House. Neither witness was back that afternoon, having gone over to the Senate to testify instead. It was just as well. There is no point in fracturing ourselves in the Committee any more than we are already with those who are fundamentally opposed to our own defense budget, to say nothing of sending more military aid to South Vietnam.

The South Vietnamese drama was far from over for the week, however. On Thursday, we had a visit from Walt Rostow of the Yale Law School, former advisor to the Kennedy and Johnson Administrations. Rostow was before us to make a plea on behalf of a Democratic organization for a stronger defense. He had sent us the report of the group, which was as strong a document as I've seen put out by a civilian organization for this cause. Rostow reflects the academic and cultural milieu of the Ivy League. His voice, his vocabulary, and his ability to debate and persuade make him a formidable figure. While I didn't buy all of his arguments, particularly those relating to Indochina, I certainly had to agree with his world view, which I thought pragmatic and terribly realistic. He wants to see us increase the military budget, not only for its own sake but as a sign to our allies and potential foes alike that we are determined to meet our commitments in spite of the reversal in Southeast Asia. He got praise from those of us who generally share his view, fenced well with those who have doubts, and was unruffled by a scathing attack by Ron Dellums, who told one and all for the umpteenth time that the real enemy is at home in the form of suppressed freedoms, government agencies like the CIA spying on American citizens, unfulfilled dreams and hopes of minorities and the poor, and so forth. Rostow smiled and agreed that Dellums had raised points that could not be adequately covered in such a short period of time, and he invited him to come to New Haven and continue the dialogue. I couldn't agree with his proposal to add another $10 billion to the military budget, but I surely don't want to see it gutted the way many of my colleagues in the House do. Dellums and Pat Schroeder both told Rostow that he was twenty-five years behind the times. In the sense that he sounded like a voice from the past, I agreed.

After Rostow finished his testimony in the afternoon, we heard from a young man representing a newly-founded organization of Americans married to South Vietnamese. I was amazed to learn that there are about 25,000 American-South Vietnamese marriages. The man before us made a plea on behalf of the families of these wives, declaring that many of them will be slaughtered if they are not evacuated. While he was talking, his own wife sat at the table with him, while seated behind were several others with children. It was clearly an ordeal for some of them. Two of the girls dabbed at their eyes with handkerchiefs throughout.

We tried to get some idea of how many people would be involved, but it was impossible. A kind of national hand-wringing is taking place, but little else. Only at the end of the week were there clear indications that the Administration is moving resolutely to get the remaining Americans out of the country. Reports of the slaying of former supporters of the government are trickling in, and it appears that with the fall of Cambodia the same pattern is occurring. Any mass evacuation of South Vietnamese is out of the question, even if we wanted to effect it. It would take a substantial number of ships and considerable organization for such an effort. Events are just taking place too fast to permit it, and even the concern about getting children and infants out is subsiding. The President and his supporters are still paying lip service to the idea of aiding the Saigon government, but the Congress seems to be stalling the game until it is too late even to talk about doing anything.

On Tuesday evening, Janie and I attended the Republican Senate-House fund raiser at the Washington Hilton. There didn't seem to be quite so many people present as in previous years, but the International Ballroom is pretty big, and it was a sizeable crowd all the same. It may have been just me, but I sensed a lack of spark about the whole affair. In the past there has been an air of excitement and enthusiasm, which ironically was present in the Nixon years. Ford was there on Tuesday night, and he made the speech that was expected of him; only it wasn't effective. What the party faithful needed to hear was a hard-hitting, fire-eating partisan message, one that would have them on their feet cheering and ready to follow their leader into battle. What they got instead was a tepid and flat performance from Jerry, which was followed not by prolonged applause but by a mass exodus for the coat-check rooms when he finished. Janie and I talked about it when we were driving home. I know that Jerry will never take any trophies home for his forensic abilities, but on one or two occasions, when he led the House, he managed to fire us up. He sure isn't doing that now. Furthermore, John Anderson told us at the Wednesday Group meeting the following day that he is worried about Jerry's chances of getting the nomination next year. He said that he has detected a "sullenness" among our Members that he hasn't seen before, reflecting a disillusionment with Ford's leadership. I've noticed it, too. I asked John Rhodes on Thursday if the President was going to veto the Youth Camp Safety Act, which a number of us had voted vainly against. "Who knows?" John replied wryly. Anderson added in his conversation that nobody at the White House appears to be making the kind of plans that ought to be made to insure that Jerry gets the nomination. The normal political preparation that should be going forward now is absent. Pete McCloskey reminded us again of Reagan's activity in California. There could be some political surprises next year, and not a little bloodshed. The only comforting thing is that the Democrats don't seem to be in any better shape.

A very busy week, this one, with the House mired down in the Energy Bill for most of the time. Some of the damnedest amendments have been offered, including one that would give a tax credit for stoves burning wood, corn husks, or, of all things, buffalo chips. Somebody called it the "Burn America First" amendment. The entire proceeding reminded me of something Bismarck is supposed to have said, "There are two things that people should never watch being made, sausages and laws." I'm very much afraid that the bill will be a hopeless maze of regulations which will have little impact on the energy shortage. So many of the amendments that have been offered follow the typical liberal formula of setting forth certain conditions to be met, and from each of these certain regulations or restrictions of taxes will follow. On paper they appear so plausible, but experience has shown that formulas of this kind tend to bog down, and enforcement becomes expensive and difficult. Many of them are not thought through sufficiently, and they can often produce results not anticipated or intended. I doubt that I will be able to vote for the bill on final passage, which looks to be at least next Tuesday at this rate.

We passed the Military Construction Bill before the Armed Services Committee on Tuesday, but it looks as if we will not get it before the House until the week after the one coming up. There is a backlog of legislation pending that must get a rule from the Rules Committee. Also, on Tuesday, I joined Sam Stratton, Sonny Montgomery, and Senator Jim McClure of Idaho for lunch with a member of the Japanese Diet named Kusaka. Several people from the Japanese Embassy were present, and, periodically, other Members of the House came by to say hello, including Bob Sikes, Dick Bolling, and George Mahon. The purpose of the luncheon was to discuss the American defense posture in the Far East vis-à-vis Japan. Kusaka proved to be an amiable person, more outgoing than the average Japanese, but he was the noisiest luncheon partner I've had in a long time. He ate his cole slaw like spaghetti, slurping in the individual shreds of cabbage and making simultaneous sounds of gastronomic approval. The conversation was less distracting. He showed a real interest in preserving our force levels in Korea and declared that Japan would view with profound alarm any significant cutback, a view that came as no surprise to me. I only wish that some of my colleagues who want a drawdown of U.S. forces abroad had heard him. I brought up the subject of increasing the Japanese armed forces, but Kusaka would say little more than that Japan was bound by constitutional restrictions, a position that I have come to believe serves more as a dodge than as a valid conviction that Japan would rearm if circumstances required them to. For what it was worth, I said that it seemed to me that Japan should participate more actively in the defense of her own homeland. The Japanese at the table nodded that they understood, even if it didn't mean they agreed.

Thursday, June 26, 1975—Tuesday, July 1, 1975

Home for an abbreviated recess which will end with a trip to Somalia this weekend. The genesis of it occurred earlier last month (June), when Secretary of Defense Schlesinger, in arguing for improving our facilities on Diego Garcia, pointed out that the Russians had established a base at Berbera in Somalia, thus improving the logistics for their naval forces operating in the Indian Ocean. Last week, the Somalis rebutted this by denying that any foreign power had a military base on their territory, and they sent a letter inviting members of the Senate and House Armed Services Committees to visit Somalia to see for themselves.

Last Thursday morning (June 26), we received a top-secret briefing by intelligence authorities in our committee room. There we saw aerial photographs confirming the Soviet presence in the vicinity of Berbera. We agreed, however, that the invitation could not be refused, but only if we were allowed to fly over any area we wished and visit on the ground those places that had our interest. Our chief counsel, Frank Slatinshek, asked me if I would go, and I said that I probably could, but I wanted assurances that we would have the guarantees of freedom of movement that we wanted. The Somalis came back affirmatively on this, and the trip was on. I talked to Frank on Friday afternoon and told him to count me in. He said that Mel would be pleased, since he wanted "a solid Republican" along. I guess I qualify. At this point, I don't know who else is going, but I don't think there will be too many of us. I think that Sam Stratton will be the senior Democrat. We leave Andrews at 8:00 p.m. on the 4th and return about the same time on Monday the 7th. We will have less than forty-eight hours in Somalia, which is probably just as well; I understand that it is a pretty primitive place.

What could make things sticky is the experience a CBS news team had there. They were also invited to come and film anything they wanted, but once they got there they found the Somalis unwilling to honor their pledge. They were not permitted to see everything they wanted. If the same thing happens to us, I think that we should leave forthwith, and I will certainly suggest it. The photographs shown us were decisive proof of lively Soviet naval activity, and they appear to be pushing forward on a long runway as well. In any event, I expect that the trip will be interesting, and I am glad that I have the opportunity to make it.

Friday, July 4, 1975—Monday, July 7, 1975

Janie took me to the Norfolk airport on Friday afternoon to catch a flight for Washington. I was met at National Airport by an Air Force major and driver and taken to our Arlington apartment to kill a couple of hours until it was time to go to Andrews Air Force Base early that evening for the first leg of our journey to Somalia. At 7:00 the driver returned, and we drove to Andrews, where I met with my colleagues in the guest lounge of the terminal. We had some last-minute changes, so that those who made the trip, finally, were Sam Stratton, who was chairman of the delegation; Lucien Nedzi, Charlie Wilson, and Bob Leggett, all on the Democratic side; plus Tony Won Pat of Guam. Floyd Spence, Dick Schulze, and I carried the Republican flag. John Ford was the principal staff member from our Committee, but there were also some DOD people along who represented specific intelligence skills, including a woman, June Crutchfield, who is a Russian language expert.

We departed Andrews about 8:15, after first being bade farewell by the Somali ambassador in Washington and taking aboard a member of his embassy staff, who accompanied us throughout our stay in his country.

The flight was a long one, broken by a refueling stop at Torrejon, the U.S. air base outside Madrid. There we secured a briefing room to go over the aerial photographs of the Berbera area, where the Russians have established facilities to enhance their logistical position in the Indian Ocean.

From Spain we flew directly to Mogadishu, the capital of Somalia, arriving there about 8:30 p.m. Somalia time on July 5. The flight had been a long one; it was seventeen hours since we had left Andrews.

As we were flying down the Red Sea, we talked by radio with Senator Dewey Bartlett, who had just left Somalia following a visit paralleling our own. He told us that the Secretary of Defense "had been correct" in what he had said about Somalia, that in fact the Russians had facilities there.

It had been raining when we landed, and the weather was warm and humid, not too different from what we experience in Washington or Virginia Beach at this time of year. As we debarked from the plane, we were greeted by a line of Somali officials, led by one of the three vice presidents of the Supreme Revolutionary Council, Major General Hussein Kulmie Afrah. In the airport terminal, he welcomed us and advised us that we would meet with their president, Major General Mohamed Siad Barre, at 11:00. It was a late hour for a conference, but since our visit was to be such a short one, we had no choice.

Then we were driven off in a fleet of Mercedes' and Fiats to our quarters at the Hotel Rugta Taleh, a sprawling complex of one-story units with three rooms and two baths, a kitchen, and a lounge to serve them. All were air-conditioned against the humid weather. I shared my unit with Bob Leggett and Dick Schulze.

Before meeting President Siad, we drove to the home of the American chargé d'affaires, Sam Hamrick. He talked about the Bartlett visit, which he felt had been effective, and speculated on the basis of the visit, on which he expressed no firm convictions. He felt that we would have to wait for a while to see whether or not Siad intended to use it as a platform for a closer relationship with the United States.

Shortly before eleven, we got in our cars again and drove to the military compound where President Siad has his quarters. It reminded me a little of our visit to Anwar Sadat in Cairo in 1973, only in this case the surroundings were considerably less posh. The building and room in which we met were unimpressive. An oscillating fan in one corner made a futile effort to bring life to the air. Inexpensive lounge chairs and sofas lined the walls. The windows were covered by modest draperies. The only similarity with the elegant room in which we had met President Sadat was the presence of the President's portrait which, like Sadat's, appears to be everywhere in the country.

Again, like our Egyptian experience, we had to wait a proper interval for the President's arrival. When he came through the door, we stood for the universal ritual of handshaking, the President moving quickly around, grasping each hand firmly. Siad is a robust man who manifests considerable vigor. He affects a small mustache, which I saw imitated by a number of other Somali officials.

The President began by telling us that the reasons for inviting us to his country were two-fold. While the Schlesinger allegation had prompted them to invite us to see for ourselves that there was no Russian base at Berbera, the principal reason for their wanting us to come was to see their country and how they are trying to develop it. Siad reviewed their problems, particularly with regard to the nomad refugees they had to care for as a result of the severe sub-Sahara drought. He talked at length about their efforts to improve the life of their people since they had gotten independence from Italy and Britain, the former colonial masters of Somaliland. At length the conversation turned to their relationship with other nations. Siad noted that originally they had tried to get arms from the West but were told that they needed only police forces. He went on to say that they had enemies on their frontier, although he did not mention the Ethiopians by name. I learned later that there are two million Somalis living within Ethiopia in the eastern part of that country, the Ogaden, and Somalia would like to exercise sovereignty over them.

When the West refused to make weapons available to them, the President said that the Somalis turned to those who would, principally the Russians. He then conceded that they have made facilities available to the Russians, but he made a distinction between facilities and bases. He emphasized that the Somalis valued freedom above anything else, and they would never compromise themselves by giving up their land to a foreign power. Furthermore, if the Russians should act provocatively, they would expel them. He added that we would be welcome to send our ships there if we showed friendship and helped them. None of this was spelled out. He urged us to visit the refugee camps and said that we should add them to our itinerary after visiting Berbera.

The revolution that brought Siad and his Revolutionary Council to power in the fall of 1969 overturned a parliamentary government. Considering the political chaos and economic stalemate at the time, there was probably no other alternative for bringing order. Western influence appears to be at a minimum. Besides the Russians, the Chinese, North Koreans, East Germans, and even Albanians and Cubans are present. The Russian influence is strongest and has taken the form of both military and economic aid. The Chinese provide mainly economic assistance.

The poverty of the country is obvious. Housing is rudimentary, and although the main streets are paved, Mogadishu gives a shoddy appearance, and flocks of goats or cattle being herded along the street were a frequent sight.

We left the President shortly after midnight for our quarters and about four hours of sleep. With a 5:30 a.m. departure for Berbera set on Sunday, there was precious little time for rest. In no way did this journey qualify as a junket. We calculated that over 60 percent of our time was spent in travel, including nearly eight hours of flying to and from Berbera on Sunday.

The main purpose of the trip was the inspection visit to Berbera. It was a two-leg flight, the first part in a Russian-built prop-jet AN-12 from Mogadishu to Hargeisa in northern Somalia. Situated on a plateau 4,400 feet above sea level, its air is clear and cool, a sharp contrast with the humidity of the capital and an even sharper contrast with the oven-like heat of Berbera eighty miles further to the north. Because the short gravel field at Berbera would not accommodate the AN-12, we had to transfer to the old reliable of world aviation of the last forty years, a DC-3. It looked like one of the first ones that Douglas ever made, with patches on the tail assembly and seats in the interior whose springs had long since abandoned resistance. This venerable machine kept faith with its legendary reputation, however, and duly transported us to and from Berbera.

It was upon reaching Hargeisa that our difficulties with the Somalis began. Several in our party began to take pictures of the ten or twelve MiG 17's positioned about the airfield, plus the rotating radar of an anti-aircraft site. The Somalis emphatically declared that photographs could only be taken at Berbera. Hargeisa's proximity to Ethiopia undoubtedly made them sensitive.

This was not the only point of friction. For some reason, the Somalis sent along a delegation whose numbers matched our own. Included were several ministers and ambassadors, among them the ambassador to Nigeria and the one to Yemen. The Minister of Commerce was also along. I had a long talk with the ambassador to Nigeria on the AN-12. He had served a stint in Washington as ambassador prior to the incumbent.

The problem was that the DC-3 couldn't take all of us, and it was necessary for it to make two trips, thus creating a delay. Sam told the Minister of Commerce, who seemed to be the spokesman for the

Somalis, that we would go ahead and the others could catch up, but he was told that we would have to wait in Berbera and tour the area as a group.

The flight to Berbera from Hargeisa lasted about forty minutes over rugged country of low mountains which gave way to desert with an occasional brown hill or peak which rises from the desert floor. It gave no hint of the intense heat that awaited us.

We came upon Berbera suddenly, a scruffy town hugging a harbor on the Gulf of Aden. Landing at the single-runway field, the plane taxied to a halt in front of what passed for a terminal. But it was when the plane door was opened that we appreciated why the place draws few inhabitants. The heat struck with the force of a blast furnace. It didn't help to be told that the temperature was 106 degrees, nor did it make us more comfortable to know that August is the hottest month, not July. One doesn't live in Berbera, one survives there.

A convoy of Land Rovers took us to the principal administration building, where we found seats in a large room to wait for the rest of the party to join us. Here occurred the rupture in what had been largely a harmonious relationship between the Americans and the Somalis. It began in a general conversation to kill time, with the Minister of Commerce repeating the theme that there was no Russian base there. We acknowledged that it might not be a base but declared that the facilities shown in our photographs indicated that the Russians were actively utilizing Somali territory for strategic purposes. It was during this discussion that we became aware of the presence and power of Colonel Muhamed Gelle Yusef, who is commander of Somalia's naval forces and also a member of the Revolutionary Council. Increasingly, he became a part of the dialogue, and what was clearer, a latent hostility appeared toward us and our mission. I learned later that he had been trained in Russia and reflects a strong pro-Soviet stance.

When we mentioned the presence of Soviet Styx surface-to-surface missiles, the Somalis wouldn't acknowledge them. The colonel wouldn't even tell us the size of the Somali Navy, although *Jane's Fighting Ships* contains data of this sort. "It is a state secret," he said.

What really wore on our nerves, and particularly Sam's, was the delay in beginning our inspection of the dock area as a result of having to wait for the rest of the party. That, plus the oppressive heat, contributed to the sour mood that began to develop. Some of our people muttered that we were getting a "fast shuffle," and finally Sam gave vent to his feelings, telling our hosts that they were obviously stalling and reducing the time we would have to investigate.

Sam's outburst caused the Somalis to fall silent, but they appeared to be doing a slow burn. After Sam had stalked out of the room, they huddled and decided to start the tour. Shortly afterwards, the others arrived and joined the inspection.

We had photographs, taken by aerial intelligence, showing the location of the specific suspicious installations. These included a Soviet barracks ship, which had been towed from Vladivostok months ago. The Russians use it as temporary quarters for their naval personnel. There were also long-range radio transmitter and receiver sites, a missile handling and storage facility, fuel storage tanks recently constructed by the Russians, a new airfield under construction, and a housing area for Russian personnel and their families.

We drove to the dock area first but saw nothing but stevedores unloading a Jordanian freighter. The Soviet barracks ship nearby proved more interesting and gave Sam an opportunity to embarrass our hosts. Still smarting from his earlier outburst, the Somalis were horrified when Sam walked up the gangway, to be confronted by the Soviet sentry on duty. The young Russian Marine, a blond-haired lad of perhaps nineteen or twenty, nervously adjusted his pistol holster but didn't draw his weapon. He held Sam back and gestured that he couldn't come aboard. At this point, Sam called for Miss Crutchfield to come up and interpret. She said the Russian kept saying, "It is not permitted," and finally, shaking his head, kept repeating, "Please." All the while, the Somalis were agitating for Sam to get off the gangway, that the ship wasn't on the tour. It struck me as ludicrous, both from our side and from theirs. What really caused me to laugh was the reaction of the crew of a Somali freighter on the opposite side of the pier. Seeing the commotion on the Russian ship, they started to pull up their own ladder to forestall Sam's boarding *them*. The Somali colonel saw it and in exasperation ordered them to lower it. Obviously we had no interest in it.

During the whole time that the incident was being played out, not a single Russian showed his face on the barracks ship. All the portholes were shielded by paper or cardboard on the inside. As far as anyone could see, the young Marine had the entire ship to himself. In keeping such a low profile, the Russians made themselves all the more conspicuous.

We then spied a military structure, apparently a naval installation with radar antennae on top. When we indicated a desire to see it, the Somalis said that we couldn't, because it was one of their own facilities, and that we ought to be "reasonable." We pointed out that the ambassador in Washington had written to us promising that we could see anything we wished in the Berbera area, but the Somalis would not be budged. The colonel now came to the fore in the discussions and became the Somali spokesman.

We drove on to the Russian housing area a few blocks away, and although we could see a few Russians in the vicinity of their apartments, we were not permitted to stop. The Somalis, after the barracks ship episode, said that they would not permit us to intrude on the privacy of their Russian guests. I really couldn't blame them, and frankly, it was the least important thing for us to see.

What followed almost led to the cancellation of the rest of the tour. The Somalis took us back to the headquarters and informed us that only the Members would be permitted to view the so-called missile facility, which they maintained was for "naval weapons." Furthermore, they declared that we could not get out of the car and no photographs would be permitted. At this, all of us protested that this was in total violation of the promise made to us before we left the United States. But the Somalis dug in their heels and said that they "could change their minds" and that we "didn't have the correct attitude." Sam suggested that the Members have a private parley to decide whether or not to accept this new development. The consensus was that we should but that we should note it in our findings. It placed the burden of proof regarding Russian military activity more squarely on the Somalis.

The missile facility was guarded by armed Somali sailors, who came to salute with their Chinese-made SKS rifles when we entered and departed. A number of low ammunition bunkers could be seen, not unlike those found at military installations in the U.S. But a building that could be used for the assembly of missiles was of more interest. We could only gaze at it from the road some fifty yards away. It was a keen disappointment not to be able to check the facility thoroughly. The Bartlett group had been given access to part of it and had seen crates for Styx missiles. Apparently the knowledge of this and the size and composition of our party prompted the Somalis to place the added restrictions, rather than Sam's display of temper and his behavior at the barracks ship.

Similarly, we never got inside the transmitter and receiving facilities, although we know from monitoring their signals that the Russians are making heavy use of them. When we asked about their operations, the Somalis said at first that they operated them. "Are there no Russians there?" we asked. "Well, yes, there are a few to train our people," they replied, "and sometimes they use the equipment." "They provide on-the-job training," they added and said that they thought this was better than sending their people to the Soviet Union to be trained. Neither Sam nor I changed expression. In an afternoon of truth-stretching, that was the most elastic statement that I'd heard.

We took a look with our staffs at the newly-constructed oil storage tanks, which were especially interesting from a construction point of view. Rather than being built by formed plates, bolted or welded together in a cylinder, these were made from spools of sheet steel which were unwound and welded in a cylinder. "Chalk one up for the Russians," we said. It is a technique we could do well to copy, making it much quicker and easier to assemble storage tanks than the old way using individual steel plates.

The airfield was the last major item on our list. Construction is just starting, and it will be some time before it is completed. The runway will extend between 16,000 and 17,000 feet, and sufficient terminal facilities are being built to service it. When we asked for what purpose such an extensive air facility was needed, the Somalis said that they were going to build a meat-processing plant and a fish freezing and processing plant nearby and that the field would be needed for these. The additional oil tanks were justified on the grounds that they were going to acquire more ships and also make Berbera into a large port to service vessels going up the Red Sea and through the Suez Canal, and that they would need the oil on hand for vessels calling at Berbera. Our intelligence people told us that these tanks are far in excess of their commercial needs for the immediate future, and it is safe to conclude that they will refuel Soviet warships.

By now it was time to start back to Mogadishu, by way of Hargeisa, where we remained for about an hour to have a late lunch and relax. Then, when the entire group had been reassembled, we boarded the AN-12 for the flight to Mogadishu, arriving at 8:00 p.m. It had been a long and very frustrating day.

The evening ended on a more positive note. Vice President Kulmie hosted a dinner for the entire party at the Hotel Juba, a new hotel in Mogadishu.

The Somalis were fearful that Sam would take the occasion for a parting shot at them, but the hospitality of the table prevailed, and Sam graciously thanked them for receiving us as friends, adding that he hoped that the visit would lead to better and closer relations between our two countries. I could almost hear our hosts sigh with relief. Sam then called upon me as the minority leader to respond, and seeking to preserve the feeling of fellowship I declared that "we did not come as adversaries, and we surely do not depart Somalia as adversaries."

Plans were made for those who wished to fly by helicopter the next morning to the refugee camp area, but it meant another early rising and I just wasn't up to another four-hour night. I begged off and got seven hours of sleep instead, which I supplemented with an additional six hours aboard the plane coming home.

We departed Mogadishu about 8:45 this morning (Monday, July 7), returning to Andrews by way of Torrejon. The changes in time over such a short period create a strange feeling, and I am glad that this is an occasional assignment and not a regular one.

In spite of the fatigue and discomfort, the journey was worth it, from both a personal and national point of view. It is still something of a puzzle as to why the Somalis invited us in the first place. Surely they must have known that we would view the Soviet facilities with considerable concern, and that if they did not meet the narrow definition of a "base," the net result of the Soviet activities was the same. As Sam pointed out in our official report, the Somalis are guilty of a "semantic quibble."

They are unquestionably a proud people, and the Schlesinger statement stung them. Half-jokingly, several of them said that they should "collect damages" from the United States. They simply do not view the Russian activities in the Indian Ocean as we do, and it is perhaps natural that they should be defensive about the relationship with a power that has befriended them. It is hard not to view their reaction as one of an unsophisticated government, young, sensitive, and inexperienced. Our chargé, Sam Hamrick, told us that Siad seemed genuinely surprised when Bartlett showed him the photographs of the Berbera facilities which had been taken by our satellites and U-2 cameras. It is possible that he issued the invitation not knowing that we already had so much information.

On the other hand, it may be that Siad honestly wants to improve his relationship with the U.S. in order to secure economic assistance and to be less dependent on his communist friends. There might even be a political tug-of-war in the Revolutionary Council, but this is purely speculative.

Depending on the Somali reaction to our report and that of Senator Bartlett, both of which confirm the Soviet military activity in Somalia, I would hope that further contact with the Somalis will be pursued, including naval visits by our Indian Ocean units. Humanitarian aid to the nomad refugees should be provided, but it should not be tied to any military or political considerations. With this as a basis, there might be room for some improvement in our relations with Somalia, but I do not believe that it will lead to a marked diminishing of Soviet influence. The Somalis have resisted the pressure of their Moslem brothers in Saudi Arabia to end their dependence on the Soviets, including offers of substantial financial help. The economic-political system, so patterned after the communists, appears to be a further safeguard.

Still, nothing is to be lost by a little exploring, and the Somalis appear to be inclined to explore with us.

Tuesday, July 8, 1975—Wednesday, July, 9, 1975

I began the morning by joining about a hundred of my colleagues at the White House for a working breakfast with the President to consider arguments in favor of ending the embargo on arms to Turkey. It was a well-orchestrated affair. The President had everyone seated at individual tables rather than at the usual E-shape that customarily prevails at large gatherings of this kind. I sat at a table with Ralph Regula and Don Clausen at either side of me, and Dan Daniel, Ken Robinson, Marjorie Holt, Floyd Spence, Shirley Pettis, and a couple of other Republicans filling it out. The President sat with the principal members of the House International Relations Committee. The breakfast matched the usual excellent standards of cuisine there, even though it wasn't fancy, just scrambled eggs, bacon, sausage, and sweet rolls and toast. The coffee at the White House is the best in the world.

The President began the session by saying that we had reached a "point of crisis" and that was why he had invited a bipartisan group to meet with him. He reviewed the events of the past year, noting that it was almost exactly twelve months ago that the Greek regulars, inspired by the junta in Athens, had attempted to overthrow President Makarios in Cyprus. Since that time, the President noted, there had been difficulty reaching a settlement because the Turkish government had been unsettled and the Greeks themselves had undergone a change. The situation was now "drifting."

Today, he said, an announcement would be made in Ankara about a $525 million economic assistance pact between Turkey and the USSR. He emphasized, however, that it was a trade agreement, not a military one. The Russians, among other things, would be providing assistance to build a steel mill.

The President said that he was worried about the impact on NATO of a Turkish drift away from its traditional allies. Next week talks will begin between the U.S. and Turkey regarding the future status of American bases there. The President had one of his military advisers point to a large map on an easel in the State Dining Room to single out the U.S. surveillance station at Sinop on the Black Sea coast. This base, he said, enables the United States to monitor the USSR and SALT I provisions. Without that base we would be unable to tell if the Russians were in violation. He then pointed to another monitoring station on the Bosporus, where we can identify the various kinds of Russian ships passing through the Straits. This, he declared, had been of inestimable value during the Mideast crisis in 1973.

Turning to the current situation, the President noted that the Turks had bought and paid for arms, which were impounded at the time the embargo was instituted. Those weapons were now being held in American warehouses and the Turks were having to pay warehouse storage fees. "There just isn't any justification for that," Ford said. He added that he would like to see a complete lifting of the embargo so that ultimately credits and sales could be resumed, but that it was absolutely necessary to get some action before negotiations begin next week. Then he turned the floor over to the Secretary of State.

Dr. Kissinger said that it was counterproductive for the United States to pursue its present course. The bases, he declared, were totally irreplaceable, and if we did not lift the embargo Turkey would likely begin to line up with the radical Arab states in order to get money to buy arms.

Kissinger admitted that the short-range impact in Greece resulting from renewed military sales to Turkey would be resented, but this action would contribute in the long run to a settlement of the Cyprus question. He said that we wanted to treat the two allies equally and not favor one over the the other. He then discussed the political situation in Turkey. He noted that Demerel, the present leader, had been the opponent of Ecevit, who had ordered the invasion of Cyprus last year. Demerel needs some success in dealing with the Americans, or he will be accused of giving Cyprus away. Finally, Kissinger repeated the President's emphasis on the importance of our bases in Turkey. Because of them, we were able to ascertain in 1973 the mobilization of seven of eight Soviet airborne divisions.

The President then called on Tom Morgan, the chairman of the International Relations Committee, to discuss the House bill. Dr. Morgan said that his bill was not as strong as the one passed by one vote in the Senate. The principal feature of it was a provision which would allow the Turks to take possession of the arms already in the pipeline, in other words, those stored in our warehouses. Aid would also be provided for the Greek Cypriot refugees. Ford said that he endorsed the House substitute bill and then told us that when he talked to Demerel in Brussels in the spring, he told him that if the U.S. lifted the embargo, Demerel had a commitment to him to make meaningful progress toward a Cyprus settlement. He added that the main issue dividing the Greeks and Turks is the amount of land occupied by the Turkish forces, but he personally felt they were close to an agreement. The President said that he told Demerel that if they made no progress, he, Ford, would be released from his pledge.

John Ashbrook asked what impact all of this might have on the drug traffic. The President said that was a good question. He said that the Turks were currently controlling production and the sale of opium, but that if we fail to get an agreement the Turks could go back to their old policy of letting the farmers sell their opium crops as they wanted and we would soon see the drug traffic out of control again.

It was a remarkable session and prompted me to call one of my Greek Cypriot leaders at home to set up a meeting with about a dozen of them this coming Sunday to review the matter. While I feel honor-bound to continue my support for their cause, I believe that these new facts need to be called to their attention. They need to be reminded that they have an American responsibility as well as one to the land of their birth. How they will react, I cannot say, but I am going to tell them that support for continuing the embargo is eroding, and many Members regard it as not only ineffective but as the Secretary said, "counterproductive."

The conference on the Defense Authorization Bill resumed today for about an hour. We spent the time on the two Jackson amendments, the one dealing with placing penalties on oil companies and their officers if they discriminate in selling oil to our armed forces, and the other pertaining to providing military aid to Israel. No final resolution was made on either, although we moved them along a little.

Scoop gave a brief review of his amendment regarding the petroleum discrimination. He circulated a letter around the table that he had received from the Secretary of Defense endorsing the amendment, and he repeated the state of helplessness of the Defense Department at the time of the nuclear alert in 1973 in dealing with those companies that wouldn't sell oil to the Department. Everyone at the table agreed that it ought to be in the bill, even though it might not be germane. It was decided to have the staffs work on the language to make it more specific, then bring it back.

We then went on to the Israeli aid amendment, and again Jackson reminded us that it had been part of three previous bills. Bill Dickinson asked him what it would cost, and Jackson replied that no figure was authorized. The Appropriations Committee would have to make that decision. It was clear that Stennis was unhappy about having the amendment in the bill, and he said that we could include it in this year but not any more. That brought Charlie Wilson into the act. He declared emphatically that the matter was clearly within the jurisdiction of the International Relations Committee and not Armed Services. He brought up the pressure that had been put on him by the Jewish community in Beverly Hills and said that he resented it. He said that he would personally raise a point of order against the amendment, even though he was sure it would be defeated on the floor. Bob Wilson, on our side, agreed and added that it wouldn't help the Middle East to have it included now. But Jackson denied this and replied that it was just a tool to make sales on long-term credits. Stennis wound things up by saying that he would have the joint legal staffs work up a memorandum that could be brought back for discussion.

With the Senate bill tied up over the vacant seat in New Hampshire, it was impossible for us to meet in the afternoon, so we adjourned until tomorrow afternoon. This thing is getting to be a marathon.

I went to the Wednesday Group meeting this afternoon and heard two particularly interesting reports, by Chuck Whalen and Peggy Heckler. Chuck had been to Cuba over the recess and met with Fidel Castro. He said that Castro seems a lot more subdued than he used to be and spoke in a moderate fashion. It was Chuck's opinion that Castro wants to reestablish relations with the United States and everyone else. He feels that the Cubans are weary of being at odds with their neighbors and just want to get on with the task of building their nation. Chuck expects some steps to be taken toward the normalization of U.S.-Cuba relations at the Organization of American States meeting later this summer in Central America.

Peggy had attended the International Women's Conference in Mexico City. It was a surprise to all of us to hear her announce that she was on the verge of never again voting for an appropriation for the United Nations. The bloc voting by the Third World and communist powers outraged her. Even on the most modest proposals, the Third World delegates were in lock step. She said that what was absolutely ludicrous was the defeat of a Western proposal condemning sexism (discrimination against women), and this at an international conference to call attention to the rights of women! The other issue that incensed her was the injection of Zionism as a cause to be condemned along with neo-colonialism and racism. Both she and Bella Abzug, who was also present, were disgusted by what transpired. The fellows at the table laughed when Peggy announced her withdrawal of support for the UN, and one or two said, "Welcome aboard." We don't often see one of our liberal collegues so openly lose faith in a cause.

Sunday, July 13, 1975

This morning I met with about ten of the leaders of the Greek-Cypriot community. I took with me my notes of the White House breakfast and also a copy of the bill that would permit the release of the arms that Turkey has already paid for, and in addition permit sale on credit if the President deems it wise. Not surprisingly, my Greek friends were hostile to the idea of relaxing the arms embargo. I told them that the new wrinkle in the move to let up on the arms embargo was the threat on the part of Turkey to close down our military bases, which have been of great help to us in maintaining surveillance on the USSR. While acknowledging that, they pleaded that any relaxation would only encourage the Turks in their "blackmail," and we should hold firm. I replied that I did not like to see the bases placed in jeopardy, but I would stand by them. I must confess to mixed feelings about it all.

I am genuinely sympathetic with these people, many of whom have relatives who have lost everything to the Turkish invasion, but I also realize that the United States, by pursuing this course, is acting in a way that is inimical to its own interests. We are becoming a party to a conflict that is centuries old, one where logic seldom finds a voice and passion rules. Morally, one can make a case for the United States refusing to make further arms available to the Turks because they have misused them. I suggested to my friends that they take this tack in seeking to persuade my colleagues in the House, but I warned them that they are going to be accused by non-Greeks of placing the interests of the land of their birth ahead of those of their adopted country. I told them that at this point I could not give them a prognosis on the outcome, that it is still too early to predict, but that I was sure it would not be the piece of cake it had been last year or even as late as last February. They despise Henry Kissinger, blaming him entirely for the failure to stop the Turks in the first place and for encouraging the Turks since the invasion began to believe that the United States was not going to persist in a course hostile to Turkish interests. Several angry confrontations with Kissinger have confirmed these views.

Wednesday, July 23, 1975

The House passed the Interior Appropriations Bill this afternoon with little difficulty. Tomorrow promises to be something else. We have the vote on the Turkish military aid bill, plus one on common situs picketing. Chalk up two No votes. The latter is nothing in the world but authority for a secondary boycott, and I'm not about to approve that. What puzzles me is that the President has said he will support a common situs bill. At the Wednesday Group this afternoon, I learned that he wants another collective bargaining measure along with it which would mitigate the effects of the common situs bill. Apparently the Senate has agreed to furnish both of them to him at the same time. Nevertheless, it doesn't change my feelings.

The military aid for Turkey is another matter. Damned if I didn't get a call today from Jim Schlesinger, the Secretary of Defense. He's getting to be a regular lobbyist for the White House, but he's a phlegmatic one. He said that he understood the political considerations, and he replied to my statements in monosyllables. I got his spirits up when I mentioned that we had made a hero out of him on the basis of our Somalia trip. "Did you make that?" he asked. I then described our dialogue with the Somali colonel as we drove by the transmitter station, and he chuckled. It was the least I could do, considering the original purpose of his call.

At the Wednesday Group meeting, the issue got a lot of conversation. Pete Biester, one of the supporters of the bill, said that there has been a lot of erosion in the support for the President's position in the last few days. The Greeks have mounted a heavy campaign against the measure, and Pete said that Members who had formerly pledged their support for the bill have come to him to say that they have had to switch their positions. There was some criticism voiced of the White House tactics, especially of their use of Wayne Hays. Sil Conte was particularly outspoken about him. He despises him. Mark Andrews said that he didn't have many Greeks in his district, but he declared that he did have a hell of a lot of farmers in North Dakota who are sick and tired of seeing American arms sent all over the world to be used indiscriminately. He said that he could just see what they would say when he went home in August when he tried to explain why he had voted to lift the embargo on the Turks. On the basis of what I heard this afternoon, it would appear that the bill will lose. Something else manifested itself this afternoon at the meeting—the stirrings of some deep mistrust of Henry Kissinger, as if he were responsible for the failure of our policy in Cyprus.

Wednesday, September 3, 1975

There is considerable interest in the latest Israeli-Egyptian disengagement agreement worked out by Henry Kissinger. It calls for the use of 200 American technicians to man the surveillance posts in the Sinai, and there is an awful lot of uneasiness in our land that this could lead to another Vietnam-type situation. I've told the press that I would have preferred that UN people be used, but one can't equate this with Vietnam. For one thing, both sides want these volunteers there. Also, we are substantially committed in that part of the world, as evidenced by the events during the Yom Kippur War in 1973. If stationing these technicians will preserve the ceasefire, we ought to agree to it. Ford is being shrewd about it and already has the assent of the Leadership on both sides of the aisle, with the exception of Mike Mansfield in the Senate. Congress will have to approve the move first, which will not only take Jerry off the hook but ease the fears of the people at large. I talked with Bill Broomfield about it in the lounge today while I was eating a sandwich. I said that I had gotten a few letters in opposition to having Americans involved, but I had made up my mind to support the President. Bill said that he was much more concerned about the enormous outlay of money, over $3 billion this year with more billions to follow, to both sides. "Imagine," he said, "a little country of three million taking us for that sum!" But Al Cederberg, who came in, said that, considering the alternatives, we will find $3 billion a small price to pay. I'm not so sure. With the economy in its present state, there's a lot of discontent about our going all out for the Israelis and paying so much money to keep them happy. I had a meeting of my little senior citizens' advisory group in Norfolk on Friday, and one of them voiced his displeasure over the drift of events there. "It would be cheaper to let every Israeli immigrate to the United States and give each one $10,000 than to continue what we're doing," he said.

The mood at home dominated the Wednesday Group today. We met in Alan Steelman's office, just across the hall from mine. Stewart McKinney, Joel Pritchard, Bill Frenzel, John Heinz, and Charlie Mosher all reported the prevailing feeling that is uniform from Connecticut to the state of Washington and points in between. Stu McKinney said that his people are just fed up. "They aren't even mad any more," he said. Bill Frenzel picked it up and repeated about the same thing from his Minnesota district. Ford, he said, is popular, but his policies aren't. Congress is regarded as incompetent. Charlie Mosher told us that in Ohio there's a "congenial ridicule of Congress," and "the people acted as though they've given up." All agreed that inflation worries people the most, and John Heinz of Pittsburgh said that he had held talks with some labor leaders who didn't like Ford, but when asked who else they would prefer, they couldn't come up with any alternatives.

What really amused us was a comment by Ralph Regula concerning Betty Ford, who has been in the news as much as her husband recently with her outspoken remarks about her daughter's having a premarital affair, or how often she sleeps with her husband. Ralph said that the people in his own district didn't like what Betty was saying and were very critical. At this the others chimed in to say that their constituents weren't complaining at all, and some in fact had declared that there was somebody in the White House they could believe at last. Ralph replied that the Republicans in his district were unhappy anyway. "Thank God," said McKinney, "they only comprise 18 percent." "You mean *both* of them disapproved, Ralph?" someone else quipped.

I did learn one tidbit at the Wednesday Group which is worth recording here, although I doubt that anything will come of it. Ralph said that the White House had done a survey in Massachusetts and discovered that Peggy Heckler would have a good chance of unseating Ted Kennedy if she ran against him next year. Kennedy's stock is awfully low in Boston right now because of his support for busing there. However, Peggy would have to take an opposite stand, and I'm not sure she would. Still, if she thought it would get her a Senate seat. . . .

Wednesday, September 10, 1975

We finished up the Military Construction conference report today, much sooner than I expected. However, it was not without some embarrassment to me. Last night, at 10:00, the Secretary of the Navy called me at my apartment to say that he was upset that we had not funded the $1.3 million for the Navy Historical Center at the Navy Yard in Washington. The matter was so minor that I didn't even bother to record it in yesterday's entry. Some months ago, Bill Middendorf had asked me to be on the lookout for the funds to restore the Tingey House at the Navy Yard. This is a very old home, used by one of the admirals for his quarters. Since it has historical significance, Bill urged me to vote the funds to have it restored. After some debate in our Military Installations and Facilities Subcommittee, we approved it and also the money for the Historical Center. The Senate, however, killed both projects, Symington telling us yesterday how important it was to reduce all but the most necessary spending. Barry Goldwater and Senator Leahy, the new senator from Vermont, joined him, though Strom Thurmond held out and said that we ought to have "a little friendly vote" on it. Our side was split, too, so in an effort to find a compromise and get Bill his restoration, I suggested that we put up the $400,000 needed for the restoration of Tingey House and put the Historical Center off till next year. I thought that I had struck a good compromise, and Symington bought it and carried the others along.

The Secretary thought otherwise. He had been alerted by somebody from the conference, which shows how confidential they are, and had gotten on the phone to Bob Wilson, Charlie Wilson, John Stennis, and me. He said that Stennis would speak to Symington. I replied that if it meant that much to him, I'd bring it back up today. He said that the D.C. subway was going out to the Navy Yard and would pick up part of the tab for the demolition of buildings and providing parking, so we really ought to fund it this year. Furthermore, we had given the Marine Corps money for their historical center last year and ought not to do less for the Navy. "I'm a history buff like you, Bill," he said. "Of such things bills are made," I thought. It struck me as an awful lot of fuss over such a small item. But that wasn't all. Admiral Gus Kinnear was in to see me at 10:30 this morning, to tell me that the Secretary had been on the phone with him at 2:00 this morning about it. Furthermore, the Secretary had left for Arizona and called while he was en route to say that he wanted a report on it. The whole business struck me as ridiculous.

Nevertheless, I dutifully went to the conference and Symington greeted me cordially, telling me that I had made a "statesmanlike contribution" to the conference. I smiled uncomfortably and replied that I hoped he would still hold me in the same esteem at the end of the meeting today. When we began, I offered a motion to reconsider the matter, reviewing the events of the night before. I'm afraid that I did nothing but open up a can of worms. Symington questioned whether we had a right to take it up again after we had already made an agreement. I got some support from Bob, Charlie, and Strom, but no one else seemed disposed to go along with it. Frankly, I couldn't blame them, and my own heart wasn't in it, although I tried to conceal my lack of enthusiasm for the Secretary's pet project. We ended up reaffirming the earlier decision, and I resolved never to be put in that position again.

The rest of our differences were ironed out fairly easily, and by 3:15 we had come to agreement and were able to sign the report. Tomorrow we take up the Military Procurement conference report, which the Senate turned down.

Wednesday, October 29, 1975

The President is going to have to work hard to turn things around. Mark Andrews told us at the Wednesday Group meeting today that a paper in his district had taken a poll and found that Ford ran behind every national figure with the exception of Wallace, and this in a district that is Republican by two to one. It doesn't look too hopeful, but it can all change overnight.

The President today was the butt of much amusement over a faux pas he committed last night at the dinner at Blair House hosted by President Anwar Sadat, who is visiting the United States. Raising his glass, Jerry extolled the virtues of the Egyptian leader and then asked everyone to stand and drink to the President of Israel. Al Quie saw it on TV, and said that the silence was deafening. Ford then caught himself and with considerable embarrassment corrected himself.

We attended the opening of the exhibit on Siberia at the Natural History Museum last night. Sure enough, Oleg Yermishkin was there to greet us. The affair was late getting started because of the tardy arrival of Ambassador Dobrynin. However, after the usual speeches by the hosts and guests, the exhibit opened. Janie and I thoroughly enjoyed it and thought that it was a balanced exhibit, neither concentrating too much on technical achievements nor showing too much arts and crafts. The buffet was excellent: tables of Russian dishes prepared at the Embassy and brought over. Oleg was up to his usual inquisitiveness. He wanted to know how I regarded the visit of Sadat. I replied that it was well that the Egyptian had indicated that he came to buy and not to beg. Oleg voiced his country's displeasure at Sadat's ingratitude, which he said was based upon Russian unwillingness to provide offensive arms to the Egyptians, and indicated that they still owed his country quite a few billions of dollars. He said that the Russians were particularly put out after having built the Aswan Dam and a steel works. "Well, welcome to the club," I said. "We've been trying to buy friendship all over the world for years, and it hasn't gotten us very far."

We then covered the Secretary of State's visit to China and kicked that around for awhile. Oleg's thesis was that the Chinese are taking a strong anti-Soviet line for home consumption. He declared that the Chinese leaders believe that they can get more sacrifices from their people if they feel threatened by the Soviet Union. He also said that he thinks the Chinese will "turn south" after having given up on expanding in the north in 1969. What he was referring to was the outbreak of fighting between Soviet and Chinese forces along their frontier that year. He recalled that he was in Ethiopia at the time and talked to an American officer at our Embassy. He said that the American told him that we were killing ten Viet Cong for every American in Vietnam, but the Russians had killed twelve Chinese for every one of their soldiers who lost his life. He smiled smugly as he said this. "No question about it," I responded, "your people gave the Chinese a bloody nose."

He asked me how I felt about a naval limitation on ships. I discouraged him and said that our people are already disturbed by the strength of the Soviet Navy. He noted that his nation had no attack carrier, which I acknowledged, but I went on to outline the kind of navy the Soviet Union has, one that is designed not to control the seas but to interdict our sea lanes, which are vital to us in any war we might have. He smiled and dropped the subject. He promised to invite us to his apartment next month for a Russian dinner prepared by Nelly. We told him to name the date. Before leaving, we had an opportunity to meet the ambassador, a bear of a man, who manifests a considerable amount of charm and mockingly complained that he had been in America so long that they had forgotten him in Moscow. Fat chance, I thought.

We're home tonight on what has turned out to be a week of few engagements. Blessedly, the rest of the week looks like this.

Monday, November 3, 1975

The big news this past weekend and today has been the firing of Jim Schlesinger as Secretary of Defense and Bill Colby as director of the CIA and their replacement by Don Rumsfeld and George Bush respectively. Also, and overshadowing these developments, Nelson Rockefeller has taken himself out of the race for vice president next year. Tonight the President held a press conference to field questions on these matters and dropped a surprise on the press corps, which had already been leaking reports on the others, by announcing that Rogers Morton was stepping down and that Elliot Richardson was being nominated to succeed him at the Department of Commerce.

Not surprisingly, there was plenty of discussion about these moves in the House today. Herm Schneebeli, who was a roommate of Rockefeller in college, said that the Vice President had called him earlier today to apprise him of what he had done. Herm said that he told him that in view of his (Rockefeller's) age, it was probably wise, that Rockefeller had served the public well and faithfully for a long time, and that no one had been more loyal to the President. John Anderson voiced his disappointment at the Vice President's decision, as did Millicent Fenwick and other Republican liberals and moderates. However, the conservatives were visibly relieved. Most of the speculation revolved around the other changes and what it portended to have George Bush back in the States from China. The reporters also scented this, and many are wondering out loud if either Rumsfeld or Bush will end up as a running mate for the President next year. I had a call from a UPI wire service reporter and told him that Rockefeller's stepping aside had to be a plus for the President but that I hoped that he would let the convention work its will next year and develop a consensus candidate. The President could certainly offer some names of individuals acceptable to him, but if he let the convention make the choice, he would go into the campaign with a broader base of support.

It is remarkable to me to see the fortunes of George Bush turn as they have. Having been impressed by him ever since my first term, and having offered his name to Nixon along with Ford's as a choice to be Vice President, I am pleased to see that my judgment has not been in error. He could well end up at or near the top before the end of his career.

Wednesday, November 5, 1975

In the House we continue to squander our time. On Monday and Tuesday we adjourned before 2:30, yet the schedule shows a flock of bills up for Thursday and Friday. Even today, we rose at 6:30 after voting on just one amendment to the controversial Consumer Protection Agency Bill. We could easily have taken up this measure on the two previous days. The House did have an important guest today. Anwar Sadat addressed a Joint Meeting of the Congress, complete with the Diplomatic Corps and Cabinet in attendance. Bella Abzug and Elizabeth Holtzman both boycotted the speech, and Senator Javits refused to applaud, but most of the Members responded in a friendly way. I personally felt that Sadat was not only candid but reasonable in his approach. He was applauded three times in the middle of his address, but met with silence when he mentioned the need for the U.S. to show sympathy and understanding for the Palestinians. Still, it was a triumph for him, and the Egyptian press in the Press Gallery applauded him just as vigorously as the Members and guests. Mrs. Sadat occupied the seat in the gallery normally taken by the President's wife, and next to her were Happy Rockefeller and Nancy Kissinger.

Speaking of foreign visitors, I had a personal one yesterday afternoon. Ambassador Addou of Somalia came by. I had missed a reception given at his Embassy a little while ago, and he said that he had wanted to come by to get acquainted. We talked about his country and our visit there last July. As he left, he indicated that Somalia is in need of U.S. aid for its nomads, driven out of the north by the drought. He asked me if I would mind writing a letter to Deputy Under Secretary of State Robert Ingersoll in support of this aid program. I smiled inwardly and replied that I would be happy to. Obviously, he was interested in something more than just getting acquainted.

1976

The weather acted capriciously this morning, remaining just around freezing and precipitating slightly so that the roads were slick as glass. What would normally have been a twenty-minute drive took forty, and we counted ourselves lucky to arrive intact. A number of cars were disabled or unable to move up a grade of any dimension.

The day itself was a busy one, but I am finally beginning to see daylight on my work. Janie reports similar progress from her desk. I had several calls to make to radio and television stations this morning to report on the President's State of the Union Address last night. Perhaps it was just the present mood of Congress, but the atmosphere in the Chamber lacked the spark of anticipation that usually accompanies this event. A fair number of Members didn't even bother to show up, and their seats were filled by the overflow from the Diplomatic Corps and by pages. Some former Members were back, including Les Arends and a colleague from my first term, Ed Foreman of New Mexico, who now lives in Dallas and works in the ready-mixed concrete business. He looked prosperous and is now completely out of politics. Mel Laird was also there. Janie and I saw him in the dining room of the Capitol Hill Club prior to the President's speech at 9:00 p.m. Mel has been bald for many years, but he has let the fringes grow, and he is now applying some kind of hair formula to keep it black. It's amazing how many people around here use a hair dye. Otto Passman has for years, and I noticed that Strom Thurmond had a new red luster about his transplanted locks last night.

The President looked well. He dresses with a more conservative flavor, and the cut of his suits reflects excellent tailoring, something that wasn't always the case when he was in the House. But that indefinable quality of a President escapes him still. It may be a concoction of reserve, majesty, and a little aloofness, or a sense of presence about the

157

office. Jerry somehow just doesn't project this, and I think it is hurting him. It is part of his difficulty in selling himself as a leader, even though these characteristics are superficial. Compared to the others running for the office, he still looks the best to me, but the weakness of his image is an obvious one.

The speech itself was one of his better efforts, I thought. He appeared strongest in calling for reform of overlapping and duplicative programs, and in asking the Congress to amend the tax laws to give breaks to Americans who invest in private enterprise. If there is to be a real recovery in our economy, it can only be through the revitalization of private industry and not through federal work programs, however massive. I thought that the weakest part of his speech was his call for an increase in the Social Security tax, even though it is minimal. Taking more tax money to keep the trust fund intact isn't going to cure what's wrong with the Social Security system. At the rate we are increasing employee contributions to it, and with the growing number of retirees, by the end of this century workers will be paying 25 to 30 percent of their income into it. There needs to be a thorough study made with a view to some alternative plan. Increasing taxes to pay for it simply postpones the day of reckoning.

There is little point in analyzing the entire speech here. We'll get a look at the specifics of his recommendations in a lot more detail in a few days. I have heard by the grapevine that the Public Health Service hospitals are in trouble again, and another attempt will be made to phase out the military commissaries.

I spent much of the day either on the phone trying to solve some of the problems I had brought back with me from the district, or in conference with people in my office for one thing or another. The House spent the afternoon on a number of bills on the Suspension Calendar, none of which were of great consequence. One of them was passed on a voice vote. It provided for a bust of the late Martin Luther King, Jr., to be placed in the Capitol. Quite a few members have mixed feelings about honoring King's memory, but he is such a symbol to the blacks that very few Members want to make waves with their black colleagues, to say nothing of their black constituents, by voting against such a project. I noticed that the money for it—$25,000—was to come out of the House contingency fund. I didn't even know that we had one.

This evening, Janie and I drove out to the northernmost corner of the District of Columbia to attend a reception at the Somali Embassy in honor of the Somali minister of finance. We had the devil's own time trying to find the address, and with ice on the side streets, it was something of a hazard. Most of the people there were from the World Bank, or had been associated with it at some time. Bob Leggett showed up, the only other Member from our congressional delegation which had made the journey to Somalia last July. The ambassador seemed genuinely pleased that we had come and greeted Janie and me with unusual warmth. I suppose he wanted to make the best possible impression on his colleague from home.

The list of Members who have announced their retirement continues to grow, and there are quite a few surprises among them. Pete Biester of Pennsylvania and Gil Gude of Maryland, both Wednesday Groupers, are leaving at the end of this year. One Member told his staff by circulating an office memo, which must take the prize for unsentimental leave-taking. Tom Downing announced his departure earlier this month, but he had the decency to come back to Washington and bring his staff into the office to break the news to them.

Wednesday, January 21, 1976

Heavy traffic slowed our drive to the office this morning, and it was nearly 10:00 when we arrived. I had a meeting of my Subcommittee on Military Installations and Facilities first thing, and it lasted until almost noon. Our business was routine, the acquisition and disposal of various real estate holdings by the three principal services.

The Wednesday Group was well attended. I think that the Members were anxious to exchange news after a month's absence. Most of it was political, centering on the Ford-Reagan contest. Pete McCloskey began by delivering a very pessimistic report on the situation in California. The Reagan people are in almost complete control of the state, and Pete was very frank to say that if Reagan was the nominee, he, Pete, would be compelled to leave the party. Stu McKinney, who seldom speaks a word of optimism, followed with an equally gloomy view of Connecticut, and John Anderson told us that Reagan had been in Rockford, Illinois, his home town, last week to speak, and the crowd packed a movie house. John added that he had been judiciously absent that evening. Joel Pritchard said that things looked a little better in Washington, but he wasn't really encouraged. But Joe McDade gave a report of solid Ford strength in Pennsylvania, and both Ralph Regula and Chuck Whalen declared he was in good shape in Ohio. I said that Reagan would get most of the delegates from Virginia, and certainly from my district. Caldwell Butler agreed that his area looked much the same. While the race looks up for grabs right now, and the Ford organization ranges from fair to poor, there is still a feeling that the President has an edge as the incumbent. No one expressed any confidence in Bo Callaway. I still feel that there are a lot of fence-sitters, waiting to see how some of the early primaries develop. If a trend begins to shape up, it could either settle the President's nomination or kill him before he goes to Kansas City.

Peggy Heckler told us about her second visit to China over the recess. She took her college-age daughter with her this time, joining the group of congresswomen who made up the party. Peggy said that she told her Chinese hosts that she had heard about Chairman Mao's slogan of "digging tunnels and storing grain," and that she would like to see some of the tunnels. The Chinese agreed, and what she saw was stupefying. The tunnels are deep and elaborate and honeycomb the earth beneath Peking. A highly sophisticated communications network ensures that the various portions of this underground will be able to keep in touch with one another in the event of an enemy nuclear attack. The Chinese repeated over and over that a war is inevitable, most likely to be started by the Russians. The enormous undertaking below the ground gives evidence of their fears, Peggy said. She told us that her daughter, a fairly sophisticated girl, broke down and wept back at the hotel after seeing the tunnel network, she was so shaken by the sight and the thought that nuclear war was being prepared for so earnestly.

Peggy went on to say that the Chinese believe that we have lost our will to act, and they were very critical of us in this regard. They expressed a strong fear of the Russian naval buildup and cited the Soviet presence in Somalia and our failure to respond to it satisfactorily. She said that she and Millicent Fenwick took the Chinese to task for lumping the U.S. with the Russians as dangers to peace,but the Chinese were quick to add that they thought the Soviets were more likely to start a war.

Everywhere that the group went, they were greeted by large crowds, and in one of the remote areas they visited, they were the first Americans that the natives had seen. Peggy said that her daughter has flaming red hair, much as Peggy's had been when she was a girl, and she was looked upon "as if she was a Martian." What fractured all of us was her account of the visit of Julie and David Eisenhower and Bella Abzug's reaction to the wide publicity the Chinese gave to Nixon's daughter's arrival. Bella told the group that she was going to complain to Deng Hsiao-ping, Mao's heir-apparent, about it. Peggy said that she wasn't able to talk her out of it until about 2:00 one morning, but she finally succeeded, much to the relief of everyone else.

We are at home this evening and will leave for the district tomorrow, there being no Friday session this week. We'll take all of the three-day weekends we can get.

Tuesday, January 27, 1976

I backed two losing efforts in the House this afternoon. The first was the vote to override the President's veto of the Health-Labor Bill. It carried, 310 to 113, easily over the margin. Bob Michel had offered a compromise of $490 million over the budget, instead of the nearly one billion dollars, but the other side had the horses. A lot of our fellows broke ranks, seeing that there was little chance of saving the veto. I came right back to my office and answered three letters from officials at Eastern Virginia Medical School and at the federally-funded welfare agency locally, advising them of my vote and my stand. I told them that while I felt there was a federal role to be played, I believed that we had to draw the line on federal spending. The total amount for this measure and the education bill passed last year comes to almost two and a half billion dollars over the budget. We just can't keep it up.

Following that vote, we got another one, on the Defense Appropriations Bill with an amendment to agree with the Senate in curtailing aid to Angola. I had mixed feelings about that one. What little we've sent has not been effective in stemming the tide, and the string is about to run out on the side we've been supporting over there. Tom Downing, Bill Wampler, and I huddled on the floor and decided that our vote would at least be a token that the U.S. is not giving the Russians carte blanche to do as they please in Africa or elsewhere. We took a licking on that one, too, and I'll probably get a going-over from part of the press at home for voting as I did.

Ironically, Oleg Yermishkin came by late this afternoon to talk about the new SALT agreement that Kissinger worked on in Moscow last week. He asked me what I thought the chances of its acceptance in the Congress were. I said that I didn't know, that Kissinger doesn't enjoy the stature he once did, and a lot of people feel that we gave away too much in SALT I and at Vladivostok. Not surprisingly, Oleg didn't agree. He said that nobody in America wanted to admit that the Russians had made a big concession to the U.S. by not counting the forward-based U.S. aircraft in Europe which can easily be launched against the USSR. He said that they hoped to make contact with the members of the International Relations Committee and the Foreign Relations Committee, to talk to them.

Yermishkin himself believes that part of the suspicion in the U.S. is due to uneasiness about ultimate Soviet world aims. I agree with him. He said that he had written a paper on this for the ambassador and the Foreign Ministry at home, and he hoped that when the Supreme Soviet met it would make a statement to allay those fears.

We talked about Secretary Rumsfeld's appearance before my Committee this morning and his citing, as other Secretaries have done, the menace of Soviet military power. "Well, Oleg," I said, "I don't think that you're going to attack us, and I've told you that before, but I am concerned about the size of your forces, the deployment of new missiles, and your Navy which grows stronger every year. In view of the decline of our own strength by our failure to replace aging ships and aircraft in the past, I believe there is a need for us to increase our budget." He replied that much of their buildup was directed against China, and he voiced the fear that the Chinese were going to attack them. "That's interesting," I replied, "because Peggy Heckler was in China last month, and she saw the vast tunnels the Chinese have built in preparation for the attack they think you're going to launch against them." He shook his head.

With the vote having occurred earlier on Angola, it was inevitable that the subject would come up. He declared categorically that his country was not going to establish a naval base in Angola. "I hope not," I said, "because you will hurt your cause in the U.S.badly, and you will vindicate those of us who voted futilely for that modest appropriation today." Having disposed of most of the world's affairs, he invited Janie and me to have dinner with Nelly and him week after next—at a Chinese restaurant, of all places.

Tuesday, February 17, 1976— Wednesday, February 18, 1976

These have been a busy two days, with appointments and meetings all day long both days. I began with a briefing from Secretary of the Army Hoffman on Tuesday morning, along with a number of my colleagues. His report showed that enlistments are running above the required number, and the caliber of men and women is continuing to improve. But what is shocking is the terrible shortage of equipment for combat units. Heading for a sixteen-division Army in just three years, we are short in every combat category, especially in tanks and to a lesser, but still serious, degree in artillery and armored personnel carriers. The outlook for buildup in these arms is bleak. We just aren't doing enough.

At 5:00, I went up to Stu McKinney's office for the Wednesday Group meeting. Politics—the Presidential variety—was still very much on everyone's mind. Peggy Heckler told us that Wallace has been packing in the Democrats at meetings in Massachusetts, that Udall has what liberal support is apparent, and Shriver is far behind with a few Kennedy die-hards. She said that although Wallace is drawing big crowds at his meetings, the press is ignoring him. She really fears that Wallace could capture the primary. "Imagine that," she said, "in a state that went for McGovern!" Joel Pritchard gave us a curious report on a poll he had taken in his district in the state of Washington. Those polled were asked what they thought of Ford by himself, and generally gave him low marks. Asked about Scoop Jackson, they scored him favorably, but when asked who they would vote for for President, they chose Ford over Jackson! Try to figure that one out. Also, Jackson outran Reagan. The consensus was that the people who seem to be making any noise are the extreme left and the extreme right. The mass in the middle aren't saying anything.

Thursday, February 19, 1976— Tuesday, February 24, 1976

The House continues with a light schedule, as if marking time for the committees to finish their work. There has been very little business on the floor in this period, but all of the committees are meeting and preparing legislation. This spring is sure to see us here not only on

Friday but at night. We'll have to if we are to take time off for the national conventions.

We left for home last Thursday (the 19th) after voting on the President's veto of the Local Public Works Bill. I voted to sustain the veto, but we got fewer than a hundred supporters in the House. The Senate, however, gave him enough to kill the bill, which was something of a turnabout.

The House calendar this week has been light, with no business on Monday and a quick vote today (the 24th) on an appropriation for the Library of Congress. Tomorrow we consider the debt limit again. By this summer, it will be well over the $600 billion mark. At this rate, we'll see it go to a trillion dollars in just a few years' time, perhaps before the end of this decade. At what point will the financial system crumble under this debt?

We had an excellent presentation yesterday afternoon by Tony Battista, who is the staff member for the Research and Development Subcommittee. He and two other staffers made a trip around the world last October, visiting our fleet units to get a picture of our readiness. The report that Tony gave was outstanding but grim. His conclusion was that although the Navy still represents a deterrent to the Soviet Navy, it is only the carrier and submarine forces that make it up. We have obsolete weapons and surface units, obsolete fire control systems, obsolete communications, and ships that are for the most part in critical need of overhaul. Furthermore, decisions are being made from the Navy Department that don't reflect input from the fleet itself, with the exception of the submarine force. Tony said that basically our Navy is prepared to fight a World War II adversary, only there aren't any around. There is no need to go on at length here, and, in fact, much of his material was secret and can not be set down. But if we do not turn things around soon, we will find ourselves in a vain game of catch-up with the Russians.

Yermishkin was by today briefly. He wanted to talk about Nixon's trip to China, which worries the Russians. In his speech to the Party Congress today, Brezhnev accused the Chinese of threatening war with the USSR. Yermishkin asked me if I knew anything about the rumor going around about the U.S. supplying China with arms. I don't know whether he was on a fishing expedition or not. I told him that I had heard nothing of the kind. Sitting in the Subcommittee meeting yesterday afternoon, however, and seeing how weakened we have become, it occurred to me that we might well give serious consideration to the Chinese overtures. It clearly disconcerts the Soviets and might serve to brake some of their adventures. In our present state, we are increasingly less able to face them down alone.

Wednesday, February 25, 1976

Although the day was a busy one, there is little of substance to report. I attended my Subcommittee on Military Installations and Facilities this morning, and we spent all of our time on the cost estimate for an Army hospital at Fort Campbell, Kentucky. Robin Beard, who has been pushing for a hospital there since last year, has taken the Army to task for the cost, which is excessive. The hospital will have fewer than 300 beds but is projected at just under $70 million. Robin had brought in several civilian witnesses, including builders of civilian hospitals around the nation. All agreed that the Army figures were way too high. There are some obvious additions that a military hospital must have, but I had to agree that the Army needs to go back and look at this one. In the middle of the afternoon we got started on a review of Navy needs, and Mike Marschall was back in. He is uniformly respected because of his openness. The entire military construction budget this year is below the 1976 request, in itself something beyond anyone's recall. At least there is a recognition that the major emphasis in military spending has to be on hardware.

The House had a short session, passing with little difficulty the extension of the debt ceiling. There was none of the pettiness that marked the last extension vote. As in the past, I dislike raising the ceiling, but the government has to pay its bills. Voting No is nothing but a demagogic position.

Tuesday, March 2, 1976—Wednesday, March 3, 1976

These have been a couple of busy and interesting days. Much of my time has been spent on the Military Construction Bill, where we have cut practically all of the requests for tennis courts, not only because we want to keep the budget austere but also because the courts are being priced in a range of about $26,000 each, far in excess of the cost quoted by civilian tennis court builders. Our foray against the Fort Campbell hospital has paid off, too. A new figure has come in $20 million below the previous one. The Subcommittee has never taken such a keen look at these projects in the past.

Late in the afternoon I joined about a dozen of my colleagues from the House and Senate for a meeting with the President and some of his staff. Among those present were Ken Robinson from my own state; Skip Bafalis, Bill Young, and Dick Kelly of Florida; Bill Brock and Howard Baker of Tennessee; Mac Mathias and Glenn Beall of Maryland, along with their House colleague, Gil Gude; and there may have been one or two others from the Congress, but I cannot recall them now. Bo Callaway and Rogers Morton were also present, plus a couple of others on the President's re-election committee. Chairs were arranged in an oval in the Blue Room for us, and drinks and sandwiches were served.

I thought that the President looked well. He greeted all of us by name, and when he saw that no one took the seat next to him, he gestured for me to do so, since I had taken a chair on his side of the room. He brought up two subjects: the first was the Defense Bill, whose fate deeply concerns him. Like Rumsfeld last December, he is worried about what the Budget Committee might do to it. I mentioned my December meeting with the Secretary of Defense, and reviewed my suggestion that Don politic the members of the Budget Committee to sell his case. The President indicated that he was going to invite them down to the White House and make a pitch, a move that all of us applauded. He said that he would like to get a "good" SALT agreement, but that if one was not forthcoming, he expected to ask for more funds. His second topic was, not surprisingly, politics, and most of the forty-five minutes we had with him was spent on the campaign. His victory in New Hampshire has only whetted his appetite, and he was high in his praises of the men like Pete McCloskey and the others who had gone up there to speak for him. The Florida Members commended him for his performance last weekend in their state. The President and Skip had braved the rain to make a number of stops, and all felt that he has made enormous strides against Reagan. Bill Young advised him to come down again this coming weekend and make a sweep across North Florida. The President said that he had talked to Bob Sikes, whose district stretches across the northern panhandle, and had gotten private assurances from him that he would get a good turnout and lots of support. Sikes, of course, can do nothing openly since he is a Democrat, but as an old-line one, he has a lot of clout in his district and can deliver a lot of support for the President.

Howard Baker said that he wanted to "play devil's advocate" and offer the President some advice. Ford puffed assent on his pipe, and Baker continued. He said that the people of America expected that Gerald Ford would need a year to become acquainted with the office. Now that time has passed, and they were prepared to "crown him." The President chuckled and shook his head from side to side. But Baker persisted and told Ford that he should now act like a President, that is, speak on national issues not like a candidate but with the authority of leadership. Baker managed to say it without seeming presumptuous, and Ford accepted it. Baker added that he thought the President's most recent statements reflected this, and he hoped that Ford would continue.

The general atmosphere was one of guarded optimism. I believe that they feel that if he can win the Florida primary next Tuesday, he will have the Reagan people on the run, and by the time Illinois is over with, only the formality of his nomination will remain. He had a good win in Massachusetts yesterday, which was expected at the afternoon meeting. This should provide him with further impetus in Florida.

Wright Patman died on Sunday. He was eighty-two, and had announced his retirement effective at the end of this session. Today (Monday) there were eulogies by the Leadership on both sides, and no business was conducted. The funeral will be held in Texarkana, Texas, on Wednesday, and no business will be taken up then either. As Dean of the House, he had over forty-seven years here. It's pretty incredible to think that he came in with the election of Herbert Hoover in 1928. The mystery is why anyone would want to stay in that long, especially in these last few years when there has been so much grief. Robin Beard of Tennessee told me last week that Patman was in Bethesda with pneumonia and was not expected to make it. He (Robin) also passed along the news that Tenny Guyer was hospitalized with a heart attack.

Aside from this somewhat grim news, things have been running along on schedule. Last Thursday was a busy day. We finished up the Military Construction Bill late in the afternoon, setting some kind of speed record for that legislation. Before the days of the Budget Committee, we never took the bill up until the summer and then dawdled over it for at least a month. No more; now everything has to be up and voted on by early spring. We'll have the Procurement Bill and Milcon before the House before the month is up. If it doesn't prove anything else, it shows that if a deadline is enforced, the Members can get the work out.

We added a few items to the Milcon Bill for the benefit of some of the Members, including some for Bob Sikes in Florida. He gave us a shopping list that totaled about $20 million. Everyone on the Subcommittee griped about Sikes' shoving these additional requests on us year in and year out, yet no one is willing to turn him down for fear of reprisal. We ended up approving three projects out of six, for a total of $6.5 million. I made a motion which was adopted, having an axe of my own to grind. In the Navy's budget request for my district is a $24.9 million pier at the Naval Station in Norfolk. I heard by the grapevine that the Military Construction Appropriations Subcommittee, of which Sikes is chairman, is thinking of cutting it, in order to "help reduce expenditures." There's no doubt about its being a big item, and it makes a large target. The hypocrisy of it all galls me, however. Sikes presides over that Subcommittee like Caesar, assured not only of getting the major items in what has been authorized for the First District of Florida, but whatever additional goodies he can shake us down for on the Subcommittee on Military Installations and Facilities. It is an enviable position. In a power situation of this kind, one can only make the best of it. After we had finished with the bill, I went up to Sikes' office to tell him that we had approved three of his requests. His receptionist told me that he was at his home in Pensacola with the flu, but she thought he might like to hear the good news. She put the call through for me, and he came on the line. As cheerily as I could, I told him that we had completed work on the bill and had approved three of his special projects, which I itemized for him. He didn't conceal his appreciation, so I then reminded him of a letter I had sent him earlier in the week, calling attention to the necessity of approving the funds for the pier at Norfolk. "Oh, yes, I got your letter, Bill," he said expansively, "and I'm going to try to help you." That sounded a lot less convincing than I would have preferred, so I didn't hesitate to lay it on him that the pier is vital if we are to provide the additional berthing space the Navy needs at Norfolk, especially as the new ships come into the fleet in the next few years. I wished him a quick recovery and hung up, feeling a little self-disgust at having to indulge in this kind of gamesmanship. Two years ago I went through much the same routine with him and got shortchanged on some funds to buy out the leaseholders on the Navy-acquired Norfolk and Western Railroad property in Sewells Point. Last year I got the rest of the money by making a deal with him on some projects he wanted authorized by us. But there's no crowding him. He understands perfectly and applies with a sure hand the power that seniority has gained for him.

Damned if everyone doesn't want something. I had colleagues lobbying me for projects in their districts. Lou Frey begged me to look out for a Navy hospital that's to be built in Orlando. Ed Forsythe asked me to get language in the bill that would transfer land at Lakehurst, New Jersey, to a Lighter-than-Air Museum. When I was home Friday evening, Admiral Gus Kinnear called me at Virginia Beach to ask me what happened to a chunk of money that had been programmed for the F-18, the new Navy single-seater fighter. It seems that it was cut in the R&D Subcommittee. I had to tell him that I didn't know, because I had been spending the last few days on the Milcon Bill.

Thursday, March 11, 1976—Monday, March 15, 1976

Not too much to report in this entry. I turned fifty-one on Friday, a figure that for some reason looks worse than it sounds. My staff helped me to celebrate on Thursday in the office, since we were leaving that afternoon for home.

We dined with friends on Sunday night and drove up this morning. The House had several bills on the Suspension Calendar, but only two of them drew recorded votes. The big item this afternoon was a meeting in Mel Price's office of those members of the Armed Services Committee who are scheduled to travel to China during the Easter recess. It has been uncertain for some weeks as to whether or not I would be included. The Chinese here in Washington have been vague about who would be invited and how many. Apparently, they decided to limit the number to six from the committee, plus wives. Frank

Slatinshek, as chief counsel, would go, along with a physician and a military aide. That being the case, Mel had planned to divide the delegation according to the majority-minority split, four Democrats and two Republicans, which would have missed me, since I'm number three on our side. But Bob Wilson told me that the Chinese preferred to have three Democrats and three Republicans. Furthermore, Bill Randall, who would have been the fourth Democrat, is a lame duck. He would serve the Chinese little purpose if he is not here next year. I've been invited down to the Chinese Mission this evening, for what is billed as "a working dinner" with them. It will give them a chance to look me over. They've already had the others down for dinner and discussion.

This afternoon, two men from the State Department, both of whom are China specialists and have traveled there since the Nixon visit four years ago, were on hand to brief us on what we might expect and to answer questions. George Bush, who headed our Mission in Peking until he came back to head the CIA, will give us an in-depth briefing tomorrow afternoon. The plan is to depart Andrews on Thursday, April 15, and fly to Japan. From there we will go to Shanghai, and the Chinese will then take over our itinerary. They will give us no clue as to what it is, although we will be spending only six days in the country, and several of those are bound to be in Peking. We will return to Washington on Sunday, April 25, by way of Hawaii, where we will spend one night to break up the trip. Janie and I are keeping our fingers crossed that nothing will happen in the meantime to scrub the trip. It will surely qualify as the most important journey we will have made in my career here.

Tuesday, March 16, 1976—Wednesday, March 17, 1976

The China trip is on. Frank Slatinshek told me this afternoon (Wednesday) that he had received confirmation on me from the Chinese. Apparently they also decided to include Bill Randall. Bill wanted to go in the worst way and had pestered Mel about it, so even though he's retiring at the end of this term, they went ahead and invited him.

The dinner at the Chinese Mission on Monday evening was an interesting experience. The Mission is located at 2300 Connecticut Avenue, the site of the old Windsor Park Hotel. As a matter of fact, Janie and I had gone to dinner there one night about six years ago. The Chinese occupy the entire building, having their living quarters and offices all in the one building. Since the downstairs had once been the lobby and dining area, the rooms are spacious. The Chinese brought over their own workmen to make the renovations, and the result is a connecting series of rooms which can be used for receptions or dinners. The most striking thing about the principal reception room was a large tapestry on one wall depicting Chairman Mao and a host of adoring Chinese clad in a variety of national dress. It was pointed out to me that there are over fifty different racial groups in China, all of whom are Chinese. From a distance it looked like countless other pieces of heroic communist art, with the benevolent, smiling Mao in the middle and several dozen equally happy and smiling comrades on either side of him. What made the tapestry so unique was the fact that it was done entirely in needlepoint. My hosts told me that it had taken a team of artists four months to make it, laboring continuously. More artistic and infinitely more pleasing were several cases of Chinese antiques, some of which were recent archeological finds dating back to 3000 B.C. There were also some pieces from the Ming era, as well as two exquisite cloisonné vases produced recently. I told Janie that I would like to bring a couple of them back from China if they are not too expensive.

Since I was the first to arrive, I had a chance to chat briefly with the head of the Chinese Mission, who is addressed as ambassador but technically isn't of that rank, since we have not yet reached agreement with the Peking government to extend full diplomatic recognition to each other. Han Hsu is properly Minister Han Hsu. He is short, appears to be in his late fifties or early sixties, and had grizzled hair, cropped close. I recall the names of only two of the other Chinese, Yang Yo-Yung and his wife, Shen Jo-Yun. There were also two other Chinese men and a woman in the group. All spoke English, but Madame Shen was by far the most fluent, and at the table, if Han Hsu was asked a question, he would usually reply in Chinese and she would translate. All were dressed in black tunics and trousers. Madame Shen's only concession to femininity was a light blue sweater worn underneath.

I was pleasantly surprised to find that only Peggy Heckler and Bill Frenzel would be there with me, which meant that we could all sit at one table and have a fairly intimate conversation. Peggy, who has been to China twice, was responsible for my invitation. She has become very friendly with the Chinese, and they have used her as a conduit to establish contact with other Members. What really surprised me during the evening was the transformation which has occurred in her thinking regarding the Soviet menace to peace and the need for the U.S. to strengthen its defense posture. Peggy has invariably voted the liberal path in the past and been opposed to defense increases, if not to the recommended budget itself. Now, by her own admission, she has undergone a change of heart. She told us that two things influenced her. One was the large Portuguese-American colony in her district, which revealed to her through reports from relatives back home the degree of Soviet penetration in Portugal. The second factor was her visits to China and her conversations with the Chinese and the preparations being made there to defend themselves against Soviet aggression. Frenzel and I ribbed her a little about it, but she took it well. The Chinese beamed at her with obvious pleasure.

The "cocktail hour," if you could call it that, consisted of sipping cups of weak tea for about twenty minutes, and then we went in to dinner, sitting at a round table with a large lazy susan in the middle, from which the various dishes were served. I sat between Han Hsu and Madame Shen. The meal was a multi-course affair, commencing with Chinese hors d'oeuvres and ending with dumplings on sweet fermented rice. Throughout the dinner, we sipped beer and a sweet Chinese wine, interspersed with slugs of one of the most potent liquors this side of the Great Wall, Mao Tai. Made from sorghum, it has a real kick. Han Hsu periodically raised his glass and wished us good health. It was the same liquor served at the Nixon and Ford banquets in Peking, and Peggy said that I could expect to encounter it in copious quantities when I go over.

The conversation at the table was lively. Our hosts were primarily interested in discussing the American political scene, with which they showed great familiarity. They asked us who we thought would emerge as the principal candidates, discussing their merits and what we might expect from them. Only in one or two instances did they manifest any ignorance of the nuances that influence our political system. They are certainly far better informed about our system that we are about theirs. At the same time, Bill and Peggy gave the Chinese a run for their money by seeking answers to the puzzling status of Deng Hsiao-ping, who has recently come under fire as "a capitalist roader" in China. Our hosts showed no embarrassment, and answered easily that Deng's acts had uncovered him. I mentioned the article that I had read of David Eisenhower's, which appeared several weeks ago in the *Wall Street Journal*, in which he gave an account of his visit with Chairman Mao. I said that I had never really comprehended until that moment the Chairman's view that if the revolution was to succeed, it would have to be kept alive for some four centuries, and that Mao himself had declared that the revolution's chance of success was only fifty-fifty. The Chinese looked at me and solemnly nodded. I then went on to say that an American historian named Crane Brinton had written a book some years ago called *Anatomy of Revolution,* in which he compared the great revolutions of modern history, including our own, the French, and the Bolshevik. Brinton's thesis is that revolutions are like physiological beings, with a life and death cycle of development, growth, and decline. I concluded that it appeared to be the case, with the current exception of the Chinese revolution of Mao Tse-tung, who was seeking to keep his revolution in ferment. Madame Shen was visibly pleased with this revolutionary dialogue and spoke of the Chairman's "unity of opposites." Briefly stated, it poses the question, "Does one divide into two, or two combine into one?" The current thinking is that one divides into two, meaning that two lines of thought emerge, one which is right and one which is wrong. The wrong one must be destroyed. When I ventured to say that this struck me as very similar to the dialectic of Hegel, which Marx had adopted, the Chinese said there was a parallel, but it wasn't precisely the same. I didn't pursue it.

They were very outspoken about the Soviet threat and wanted to know if our defense budget was going to remain intact this year. We told them that we thought that it would not undergo the kind of wholesale cut it suffered last year. I said that I thought that the American people were becoming increasingly aware of our decline in strength vis-à-vis the Soviet Union, and that this feeling was being transmitted back to Congress. The Chinese then asked us what kind of a response we might make to further Soviet adventures. I replied that we would certainly move vigorously in areas that we considered vital to our national interests. This was too vague for them, and they pressed for specifics. I mentioned Europe and the Middle East. "What about Rhodesia?" they asked. "No, not there," I replied. Peggy and Bill agreed that we would not move to intervene in South Africa. I recounted my visit to Somalia last July, which held their interest, and they nodded approval when I added that the U.S. ought to improve its logistical position in the Indian Ocean by deepening the harbor and lengthening the runway at Diego Garcia.

Toward the end of the evening, I turned to Madame Shen and quietly said that it was my earnest hope that, following the election, Ford would further develop the relationship between our two countries. "We have a common foe," I declared, "and the need to strengthen the bonds between us is great." Then, gesturing toward Han Hsu, I added, "We should make him a real ambassador." She said nothing, but she nodded imperceptibly. On that note, the dinner ended.

The sequel to the evening at the Mission occurred on Tuesday afternoon, when those of us who are to make the trip met with George Bush, who represented us in Peking for fourteen months. With him was Jim Lilley, a China expert with George at the CIA and a veteran of twenty-one months with the U.S. Liaison Office in Peking. We talked about the forthcoming trip and some of the things we might expect. George strongly recommended that we use the services of Bill Thomas and his wife, who are with USLO in Peking. Both are fluent in Chinese and can be a big help to us during our week in China.

George told us to ask plenty of questions while we are there. "Be disarmingly frank," he said. "The Chinese will expect it from American congressmen." Both he and Lilley said that the attack on Deng has caused a shakeup in the defense establishment. Deng held three positions of leadership: one in the party, another in the government, and the last as chief of staff. He now holds only his party position. Lilley gave us a review of their military posture, some of which was classified. He said that the Army had undergone a major program of modernization recently, but that in the last few years it had been through a cycle. After Lin Piao's fall, little money was spent on improving defense. Last year, after a modest start, the appropriations were much greater. They are spending much more on planes and ships, building eight to nine submarines a year. Their land-based missiles can hit any Siberian targets, and preparations are going forward on a larger one which will have Moscow within range. The Chinese are in severe need of Western technology and have purchased British jet engines as well as some electronic equipment from the Japanese. But they will need much more if they are ever to have a modern, sophisticated force.

In discussing the current political crisis surrounding Deng, Lilley said that Deng was brought down because in the eyes of his foes, he was trying to bring back Mao's critics, men who had been laid low during the Cultural Revolution but were more recently being elevated to positions of influence. According to Lilley, Mao was told that Deng wanted to change Mao's cherished educational system and bring back "long-nail Mandarins." For all of this, Mao decided to put him down, and when Deng tried to put one of his cronies in as head of the Peking Military District, the Army leaders became unhappy, a fact that Mao's people capitalized on.

We asked about the future. Lilley said that all of the factions in China, no matter what their persuasion, believed in two principles. First, China must be a great power by the year 2000. Second, China needs Western technology to do this. Where they disagree with one another is over how fast they should go about it. Deng is a pragmatist and felt that revolutionary idealism should take second place to engineering and the acquisition of skills and leadership to move China forward as quickly as possible. This brought him on a collision course with the more pure revolutionists.

Before leaving, Dick Ichord asked George how he assessed the Nixon visit to China last month. George said that the Chinese place great stock in the Shanghai Communiqué, which was issued jointly when Nixon first went to China four years ago. That document gave birth to American agreement with the "one China" concept. The Chinese recalled what Nixon had said to them when he first came, that he was there because it was in his country's interest. Therefore, they felt that he had acted with courage and foresight, and having him back on the fourth anniversary of the Communiqué seemed natural. Watergate for them was an internal affair of the U.S., and thus meaningless. Inviting Nixon back was a symbolic move, reminding America of Nixon's stand of drawing closer to China. To be sure, they misgauged the reaction in the U.S. Frankly, it surprised them that there was so much residual hatred of Nixon, and they have probably had some second thoughts. But George emphasized that Mao rests his hopes upon the Shanghai Communiqué and significantly has indicated that it is in no way to be jeopardized in the movement against Deng.

Thursday, April 15, 1976—Sunday, April 25, 1976

With the visit to China behind us, I am reminded of the words of Napoleon seven generations ago: "China—there lies a sleeping giant. But let her sleep, for when she awakes, she will move the world." The chairman of our Committee, Mel Price, put it well in his toast at our farewell banquet on our last night in Shanghai. No nation that we have ever visited for so short a period has left such a lasting impression.

In composing this entry, it is difficult to know where to begin. Our experiences have been compressed into a mosaic of memories. For the sake of order, it might be best to develop this chronologically and relate the daily events, and yet it is hard not to set down a panorama of impressions, because that is our principal reaction to these past ten days.

We departed Andrews Air Force Base at 9:00 a.m. on the 15th. In the party were seven of us from the Armed Services Committee: Mel Price, Sam Stratton, Dick Ichord, and Bill Randall, all Democrats; and on the Republican side, Bob Wilson, Bill Dickinson, and me. From the International Relations Committee we had Lester Wolff, a Democrat, and Herb Burke, a Republican. All of us had our wives with us except Bill Dickinson, who is divorced, and Lester Wolff, whose wife is not well. His son, a young attorney in New York, accompanied him. Frank Slatinshek, our chief counsel, and his wife were in the group, along with Joyce Shub, a staffer from Wolff's Committee. The party was rounded out by Stapleton Roy from the State Department, and Dr. Raymond Johnson, a Navy physician who heads the Department of Internal Medicine at Bethesda. Our military escort was a retired Air Force Colonel, Joe Clark.

Both Deputy Minister Han Hsu and Madame Shen, from the Chinese Liaison Office in Washington, came out to see us off. They seemed particularly pleased that we were going and joked with us in good humor about our journey.

The flight brought back memories of my trip to Vietnam in 1970, during my freshman term. We flew the same Great Circle route, the first leg of seven and one-half hours to Anchorage, Alaska, where we lunched with the Air Wing Commander at Elmendorf AFB before beginning the second half of the flight, to Tokyo. Crossing the International Date Line, we lost a day, but Janie and I beat the jet lag by going to bed at 7:30 that evening, and we woke refreshed the next morning from a ten-hour sleep. Then it was on to Shanghai Saturday morning, April 17, a three-hour flight to Hung Chiao Airport.

It was raining when we arrived, and in fact the weather was seldom clear during our entire stay. Most of the time it was overcast, with occasional rain, with only one sunny day, fortunately on Sunday, when we drove out to the Great Wall.

Our introduction to China began at the Shanghai Airport with the first of many seemingly interminable multi-course meals. It was a luncheon hosted by Shanghai officials from the Peoples Institute for Foreign Affairs. All wore the national uniform of China, the Mao tunic, in black, blue, or gray. In keeping with their own revolution, the women wore trousers, too, which made the pants suits of our ladies complementary. The luncheon was preceded by a briefing—the first of many— at which the national beverage, tea, was served in steaming covered cups. The uniformity of the country, in dress and behavior, made every occasion predictable. Whether it was a meeting with the Foreign Minister or the chairman of the Revolutionary Committee of a People's Commune, the cups of tea, constantly refilled by waiters or attendants, were on the table.

After lunch, there was a considerable wait until the weather cleared enough for the plane to land which was scheduled to take us to Peking. We used the time to buy and write postcards and to shop. Chinese stamps are unusual: they have no glue on them, and have to be pasted on individually, using a pot of glue available at each post office. Our American crew and plane left us in Shanghai and flew back to Tokyo, and everyone felt more than a little strange to see the big bird with "United States of America" on the side disappear into the mist.

Several of the Chinese from the Peoples Institute for Foreign Affairs accompanied us for the remainder of our stay. Since we were the eleventh group from the Congress to visit China, they were familiar with our customs and habits. Americans generally adopt an easy familiarity in travel abroad, and the Chinese had fortunately been exposed to it. Normally reserved, they indulged in the quick friendship of our group.

We were advised that after we reached Peking that afternoon, we would be the guests at a dinner that evening, hosted by Chou Pei-yuan, vice chairman of the Peoples Institute for Foreign Affairs. We landed at dusk and were driven to the Peking Hotel, a vast interlocking establishment which had grown from a gracious old hotel of the 1920s with successive wings to include the high-rise section in which we were housed, built about a decade ago. Altogether it contained 900 rooms, and with the polyglot nationalities making their pilgrimages to China, it appeared that all the rooms were booked.

As I mentioned in an earlier entry, the Chinese had given us no hint of our itinerary prior to our departure. It was not until after dinner that evening that we were told what our schedule would be: three days in Peking, a day and a half in Dairen (renamed Dalien by the Chinese), and a day and a half back in Shanghai. The Chinese told us that we would be the first American delegation to visit Dairen, and in keeping with our Committee's responsibilities, they had arranged for a visit on Monday to the headquarters of an infantry division of the People's Liberation Army, also a first. In Dairen, we were scheduled to view the extensive tunnel network, which is the heart of the Chinese civil defense program. It whetted our appetite for the balance of the visit.

The following morning (Sunday), we drove out to the Great Wall, about forty miles from Peking, but Janie and I took an hour beforehand and walked up to Tien An Men Square, a vast open plaza which is the Chinese equivalent of Red Square in Moscow, only incomparably larger. It was our first real encounter with the city and its people, and at this point it might be well to make some general observations.

Peking has a grubby appearance. A haze obscures the city, giving it a grayish cast. The soft coal burned by the Chinese is the villain to a

174

large extent. The smoke and dust permeate and penetrate, but the winter is also hard and dry in North China. Even in mid-April, spring was struggling for rebirth. Not a blade of grass was to be seen, and the Chinese constantly swept the bare ground, scouring the soil so that the slightest breeze produced swirls of dust. The countryside was equally barren. The land had a worn-out look, as if centuries of exploitation by generations of peasants had robbed it of its last vestige of fertility. Yet the late spring and summer rains will revive it. Trees bloom, and crops will come forth.

By contrast, Shanghai, in the south, has considerably more moisture, and the winter is not nearly so severe. There, the fields and parks were green and life seemed less of a struggle.

Housing there, by any standards, is spartan at best, and millions still live in primitive conditions. A visit to a commune outside of Shanghai gave first-hand evidence of this. The multi-family building housing the workers lacked both central heating and indoor plumbing. The rooms were small and cramped, crowded with the little furniture available. The workers' apartments that we visited in the city of Shanghai were only a step above their rural counterparts, and although less than twenty years old, they would not even have met tenement standards in New York. Toilet and kitchen facilities, small and restricted, were shared by two or more families.

The Chinese made no attempt to hide the inferiority of their housing. They were frank to say that it was far behind the West, but they emphasized that it was at least shelter, and before the Liberation in 1949, millions didn't even have that.

One curious aspect of the cities was that although no litter was to be seen, nothing seemed really clean. The country appeared to have been swept, but never scrubbed. Yet the people themselves, without exception, were clean. The children and young people were particularly neat in appearance, their clothing often bright in comparison to the blue, black, and gray Mao tunics of their parents. There were cuspidors everywhere, but if none was within reach, people would spit on the streets, the sidewalks, even on the terrazzo floors inside the buildings.

However, if housing is inferior, the Chinese are at least adequately fed, which certainly ranks as the revolution's greatest achievement. Much has been written about the beggars and famine in pre-war China. No one starves any more, and everyone except the very old and infirm works. Even in elementary school, half an hour is set aside each day for work. We saw six-year-olds placing tiny circles of cork into the hollows of plastic caps which would be used later in a neighborhood factory or workshop. They and their parents and neighbors are all bees in Chairman Mao's hive, and they are never out of sight or unmindful of him. Department stores are topped with his slogans or exhortations. Billboards admonish one and all to strive harder for the socialist motherland, and gazing benignly down on all of this activity is the face of the Great Teacher, complete with the mole on his chin. His portrait or statue—larger than life—is everywhere—to greet the visitor on his arrival at the airport or bid farewell on his departure, in every school and public building, in the communes, and in the military encampments. His presence is felt in every corner of China, a deity in whose name every truth is uttered and whose inspiration has brought about every achievement. "Praise Mao, from Whom all blessings flow...." It was 1984 eight years early.

I suppose that Shanghai and Peking are no more dense than Tokyo, but they seem so. Swarms of people are on the sidewalks and squeeze into stores and shops. Bicycles create a traffic jam that has no parallel anywhere else. From dawn to dusk they form a continuous stream flowing in opposite currents on the streets of the cities. The relatively few cars, buses, and trucks weave among the cyclists, their horns blowing constantly, creating a frantic urban cacophony. Furthermore, cars and other such vehicles are not permitted to use their lights in the cities at night, in order not to blind the cyclists, and this creates a real hazard from bicycles darting out unexpectedly from the shadows.

China is on the move—literally. The emphasis on self-reliance and the spirit of make-do are reflected in every type of conveyance to be seen. On the streets and roads were everything from trucks of various sizes and vintage to two- and four-wheeled carts drawn by donkeys, ponies, oxen, and men—China's oldest source of power.

Our own transportation in every city was provided by private cars made up into a convoy to which we were assigned on the basis of seniority, with the chairman (Mel, not Mao) in the lead car, always a large, black one. Every time we set out, I felt as though I was in a high-speed funeral procession.

The Sunday excursion to the Great Wall and the Ming Tombs was not a disappointment. The wall has captured the imagination of schoolchildren the world over, and no visitor to China should pass it up. Built in the rugged mountains that rise suddenly from the arid plain outside Peking, the Great Wall, for most of its 4,000 mile length, has fallen into disrepair, and in many stretches is only a trace of stone and rubble. The current rulers have wisely restored a portion of it. It is a national treasure to be preserved and now looks as it did 2,000 years ago, a stone snake coiling its way across the ridges of China's northern mountains. It is a tourist mecca for the Chinese as well as for foreigners. Busloads of soldiers, families, and. children thronged the plaza below the steps leading to the roadway along the crest of the wall. Most walked short distances along the top, and a few adventurous ones climbed the steep elevation to one of the towers at the peak of a ridge.

The afternoon drive to the Ming Tombs, while impressive, was something of an anticlimax. By late afternoon, we were back in Peking and ready to begin the substantive part of our visit to the Peoples Republic of China, a conference with Foreign Minister Chiao.

The meeting was held in a guest house just behind Tien An Men Square. Chiao is in his early sixties and is tall for a Chinese, a shade over six feet. His gray Mao tunic was tailored of superior cloth, and he had a quiet grace about him. Like many Chinese, he is addicted to smoking, and he lit a succession of cigarettes, holding them delicately between his thumb and forefinger.

We sat in large easy chairs placed around the room, the interpreter between Mel and Chiao. Tea was poured continuously. The pattern of the conference was one that we would follow in successive meetings with Chinese officials. Mel would introduce each of us and tell where we were from and perhaps something about our past. The Foreign Minister took note of this and began by saying, "I imagine that this is your first visit since the liberation of our country. It is precisely for this that we have invited you—to see our progress." At this, Dick Ichord said that he had been a flyer after World War II, bringing medical supplies to Shanghai. Chiao smiled and said that he had been there then. Then Bob Wilson quipped, "He hopes to find the girl he knew," at which the Foreign Minister chuckled, "Maybe she's an old woman now."

Then Bob, in a more serious vein, reviewed past relations between China and the U.S.: There had been unpleasantness in recent years, but now it was necessary for friendship. Bob added that recent events in China were of interest to us, particularly the changes in the government, military problems, and the like.

When this was translated, Chiao nodded and then replied, "I agree with the observations of Mr. Wilson. The American and Chinese people have been friendly in the past. Your state (California) is well known to us. San Francisco is known as 'old gold mountain' from the time in the last century. Of course, later on, certain incidents happened in the Second World War and the Korean War, but that is part of the past now. In our view, friendship between the people of our countries will last forever, and since the visit of President Nixon, state relations have improved. We have many common points of view now." He went on to extol the Shanghai Communiqué, the joint statement agreed to at the time of Nixon's visit in 1972.

"Both sides should oppose hegemony," he said. "We think the Soviet imperialists constitute the main danger, and all of you from the Armed Services Committee should be concerned for your own military affairs. China is a country under the leadership of Chairman Mao and the Chinese Communist Party. We rely upon the people for our national defense. 'Millet plus the rifle' served as our motto in the struggle for independence and now." It was a phrase that would be repeated over and over to us, recited as if by rote.

Chiao went on: "Though we possess few new weapons, we rely little upon them. On the contrary, what we pay more attention to are underground tunnels. You have been to the Great Wall. It was built to protect the people in the south from the nomads of the north. In modern warfare, it could avail little. Our tunnels are our 'Underground Great Wall,' but will be greater." Then he quoted another oft-repeated slogan from Chairman Mao: "'Dig tunnels deep. Store grain everywhere. And never seek hegemony.' This is our foreign policy." he said.

Mel replied that he had the impression from the Chinese that there is an imminent threat of war. "Do you feel there is one?" he asked. "How do you look at prospects for maintaining peace in this part of the world?"

"On this point," Chiao answered, "maybe our views are slightly different from yours. We hold that the danger of war has increased, but we don't believe it's imminent. We believe that war can not be averted, only postponed." He said that they regarded the possibility of nuclear war as less than that of a conventional one, citing the Soviet military build-up as proof.

At this point, I reminded him that we in the House of Representatives had increased by $2 billion the authorization for defense expenditures over the military budget recommended by the President. Chiao replied that they had taken note of the defense increase in the U.S. to counter the Soviet threat, but he compared this period to that of the late 1930s when the West sought to avoid war at any price. "This thinking accelerates the outbreak of war," he said.

Then Lester Wolff noted that changes had recently occurred in the government and asked what effect this might have on China's policy toward Russia. Chiao replied that China's foreign policy since Liberation had stemmed from Chairman Mao's thought ("What doesn't in China?" I wondered), "and whether this person or that person implements policy, including our policy toward the United States."

But Wolff persisted. "We're concerned that China will turn inward again. We're concerned that China and Russia will be friendly as they were in the past, and we will be left out once more." Chiao answered, "The question of 'inwardness' doesn't exist. We all live on this planet, so on that point there is no ground for worry. Our policy toward the U.S. was personally formulated by Chairman Mao and expressed in the Shanghai Communiqué, and this policy will not change. Our relationship with the Soviet Union is a long and complicated story. For a certain period of time after the Liberation, our relations with the Soviet Union were relatively good—from 1949 to 1954. Why do I say, '1954'? Because the Soviet Union's Communist Party changed its nature and its policy. It became revisionist. For this, Krushchev was responsible. And then, from 1954 to 1964, we had a long period of observation and debate with them, and we concluded that the people in their upper strata were incorrect. They betrayed socialism, Marxism, and Leninism. Our differences with them covered two aspects: ideology and practical policy. After ten years of observation, it was apparent that the Soviet Union tried to dominate and control China and turn China into a satellite of the Soviet Union. In 1964, when Krushchev fell and Brezhnev came to power, did they change their policy? They did not. They went on in a bigger way.

"We don't agree with the West that Brezhnev is a moderate. I met many persons in Europe who told me this. I told them that their view is superficial. As a matter of fact, Brezhnev went even further than Krushchev in expansionism and Soviet imperialism. We have a label for him: we call him 'the new Czar.' All of you are familiar with the history of Russia. In the fifteenth century, the Slavic people occupied only a small area around Moscow and Kiev. But under the Czar they expanded and now they are much bigger. In our view, even without Brezhnev they will never change their ways.

"Why does this phenomenon occur? Because in the Soviet Union a privileged class has emerged, and it is the privileged class that is exercising control over the Soviet Union. I don't know if you have read Brezhnev's speech to the 25th Party Congress. It is long and not a good speech, but you should read it. In it, he called upon his own people to tighten their belts to accelerate war preparations. He has such a desire to seek world hegemony. How will this not lead to war?

"In our relations with the Soviet Union we will debate our ideology. Chairman Mao has said that the debate would go on for 10,000 years, or a minimum of 8,000 years. But this should not affect normal state relations. Yet the Soviet Union wants to link state relations with ideological debate, so on their part it is difficult to maintain normal state relations.

"China will not return to the early 1950s. The Soviet Union is seeking world hegemony and actually preparing for war. This is a reality, and in this both of us have common points. Both of us are opposed to hegemony."

Following this rather long monologue, which was an overview of the party line, Sam Stratton raised the question of the possiblity of some kind of cooperation between the U.S. and China to postpone war. "Where could we work together in the military field?" This was a speculation that we had shared when the Chinese extended the invitation to visit their country, but the Foreign Minister threw cold water on it when he replied, "The social systems in our two countries are different, but in international affairs we have many common points. You exert your efforts, and we will exert ours. It is our policy to be self-reliant."

By this time, Chiao had begun to wiggle his knees, which I had heard the Chinese do when they are anxious to end a conversation or are impatient. We had been with him for two hours, and it was clear that he wished to terminate the discussion and move on to the dinner that was set in the next room. The wives, who were not present for the conference, had arrived, and so we adjourned for a session of official photographs and then the customary ten-course meal.

On Monday, April 19, we drove for nearly two hours to the east to a village called Yang Chuan, where the 196th Infantry Division is headquartered. In a conference room on the second floor of the main building we were welcomed soberly by the deputy commander of the division, Chang Sheng-huei. The uniform of the Peoples Liberation Army consists of an olive green Mao tunic and green trousers. All soldiers have a plastic red star on the front of their Mao cap. Red tabs on the collar complete the uniform. Uniforms are nearly identical, with no distinction among the ranks. The only difference between officers and men is in the pockets of the tunics. The officers have four and the enlisted men just the two breast pockets. At lunch that day, I asked one of the Chinese at my table how the men knew who was in command or who could give an order. He replied that the officers lived in the barracks with their troops and were personally known to them. Further, I learned that men stay in the same unit for a number of years—one of the men I talked to had been there for eleven years—and this would certainly help make it clear who was who. Also, despite the equality of the sexes in China, women are not permitted in combat, just as is the case in the U.S.

Chang looked to be about sixty. He told us that the division had its origins in several guerrilla units, which had fought against the Japanese in 1936-37. By the time of the civil war with Kuomintang forces in 1946, it was a full division.

I wondered when the division's record was going to include combat operations against the U.S. Chang got around to that shortly. "Not long after the establishment of the Peoples Republic of China, the imperialists unleashed war in Korea, and this unit volunteered to fight. During that time the aggressors not only crossed the Yalu and spread war flames to our border, but they occupied our territory, including the island of Taiwan. While we were in Korea, we not only carried on combat along the Yalu, but down to the 38th parallel and south of it, and smashed the scheme of the imperialists in Korea, who used it as a bridgehead against our country."

The Peoples Liberation Army doesn't just sit in its barracks or hold field training. Units work in the fields and factories, and train the people's militia, an enormous reserve of tens of millions. The 196th Division raises most of its own food and operates a small pharmaceutical production unit, employing the wives of soldiers. On a tour of the encampment, we saw soldiers making soy sauce and bean curd, hulling rice, sewing and repairing uniforms and shoes, and digging a drainage canal. The military hospital had patients from both the unit and the civilian community; some were being treated by acupuncture. Again, the grime on walls and hallways was disconcerting, but the health care, like everything else, has to be compared to the pre-Liberation days. Then it was practically nonexistent, except for the missionary hospitals.

The PLA is highly politicized, like all communist armies, and it was inevitable that the political commissar was given a chance to deliver a message. Short and stocky, with a belligerent appearance, he looked the role of Mao's apostle. Speaking in the soldiers' meeting hall, he barked out his sentences, reciting the revolutionary litany, "We have resolutely implemented the principles on lines of proletarian strength. We have carried out our work, opposing various bourgeois political

lines in the Army, so that our Army will always remain a Peoples Army."
Nor did he forget to take a swipe at the now-disgraced Deng Hsiao-ping
and the demonstration of April 4 in Tien An Men Square. While the
monologue was being delivered, I wandered over to a display of captured enemy weapons. Of the seven in the case, I recognized four as
U.S.-made, a Springfield rifle, a Thompson sub-machine gun, an M-1,
and a carbine, all circa World War II with the exception of the
Springfield. The M-1 had obviously been taken from an American. The
soldier had carved his girl's name, "Susie," on the stock.

The barracks looked like those of countless other armies. Double-
decker bunks were arranged in rows, all smartly made up to pass
inspection. The soldiers' rifles, SKS semi-automatic, were in their
racks, the metal gleaming from their last polishing. Following lunch, we
were given a display of firing by militia and regular PLA soldiers. Using
rifles and machine guns, they showed considerable marksmanship,
each unit performing in turn.

The day concluded with a performance of singing and dancing by
male and female members of the division. Both songs and dances
centered on a revolutionary theme, in keeping with Chairman Mao's
dictum that culture must be revolutionary, too. The performers were
excellent, especially four young ballet dancers who could easily have
made it in American ballet professionally.

The next day, Tuesday, we drove out to Peking University to meet
with Vice Chairman Huan of the Revolutionary Committee of the
University. Huan began with the history of Peking University, telling us
that it was established in 1898. What he omitted was that the Americans
were responsible for its birth and funding. It was the first university
established in China, and it has had a remarkable history. Mao Tse-tung
studied there on two occasions, and during the Japanese occupation of
China, the university was a focal point of student resistance. Huan told
us that the Great Cultural Revolution began there.

At this juncture, Huan lapsed into the revolutionary vernacular.
"Education," he said, "must serve the proletariat. Feudal education
served feudal rulers, while the education of the bourgeoisie served the
interests of the bourgeoisie. Our education should serve the dictator-
ship of the proletariat, and those educated should serve the people."

He told us that Peking University has twenty departments divided
into three categories: the social sciences, natural sciences, and foreign
languages. Students are drawn from the workers, peasants, and
soldiers, who may apply after two years of labor in any of these
categories. But not everyone can apply. The people in the communes,
factories, and the Army meet to recommend those they believe fit for
college enrollment. Selection is made on the basis of "Moral, intellectual,
and physical qualifications." It sounded reasonable, but then, the
definitions of "moral" and "intellectual" have a different dimension in
Mao's China.

Lester Wolff inquired if this system of selection would not lead to the creation of a small elite class. In the U.S., he stated, we have open enrollment and anyone can apply and be admitted to at least one college.

Huan said no, that "the broad masses are represented by workers and soldiers. These children constitute a majority of the people." And then, as an afterthought, he added, "The children of the bourgeoisie, if they behave, can be admitted."

Since the number of universities is limited, the government has encouraged the establishment of higher education units in factories, and great numbers of these have been set up. It is an effective way to expose more people to education. The Chinese have also experimented with the length of school terms, shortening most to three years and some to two. For example, library science is now a two-year program.

Bob Wilson asked, "What about your physicists and scientists? Surely you are not able to cut them without sacrificing instruction." Huan replied that their physics program was for three years, with four years for theoretical and nuclear physics. The Chinese don't grant the long summer vacations and take the other holidays to the extent that American institutions do, so the cutting of the number of years is not really a revolutionary development, educationally or politically. But their students are required to spend about a third of their time in factories, communes, work institutions, and so forth. Huan said that before the Cultural Revolution, in the late 1950s and early '60s, computer science students never saw a computer, but only a blackboard. Now they have contact with the research and manufacture of real computers, and indeed the one in use at the university was also made there.

Bob asked Huan about how much time was spent in political discussions "to beat back right wing deviationists." Huan replied that two half-days a week in ordinary times, but recently, with the necessity "to reverse right deviationism," two evenings have been added. That totals up to an intense amount of political indoctrination, and since these students were chosen by their associates in the factories, communes, and the Army, it is obvious that they come to the university already politically primed. An elite class is certainly being turned out, but one that is dedicated to the cause of revolution and Maoist thought.

All of us had been speculating on what will happen after Mao's passing. Even the Chinese realize that he is a mortal deity. Herb Burke put the question to Huan. "Will not the revisionists reverse his policies?" Huan said that it was precisely this that gave the present campaign its significance. "What is important is not in dismissing them from their posts, but to heighten the understanding of the broad masses in the future so that the people will recognize revisionism if it should reappear. The people must recognize and expose it." He added that the recent incident in Tien An Men Square, once denounced by the Central Committee, prompted "broad support from the masses." It was an unwitting admission that the "broad masses" are getting their signals from the Central Committee, and it is there that the policy after Mao will be decided.

The role of Chou En-lai in the Tien An Men Square episode was questioned by Les Wolff. Huan replied that there was a great feeling of "commemoration" for Chou. Indeed, we saw numerous bulletin cases along the walls with pictures of Chou in them, showing him at various times of his life. Huan said that there was nothing unusual about the people laying wreaths to his memory at Tien An Men on April 4. It is a tradition of festival time when the graves of relatives are honored. The government does not encourage this, but neither does it forbid it. It is just a custom that has lingered on. According to Huan, "Certain bad elements made use of the occasion and spread rumors that the present leaders had been against Chou. Those counter-revolutionaries took advantage to push their counter-revolutionary activities. After we arrested them, we found that they were hooligans and bad elements. They opposed Chairman Mao, the Central Committee, and even Chou En-lai. They took advantage of the feeling for Chou, but they were caught in a spot. Now we can see their reactionary feeling and their vicious, cheating, and arrogant nature."

He went on to say that the important thing for the people was to study Marxism, Leninism, and Chairman Mao's teachings to understand how to root out Deng Hsiao-ping. "In this way, we will be more vigilant to the trouble made by bad elements and class enemies." They suspected trouble when the wreaths were sent and "shouldn't have been taken in by them. After the incident there, our consciousness has been heightened. We know that Deng Hsiao-ping was supported by the counter-revolutionaries and they, in turn, by the counter-revolutionaries on Taiwan, who called them their 'spiritual brothers.'" Despite all of the verbiage, it was something of a revelation.

There was one final colloquy between Sam Stratton and Huan that is worth recording. Sam said that "truth in science must be found wherever it leads, and that the purpose of education is to find the truth." He mentioned the example of Galileo's experience with the Inquisition, which brought him to account and made him recant under penalty of death that the earth circled the sun. He recanted, but to himself said, "Yet it *does* move." Huan's reply was, "What you say I feel is not the essence of education. American education supposedly passes along knowledge, but I think that education in the U.S. is to have the students support the capitalist system as everlasting. We obviously have a different view, but in natural science we do seek the truth, and we've launched satellites, which proves our scientific capability."

Bob Wilson then noted that we knew very little about China, that it was like an egg: we could see what was on the outside but not what was on the inside. Huan's comeback brought a laugh, because it was clever. He said "We believe that the U.S. and China should cooperate. If we do, then we shall see the egg hatch into a small chicken of friendship."

On this note we adjourned for a very quick tour of the campus, which still retains much of its old charm. Gravel paths led past traditional Chinese buildings with their bright-tiled roofs, upturned at the corners. Pines and evergreens surrounding a placid pond lent a tranquil note. Superficially, it was a Mandarin setting, not a revolutionary one. Even the water tower was disguised to look like a pagoda. The most visible incongruity was a modern instructional computer in an old, traditional Chinese-style building. English-speaking students served as hosts, and they chattered merrily along, showing no inhibitions. Most were girls in their twenties, although they looked to be no more than fifteen. I might add that the young people almost uniformly had a wholesome and attractive appearance, and really pretty girls were the rule, not the exception.

That afternoon, we were given a tour of the Great Hall of the People, which bounds one side of Tien An Men Square. It faces the National Museum on the other. The square opens into Peking's main thoroughfare, Changan Avenue, with the Forbidden City of the past emperors just beyond it. In this area occur the vast parades held on May Day and in October to celebrate the Liberation. Here, too, are the portraits of the only other figures who share the spotlight with Mao Tse-tung. They are hardly rivals, since they are all dead. But in death they support the legitimacy of his cause. Marx, Engels, Lenin, and Stalin, in that order, are to be seen in schools and public buildings, factories, and communes. They are the tangible signs of the ideological struggle with the Soviet Union. And it is no wonder that the Russians do not separate ideology from state relations. In their eyes, the Chinese have not only usurped Marx and Engels to validate the truth according to Mao, they have taken the beloved and sanctified Lenin and the less-beloved but nevertheless bona fide Russian Stalin and exploited them in their heresy. Mao thus lays claim not only to the mantle of Communist China but in the whole world. It is he who has remained the pure and true believer and the current generation of Soviet leaders who have departed from the fold. The exasperation of the Russians in the face of this self-righteousness is, to a degree, understandable, and the Russian ambassador in Peking must do a slow burn every time he drives past Tien An Men and sees the large, garishly-tinted portraits of the four communist saints facing the square.

The Great Hall of the People is an immense structure, with marble floors and alabaster pillars inside. Supposedly built in the incredibly short time of ten months, it has wide staircases leading to reception rooms named for China's thirty provinces which are decorated with the distinctive art and other features of each of those provinces. The Assembly Hall, where the National Party Congress meets, has 10,000 seats. Folds of red velvet are draped on either side of the Chairman's face at the back of the stage. Pinpoint lights in the ceiling form a galaxy around a massive red star. I told Janie afterward that it reminded me of Albert Speer's recollections of the architecture during the Third Reich, all of it so massive and designed to impress by its size and a sense of permanency. The delegates who gather under the great ruby star in the vast auditorium must surely share the same emotions felt by the party faithful at the Nuremberg stadium on those September nights in the 1930s when Hitler spoke of the power and achievements of the Reich.

A conference with Vice Premier Chang Chun-chiao, second in power to the new Deputy Premier Hua Kuo-feng, rounded out the day. Some say that Chang is the strongest force in the Central Committee, more powerful than Hua, who was a compromise choice to succeed the deposed Deng Hsiao-ping. Barring any misstep, he will certainly be a contender when Mao passes. He is fifty-seven, still young enough to make the transition. Like Foreign Minister Chiao, he wore a well-tailored gray tunic, but he is shorter and appeared more jovial. He said that he understood that we had toured the Great Hall of the People and noted that the room in which we were meeting was adjacent to the Taiwan Room, and then chuckled at his own pointed subtlety.

Mel began by noting the composition of our group and pointing out that we were interested in security, and then asked where we could work together in this area. Chang was quick to respond. He reminded us that the Foreign Minister had already talked to us and advised us that the military were subordinate to the PRC's political line. "The biggest threat to China comes from our neighbor to the north. For this threat, we have to rely mainly on ourselves. It is clearly stated in our constitution that China favors socialist countries and will support revolutionary struggles throughout the world and will take measures against imperialist wars." And then he added, "I have a question for you: What is the U.S. doing in the Pacific since the Soviet Union is building up its strength there?" Mel replied that we weren't doing enough, because Congress had cut defense expenditures in the past. He asked Chang what he felt we should be doing there and in the Indian Ocean.

Chang's reply was interesting. "In our view, your focus lies in Europe, and you should pay more attention to Europe." It was a curious answer since he had raised the question of the Pacific in the first place, but he went on: "In my view, the focus of the Soviet Union is in the West. In the Pacific and Asian region, the Soviet Union has attained the least, and it has made the greatest gains in Europe and Africa. Some people say that the Soviet Union is trying to encircle China in Asia, but we don't think there's anything terrible about this. We don't believe it."

Mel asked about the Indian Ocean and Soviet activity there, to which Chang replied that this was a U.S. problem. The growth of the Soviet Navy simply showed that the danger of war was growing.

Lester Wolff got a little bit exasperated and reminded Chang that there were many Soviet troops on the Chinese border. If we had fewer troops in the West, more would be facing China. Therefore there was a relationship between the two parts of the world. Chang smiled and replied that obviously there was a connection of sorts, but the point that he was trying to make was that the focus of Soviet strategy was not in Asia but in Europe.

At this point a small debate developed, with Sam Stratton arguing that since both China and the U.S. recognized that the Soviet Union was a threat, why quarrel about where the focus was? All of us should work together to blunt the threat. That was the purpose of our visit, to see what we could do and exchange ideas on this. Chang paused for a moment, sensing the trend of the dialogue, and then replied, "We agree that the Soviet Union poses a threat to the whole world and not to a specific region, but the focus is in Europe. This is very important. Our two countries have to do in their own way what they can to develop their national defense. China and the U.S. have different social systems, and each must deal with his defense in his own way."

Sam answered, "The feeling of previous delegations to China was that China wanted the U.S. to remain in the western Pacific. What the Vice Premier was now saying seemed at variance, since he was saying that we should go our own way, and it didn't really make any difference what we did. Has China's policy changed?" Chang replied that they had stated many times that their views had not changed. "With respect to Korea, we've stated that the Korean people don't approve of your presence in South Korea, so how can we say that we approve? In the Pacific, the spearhead of the Soviet Union is aimed at the U.S. They are trying to squeeze you out. This is a question of the Soviet Union and not of us. We favor your maintaining a friendly relation with Japan."

Sam said that if we withdrew from Korea and Japan, it would be an invitation for the Soviet Union to move in. Now it was Chang's turn to lose patience. He said, "I think we will do well not to argue this point. We have never believed that there is a vacuum in Korea."

And then Bill Dickinson put the question squarely, because the Chinese have been so obviously ambiguous about our Korean presence. "Some people," he said, "want us to withdraw from our overseas bases. Certain members of Congress advocate this. Specifically, if we withdraw all of our forces from Korea, what would your attitude be? Would China welcome this?" Chang knew we were baiting him, and he just wasn't going to make a statement that would be at variance with the Chinese ideological position. His answer was skillful, all the same. "At present you are not preparing to withdraw, but if you did, the North Korean people would be pleased. I'm not in a position to advise whether the U.S. should withdraw or not, but we feel that the U.S. has scattered its strength. One needs to know where the focus is. The real question is whether America should try to keep down ten fleas with ten fingers or close its fingers into a fist."

At this, Wolff decided to employ a little allegory of his own. "If the dogs of war are unleashed, the bite of the dog will not be restricted. World War II started with a few belligerents and ended with many. If war is inevitable, as you say, then it will engulf everyone. How do we prevent it? China will not be able to stay out." Chang seemed to welcome the allegorical dialogue. It put him in his natural element. "When war breaks out, it will develop according to its own law. There is also a law of development as to where the dog will bite. We should not pacify the Soviet Union; appeasement will only accelerate the outbreak of war. Our purpose is to remain strong. China is a piece of meat that the Soviet Union wants very much to bite, but this piece of meat has bones in it which will cause the dog of the Soviet Union to break its teeth."

I then spoke up and asked where the Chinese would concentrate their defense effort. I noted our visit with the 196th Infantry Division and its skillful use of small arms. "Will China fight a guerrilla war or use more sophisticated weapons?" Chang said that they would fight "a people's war," which would be fought along conventional as well as guerrilla lines. "As far as the Army is concerned, it will fight a regular war, but the greatest units of our armed forces are our militiamen. We can mobilize tens of millions of troops in a short time. As to how we shall fight, it depends on how they will come in. It is no secret that we have concentrated our forces in the north. Our focus is in the north."

I also asked him if China intended to increase her defense spending as we are doing. Chang's reply was ambiguous. He said that it was difficult to differentiate between civilian and military spending. The military manufacture civilian goods, and vice versa. On the whole, there were little fluctuations in their military budget, but massive increases in building air raid shelters. "In China," he said, "there is no debate on the military budget. Our system is different from yours." There was nothing ambiguous about that, I thought, remembering the debate we had in the House two weeks ago.

Dick Ichord asked if Deng's removal as chief of staff of the Army had resulted in a new appointment to the vacancy, and also what method is used in determining appointments. Either they were embarrassed, or the Chinese in the room thought the question genuinely funny, because they all broke into laughter. Then Cheng answered, "As our Army was founded by Chairman Mao, and is under the leadership of the Party and the Central Committee, it is the Central Committee that is in charge of appointments. It has a military commission chaired by Mao Tse-tung. No one has succeeded Deng, but it doesn't make any difference. For several years we didn't have a chief of staff, and when Deng held the post, he didn't do much work—but please don't put that on the record."

Bob Wilson asked him if he considered his country to be a major nation as far as nuclear strategy is concerned. Chang replied that they needed to protect themselves from air raids, and in addition, every single city would have to fight. "During the Japanese occupation, many villages had underground tunnels, and the Japanese were unable to control these villages. We are also working on nuclear research, because if we don't have nuclear weapons, some nations will try to bully us, but we only have a small number. Even in the future, our nuclear weapons will not equal those you have, or the Soviet Union's. Too many are not of much use anyway."

Then Chang betrayed his anxiety over something that has worried the Chinese since it happened—the April 4 riots in Tien An Men Square. The Chinese were greatly embarrassed, because it flawed the image of an orderly, disciplined nation. "I have a question," he began. "Now that you have been in Peking several days, do you think there is much turmoil?" He was more transparent than he thought, but we laughed and replied that we had encountered only hospitality. Chang beamed and then said, "The reason I asked this question is that when you left the U.S. I read many news dispatches about the turmoil in Tien An Men Square. As for the change in government, this has created speculation of a change in policy. As a matter of fact, the change in the premiership came because Chou En-lai passed away, and not because of any big changes in China." He added that the lines of policy are laid down by Chairman Mao and that a change in personnel will not bring a change in policy.

"When we had friendly relations with the Soviet Union, it was during the premiership of Chou En-lai, and also when we had the falling out. This was due to the change of policy by the Soviet Union, and not because of a change in China. Brezhnev has replaced Krushchev, but the policies of the Soviet Union are unchanged. So on this question one should look at the line of policy the government pursues, and not the person. Also," he noted, "during Chou En-lai's life, the policy toward the U.S. changed."

The conference was coming to a close, but Bill Randall asked him one last question. He asked if China was making an effort to purchase arms elsewhere. Chang replied that China herself sold some military goods, but again, it was hard to define what was military and what was not. Some people, he noted, did not regard certain materials as being strategic in nature, but they did. "We think grain is a strategic commodity, but mainly," he said, "we rely on ourselves. In our experience over the last two decades, we mainly relied on ourselves. If a blockade was ever made, the Chinese people will realize that they must rely on themselves. Nothing is hard in this world if you dare to scale the heights." He had appropriately ended his answer with a quotation from the Great Teacher.

As we stood to go, he said he was glad that we had come to exchange views which would improve understanding, but he was rather emphatic in repeating that the conversation was entirely off the record. "If you don't publish, we will be able to exchange views again. If not, we won't." There was certainly nothing ambiguous about that.

That evening we hosted a ten-course dinner for our Chinese friends, especially those in Peking who had met with us and made the arrangements there. In the true spirit of potlatch, our banquet consisted of more courses than any of the ones at which we had been guests. By this time, I was fully familiar with the white lightning liquor Mao-Tai, and the Chinese toast, "Gan bei," which means "bottoms up." Mao Tse-tung should be the healthiest person in China by now.

Bad weather delayed our departure from Peking on Wednesday;

fog and rain in Dairen had socked in the airport there, so we spent the extra time in Peking visiting the Forbidden City, the Winter Palace, and the grounds of the emperors. It was well worth shaving a few hours from Dairen. The buildings and parks within the Forbidden City and the treasures of the emperors are beyond description. Like the Great Wall, it is something no visitor should miss.

Finally, in the early afternoon, we received clearance and left in a Soviet-built Ilyushin prop-jet for Dairen. In Peking we had been only mild curiosities; the Chinese there are used to foreigners. But in Dairen, we were celebrities and the object of intense interest. Throngs of people lined the streets leading from the airport, waving and clapping their hands. When we pulled into the main square for a meeting at a guest house, several thousand were present. We applauded back, which is the Chinese custom, and waved. Bill Randall wanted to wade into the crowd and shake hands, but Dickinson told him there weren't any votes for him there.

Dairen is at the end of the Laiotung Peninsula and reflects the presence of its former occupiers, the Russians and the Japanese. Not until 1945, with the defeat and expulsion of the Japanese, did the Chinese get it back, and during the Sino-Soviet honeymoon, the Russians used it as a naval base. That ended in the mid-1950s. Nevertheless, much of the city has a Western flavor, particularly the architecture, and many buildings, just as in Shanghai, are a legacy from imperialist times. In the countryside, most of the homes were of stone with tile roofs, strikingly and curiously similar to coal-mining regions in Wales or Scotland. Industry and shipping dominate the economy.

We were quartered in several guest houses overlooking the Yellow Sea, some miles outside the city. The view was stunning; with fishing boats riding at anchor in the mist and one huge rock thrusting precipitously up out of the sea just a few hundred yards offshore, the scene could not have been more beautiful in an Oriental brush painting. The Chinese told us that these houses were built in the 1950s. They should have known better. The fixtures were no less than fifty years old, and there hasn't been a chain toilet installed anyplace since well before 1930. A more modern assembly hall nearby more nearly fit the Chinese statement.

If the substance of the Peking stay was in the meetings with senior officials of the Central Committee, the few hours in Dairen were a revelation in herculean effort the Chinese have made to defend themselves from both a nuclear attack and from invasion. We saw not one but several of the much-talked-about tunnels, China's "Civil Defense Ark."

We were driven to a glass factory first, where it was interesting to watch the skill of the workers in making various glass table ornaments, but unimpressive from the point of view of modern production. The inevitable briefing followed, with a recitation of statistics by the chairman of the Revolutionary Committee of the factory, was something to be endured. Nevertheless, I noted in all such briefings, whether there, in the commune, or in a textile shop, that three points of reference were made: first, the production output in 1949 before the Liberation; next, the output at the time of the Great Proletarian Cultural Revolution; and finally, the current figures. Comparison can thus be made with the old days and also with the pre-Cultural Revolution era, in order to show that, in keeping with the party line, the Cultural Revolution did wonders for the productive spirit of the workers. It is the tangible evidence of good Maoist orthodoxy, and the implication is that "right deviationists" and "capitalist roaders" would reverse these socialist gains.

From the glass factory we departed for the guest house in the heart of Dairen where we were first briefed and then taken to an entrance of one of the tunnels located in the building itself. The chairman of the Revolutionary Committee of the city told us how they had undertaken the first maxim of Chairman Mao's formula. The tunnels had indeed been dug deep—from twenty-four to sixty feet below the surface. Each section of Dairen was responsible for its own share of the network, which interconnects like a honeycomb beneath the city. The particular portion that we would see is located in the Sun Yat Sen section. It is twelve miles long and can accommodate 60,000 people. Food and water are stored in various shelters, and a ventilation system provides fresh air. Underground generators provide light and power. The present tunnel was built in three years and is still being expanded.

When it was time to enter, we filed down the steps to the basement level of the building. A switch was thrown, and a section of the floor slid back. It was a melodramatic introduction to Mao's ark for survival.

We descended into what looked like a grotto, about six and one-half feet high and five feet wide. The walls had been bricked to about shoulder level, and the vaulted ceiling was of concrete block. All was whitewashed. On either side there were occasional alcoves, somewhat larger. In these were located classrooms, dining halls, an infirmary, and even a barbershop! It was a city beneath a city. As we descended further, the tunnel increased in size, becoming broader and higher. Toward the exit, there were steel plates studded with sharp spikes, which could be placed on the floor to discourage enemy infantry. Coils of barbed wire were piled nearby. Concrete shields with gun ports were available—all for immediate defense. The irony of it all was a Russian war memorial which we had passed when driving into the city, commemorating the liberation of Dairen by the Red Army in 1945. The Chinese surely have a different reception in mind should the Russians come again.

Following dinner that evening, we attended an acrobatic performance at the principal theater. The auditorium was filled when we arrived, except for several rows reserved for us near the front. My first two impressions were the absolute silence that greeted us, in contrast to the warm reception in the streets: the hundreds of Chinese in the theater were totally quiet, their faces impassive; and the smell of the proletariat, a combination of collective body odors and the effluvium of garlic.

The performers, however, were superb. Their costumes were gay, and the juggling, dancing, and wire walking as good as I've seen. All hailed from Dairen, and the Chinese said that this wasn't the first team; that group was in Shanghai on tour.

The next day exposed us to the most chilling aspect of the Chinese preparations for defense. We visited the Red Guard Primary School. It was a fairly large building, though old, but we were not there to view educational activities. The Chinese had told us that schoolchildren were involved in the tunnel program and in civil defense, but I don't think any of us were prepared for what followed. After the usual introduction, a twelve-year-old girl got up and proceeded to brief us on the tunnel that had been dug by the students at the school. Close to a mile long, the project had been started in 1964. Her recitation began with the familiar Mao slogan about digging tunnels, and then she told us how they had gone about it. "In the course of digging, we overcame many kinds of difficulties. We did not have the technical knowledge, and we did not know how to survey, so we asked the advice of workers and PLA soldiers. We did not have any tools, so we brought from home picks and shovels. Finally we succeeded. The tunnel digging greatly raised our political consciousness. Besides, the digging of tunnels gave impetus to teaching in our school." Pointing to a chart of the tunnel on the wall, she said, "New teaching materials appeared. In our mathematics class, we combined the problems of digging tunnels with our math problems. In courses like health, we learned how to combat germ and chemical warfare and how to conduct guerrilla warfare." Most of us were speechless at the spectacle of this little girl in a brightly-colored smock, her hair in two ponytails tied with red ribbons, lecturing a room full of adults on such a grim topic. Her shrill and high-pitched voice echoed in the room as she solemnly reviewed the preparation her classmates had made.

Outside, we entered one of the openings in a hillside, moving down the vaulted passageway, again noting the classrooms in alcoves to one side or the other. Although it did not have the finished appearance of the one of the day before, it was nevertheless skillfully done. We made only a short tour, exiting on a target range one level above the school playground. Here occurred the second shock. Drawn up in a double rank were twenty boys and girls ranging in age from eight to twelve, standing at attention with SKS semi-automatic rifles at their sides. Targets were set up about one hundred yards away. The boys wore army-type uniforms with red kerchiefs, the girls flower-print smocks. We took seats at tables behind the firing line and witnessed the most incredible scene imaginable. The leader of the squad, a fairly tall lad, barked out the orders and in turn first the girls and then the boys took their places, shooting from a prone position. At each sharp command, they marched smartly to their positions, fixed bayonets, lay down, loaded clips of bullets, and commenced firing. The metal man-shaped targets fell like tenpins. The second group fired at multi-colored balloons, popping them in rapid succession, and when one balloon broke loose and started to skitter up the hillside, one of the boys calmly popped it with a single moving shot. We applauded in disbelief. As they marched back to form ranks, I couldn't take my eyes off a little eight-year-old. The rifle with bayonet affixed was almost as tall as she was. If we had ever had any doubts about the seriousness of purpose, the literally deadly dedication of the Chinese to preparation of war, it was dispelled by this exercise.

As we left the field, the Chinese could see the reaction on our faces. Janie called the littlest one "a tiger," and the translation of this was greeted with delight by our hosts. Madame Chu, one of the interpreters and officials with the Foreign Ministry, who rode in our car with us quite often, said proudly, "You know that these rifles are made here in Dairen?" "Really?" I replied. "Well, we are quite familiar with that weapon. Our soldiers in Vietnam told us what a great rifle it is." Her mouth dropped open in surprise, and then she broke into laughter and chattered away in Chinese to one of her colleagues, who laughed too.

We were not through with tunnel indoctrination, however. From the school, we drove outside Dairen and entered another tunnel on a hillside. It was by far the most spacious and elaborate one we had seen. An entire store had been built within, including a restaurant, and it made a complete circle inside the hill. Some of us made the circuit and shopped, and then we assembled in a large hall in the center to see a performance of workers accompanied by a Chinese string orchestra. The singers were excellent. There just aren't any poor performers to be found, and the songs, in Chinese quarter-tones, were pleasing. The titles of the songs were something else: "Chairman Mao Praises the Militia Women"; "The Ping Pong Ball Carries Friendship," an allusion to the first contact made with the PRC by the U.S.; and one song, sung by a PLA man, was entitled "Praise of Chairman Mao," and sounded like an aria from "Madame Butterfly." Finally, we heard from a female vocalist, "The People of Taiwan Are Our Brothers." Either it's a popular song, or we were being given a subtle message, because we had heard it at the performance of the PLA unit several days before. The PRC, of course, talks of "liberating" Taiwan, and later, chatting with Madame Chu in the car, I mentioned their "invading" Taiwan. She smiled and corrected me, saying, "We say 'liberate.'" But her smile was such that it made it very clear that we were dealing only in semantics—and she knew that I knew it.

In attending the several performances, we learned that the introductions are done in a carefully stylized fashion. The young lady announcing the next act would stride out swinging her arms, and then, with her fists rigidly at her side, standing in what Janie described as the third position in ballet, would make her announcement in almost a sing-song, pitched fully an octave above her normal speaking voice. Any gestures during the songs or recitations were reminiscent of the elocution lessons of a couple of generations ago.

The last stop in Dairen was at a locomotive factory, laid on largely at the insistence of Sam Stratton, who has a locomotive factory in his district in Schenectady, New York. Since none of us were technically qualified to judge, the walk-through was relatively meaningless. But the finished machines were impressive, 4,000-HP monsters powered by diesel engines. Sam had a closer inspection and said that the plant would be a credit to any industrial nation. The engine blocks were precision-ground and cut by a computer-controlled machine.

The spokesman, as usual, was the chairman of the Revolutionary Committee, and he reeled off the statistics of production. The only interesting part of his monologue was the portion relating to the Russians, who had provided equipment initially and one locomotive as a model. When the Russians pulled out, the Chinese were thrown on their own resources. They upgraded the locomotive from 2,000-HP to 4,000 and began to import and develop new machinery. We noticed that some was new, with the dates 1975 and 1976 visible. Some of it was of Japanese manufacture. Apparently they copy much of the machinery that they import. They were bitter over what they called Krushchev's treachery, but proud of their victory in self-reliance.

At mid-day we flew to Shanghai, China's largest city with a population of ten million, with half in the city proper and the other half in the suburbs. It has a lot of the flavor of Hong Kong, left over, perhaps, from the years of the International Settlement and heavy foreign presence. Heavy industrial development followed Liberation, and hundreds of needle-like smokestacks prick the sky.

Our hotel, built by a wealthy Englishman named Sassoon who made a fortune in opium and guns, was erected in 1928 and is located in the old French Concession. It still has a stately grace about it, with dark wood paneling and white walls.

For the communists, Shanghai has special memories, for it was here that the first Communist Party Congress was held in 1921. It was also one of the last Kuomintang strongholds to fall, in May 1949. There is also a Shanghai faction in the Central Committee, which is generally thought to be the most radical.

After a tour of the Exhibition Hall where the products of China are exhibited, and which will ultimately be housed in the Stalin-wedding-cake building given to the Chinese by the Soviets, we returned to our hotel for a meeting and dinner with Hsu Ching-hsin, vice chairman of the Revolutionary Committee of the Shanghai Municipality. Hsu began by saying that he was happy that we were in the city where the Shanghai Communiqué was issued, and he hoped that contacts and friendship could continue smoothly. He went on to express his belief in underground shelters for defense, not for attack, saying that if the Russian bear decided to bite, he would not be able to do so easily, adding that,

"When the Soviet fleet passes through the Taiwan Straits, it is clear that they have no good intention toward us. When we sleep, we keep one eye open." His comments on crime were particularly interesting. He indicated that they have few policemen in China, because they cannot be relied upon to keep public order. "Even though U.S. visitors to China return home and say you can't lose anything, that everything is found and returned, and everyone is honest, unfortunately, while that is nice, it isn't entirely true," Hsu said. "There are still thieves in China, and it is still wise to keep an eye on your belongings."

In addition, Hsu told us how bad things had been before Liberation. Unemployment was widespread, and there were "100,000 prostitutes; 6,000 gambling dens; 10,000 opium houses." One cold night in 1948 in Shanghai, 800 people froze to death in the streets. Now, he said, the prostitutes have been taught other skills, and the opium addicts have been rehabilitated.

Following Hsu's remarks, Mel indicated that we were concerned with the education problem that exists after the events on Tien An Men Square, asking how their system would provide more doctors and scientists. Hsu replied, "Don't worry about it. In old China, 90 percent of the people were illiterate. Then our talent was really wasted. Today we have 1,000 universities in Shanghai alone. We have made great progress here except for those such as Liu Shao-chi, Lin Piao, and Deng Hsiao-ping, who want to retrogress to capitalism. Today we have one million in the People's Militia. They have arms, too. There are two purposes of the militia: to protect against foreign enemies, and also against domestic enemies."

On Friday, April 23, our last day in China, we were driven to a people's commune about thirty minutes' drive from Shanghai. It is named Ma Chiao, was founded in September 1958, and has a population of 36,000. There is little point in setting down the statistics given by the chairman of the Revolutionary Committee, Mr. Wong. Suffice it to say that it was an extensive agricultural community, and largely self-sufficient, growing food grains, cotton, fruit trees, melons, medicinal herbs, and oil-bearing vegetables. Pigs, poultry, and milk cows are raised, particularly pigs, in large numbers. This commune is making the transition to chemical fertilizers and mechanized plowing and harvesting.

Small private plots are available to each family, and all share in the profits of the commune at the end of the year. In addition to agriculture, the commune operated some light industry, including the building of small cement boats, which we saw. The commune has its own hospital and doctors, schools, and teachers, and sends a number of its students to the universities.

We had considerable dialogue on the distribution of income, private plots versus commune production, and related topics. Wong answered as frankly as we could expect within the limits of his ideological walls. A tour of some of the shops revealed an industrious spirit, with children and adults alike operating machinery. The lack of safety devices was most obvious, and we commented on this to the Chinese. "These," they said, "will have to come later."

After lunch we made a tour of a primary school and a workers' apartment community within Shanghai. It provided us the most rewarding and heartwarming experience of the entire trip, perhaps because it was so unexpected.

These urban units are not so self-sufficient as the rural communes, but their organizational lines are much the same. For example, a neighborhood factory making handkerchiefs employed the wives of other factory workers, some working in the neighborhood and others elsewhere. The women formerly did piecework in their homes, but after Liberation they brought their sewing machines to a central building. Here the work is broken down into an assembly-line technique. Several women cut the cloth, others stitch designs, others the hems, and others press or pack the finished handkerchiefs. They barely looked up from their work as we passed through.

The particular neighborhood community that we visited was built in 1952 and contains 56,000 people. Besides the factories, it operates shops, schools, and a hospital and clinics. The Revolutionary Committee manages every facet of the residents' lives as tightly as those in the countryside. The apartments and courtyards teem with people like a Puerto Rican tenement section in New York. We were invited in groups to meet some of the residents, so Janie and I, with Lester and his son, joined an interpreter and entered one of the buildings. The young man who met us was twenty-nine and lived with his parents, sister, and grandmother. The parents were working, but grandmother, a toothless old lady of eighty-four, was there to greet us. I have described living conditions previously and need not repeat them here. Six people shared two rooms, and, with another family, the bathroom and kitchen. By our standards, it was a slum, by theirs, adequate shelter and far superior to what his grandmother and parents had known before Liberation. They showed no shame in these conditions and served tea in their best glasses, indicating thereby that we were honored guests. We forgot the shabby surroundings and enjoyed the warm hospitality which is legendary in China.

Yet what capped that afternoon for us was the visit to the primary school. Our coming was known, so a crowd of several hundred were jammed along the curb across the street from the school when we drove up. It was Dairen all over again, with applause and hand-waving in greeting. At the entrance to the school, about a dozen children from four to eight years old were lined up, dressed in national costumes from the various provinces, chanting in Chinese, "Welcome, aunts and uncles." They captured our hearts. I have never seen more appealing children.

Moving from classroom to classroom, we were greeted with the same chant, but the strict regimentation practiced even on these little ones betrayed itself. The chanting, which sounded spontaneous when we entered each room, stopped on signal by the teacher as abruptly as the turning off of a radio. Each class performed some activity like tumbling or ping pong (on miniature tables) or playing ball, and one group was even doing production work. Even the youngest spend half an hour each day at this.

A performance by the youngsters in their assembly room ended the visit. Again, the singing and dancing charmed us, although all of it was politically oriented, including a dance done by one group denouncing Deng Hsiao-ping. Standing defiantly and gesturing menacingly, they called down what wrath they could muster on the former vice premier. In the Peoples Republic of China, it is never too early to learn to attack right-wing deviationists.

Late in the afternoon our motorcade made for the airport. There we said a cheerful farewell to our hosts of the past week and boarded "The United States of America" for the flight to Hawaii and then home. A day and a half in Honolulu helped break the long journey.

I wish that it were possible to write a final verdict on our stay in China, but I cannot. My mind is still a kaleidoscope of memories and impressions.

In her long history, China has been influenced by many forces, from Buddha and Confucius to Tao and Mao. And for most of her history, China has been content to live as a neighbor apart from the rest of the world. To a degree, this characteristic is ingrained in the nation. There is a thread that connects the self-imposed isolation of the emperors who sleep in the Ming Tombs and the self-reliance ordained by Mao Tse-tung. There is a parallel between the self-assuredness and ancient belief of the Chinese a millennium ago that their nation was the center of the earth and the rest of the world peopled by barbarians and the smug dogma of Mao in laying claim to the possession of Marxist truth.

It is true that Mao has rooted out many of China's traditional institutions, but he has really simply remolded them with his own teachings. There is a remarkable constancy in his revolution. But in the technical environment of the twentieth century, he has employed its tools and instruments to unify and dominate the lives of his people as no previous Chinese ruler has ever done. The self-discipline has brought enormous gains. Given another generation of uninterrupted development, China will easily be a superpower. Much will depend upon how the transition is made when Mao Tse-tung passes. But if Mao is old and growing feeble, his revolution is not. It is filled with vitality and self-confidence. Brinton, the historian, would surely see it as still in its youth. If it is not cut down by the war the Chinese see as inevitable, nuclear or otherwise, and if it does not shatter itself in bitter divisions when Mao dies, China's impact upon its neighbors will be profound.

Most ominous was a large crimson sign at the entrance to Shanghai Airport, which no visitor leaving China can fail to see. In

Chinese and English, the words boldly proclaimed: COUNTRIES WANT INDEPENDENCE. NATIONS WANT LIBERATION. PEOPLE WANT REVOLUTION. THIS IS THE IRRESISTIBLE TREND OF HISTORY.

Sunday, April 25, 1976—Tuesday, May 4, 1976

We've been back from our China venture for about ten days and have finally caught up on our sleep. Jet lag affected most of us, and I know that it contributed to a cold I came down with the day we arrived home. Nevertheless, I would not have missed the trip for anything, and we regard it as an unforgettable experience.

Friday at home was unusually active. I spoke at a luncheon honoring Susan Ford and the other Azalea Festival participants. I sat next to Susan during lunch and had a chance to talk to her. She is an unassuming, remarkably mature eighteen-year-old. I told her the story of how I learned of my appointment to the Armed Services Committee during my first few days in the House in January 1969, and how grateful I was to her father for placing me on the Committee. We discussed the Texas primary to be held the next day, in which, as it turned out, Jerry did poorly, and I asked her the to-be-expected question of how she liked living in the White House. She said that during the first few weeks she couldn't believe it, and she went around picking up matchbooks and stationery like any visitor, before realizing that she actually lived there and was the President's daughter. I asked her how she felt about her father running for reelection, and she told me that personally she would rather return to private life, but that all of the Ford family stood behind her father's decision to seek election in his own right. And then she told me a humorous story. She said that a few weeks ago her mother was away and her father was alone in the study, working on some papers and watching television. On such occasions, her mother has left standing instructions for Susan to "look after" her father. She said that she asked him what he would do if he lost the election this fall. Her father paused and then said with a grin that he guessed he would become a professional golfer. Susan was exasperated and asked, "Dad, what would you really do?" "Well," he responded, "I might practice some law." She said that she told him she hoped he would do something like that, because her mother had said that if Jerry had to stay home, she would leave him. Apparently, he feels the need to be "doing something" all the time.

The President faces a critical test today in Indiana. Having been beaten badly in Texas, he needs a good win in Indiana to stave off the Reagan challenge. I still think that Ford will win it on the first ballot in Kansas City in August, despite the hoopla in the press, because it boils down to a game of numbers. Reagan has won in two Southern states. If he can't win in the North and Midwest, he can't win, period. The

197

Members from Indiana all say that Ford will win but that his margin will be less than it would have been had he won in Texas. Also, a heavy turnout would favor Ford, since the Reagan people appear to be better organized, and a small vote would aid them. John Myers told some of us in the Republican lounge this afternoon that he was mystified by some of the things that the President was saying. He said that he had told him before one of his speeches in Indiana to play down the Panama issue by assuring the audience that the U.S. was not going to abandon the Canal. Instead, he said, the President took an ambiguous route and left everyone with the impression that the Canal is, in fact, going to be abandoned. What brought boos was Ford's statement that Kissinger would remain on as Secretary of State as long as he was President. There is a lot of feeling against the Secretary of State in the Midwest, but Jerry toughed it out.

The big surprise, of course, is Carter. His win in Pennsylvania and Humphrey's announcement that he would stand pat and not actively enter the primaries has led everyone to the conviction that nothing can stop Carter now from getting the nomination. I would not have believed it possible as late as three weeks ago. This has all of the earmarks of a peculiar election year, with a yearning for someone who can be trusted and who reflects virtues that until recently were thought to be a part of the American past. It certainly isn't liberal, but neither is it totally conservative, else Ronald Reagan would have done better than he has. It is a curious mixture, a reaction against promises unfulfilled, too much government, political cynicism, and some old-fashioned patriotism, which may stem from Bicentennial consciousness. I'm not sure yet what impact it will have on the congressional races.

Before concluding, I should mention that Oleg Yermishkin came by last Tuesday to see me. His call hardly came as a surprise. I knew that he was itching to learn my impressions and any information that he could glean from our conversations with the Chinese. I kept confidential our conversations with Chang, the vice premier, but used some vernacular speech in relating what we had witnessed. "To begin with," I said, "those folks don't really like you at all." He got a sickly grin on his face and nodded. "The other thing is," I added, "you had better leave them alone." And then I described briefly the tunnels and other preparations for war. "We aren't going to attack them," he protested. "They are preparing to attack us." "Not very likely," I answered. "Their preparations are purely defensive. But if you invade them, they will swallow you, take my word for it." I added, "You know, I'm somewhat sympathetic, but I'm glad that they're your neighbors and not ours. It would be as if Mexico had a population of one billion, was building nuclear weapons, and wanted us to give back Texas, Arizona, New Mexico, and the southern half of California." "You're right," he groaned. "All they want is all of Siberia east of Lake Baikal!" We made a date to dine with them in a few days, and I told him that I would bring my film along.

Wednesday, May 5, 1976

What a difference a day can make. Yesterday I commented on the near certainty of Ford's winning the Indiana primary, and today he's a loser by two percentage points. A few weeks ago, everyone was predicting that it would be the Democrats who would be tearing themselves apart by convention time. Now the talk is about a replay of 1964, when the Republicans did the Democrats a favor by dividing themselves. Part of Ford's defeat is ascribed to a large crossover by Wallace Democrats, that if Wallace hadn't faded so quickly in the race for the Democratic nomination, Ford would be the winner already. Tiger Teague, who had a rough race for renomination down in Texas, told some of our people that thousands of Texans had crossed over and voted for Reagan. Bud Hillis, who had felt yesterday that Ford would shade Reagan, was at a loss today to explain what happened. There was a good turnout, and crowds had been large when Ford appeared. "Everything went his way except the results," Bud said. He told the Wednesday Group that if the election had been held three weeks ago, Ford would have won with 60 percent of the vote. He said that that figure had been eroding steadily, and the Texas loss kicked it over to Reagan completely. John Anderson thinks that things are going to get worse. He noted that months ago, predictions in Nebraska were poor for Ford, and this defeat will only aggravate the diminishing of Ford's chances. The Wednesday Group, being solid for the President, was understandably a gloomy place today.

Tuesday, May 11, 1976

The aftermath of the trip to China continues. This afternoon, Ambassador James Shen of the Republic of China (Taiwan) came by. Kathy had thought that he was from the PRC Liaison Office, since the call came from "the Chinese Embassy." When I greeted Mr. Shen and saw him in a Western business suit, I knew immediately that he wasn't a PRC official. He had been to see several of the others who had gone, and he wanted to pick my brains as well. I went over the discussions that we had had, none of which seemed to surprise him. He seemed reassured that the PRC people were not interested in acquiring U.S. weapons or seeking military occupation, but he was a little puzzled as to why they had invited us. We agreed that it was probably to persuade us that our attention ought to be focused on Europe and their own conviction that preparations to take on the Russians if necessary are very real to them—hence the visits to the tunnels and the military. He asked me about the vice premier and the foreign minister, their bearing, persuasiveness, and impact. I mentioned that the foreign minister reminded me of a Mandarin. "He studied in Germany, you know," he replied. "Perhaps that explains it," I smiled.

At the end of our meeting, he asked me what my opinion was of the future. I repeated what I have recorded elsewhere. "Left to themselves," I said, "without war to disrupt their progress, and if they are successful in making the political transition after Mao's death, they are bound to make enormous strides. They will largely complete the mechanization of agriculture, greatly broaden their industrial and technological base, and their population will have increased easily to 1.3 or 1.4 billion. All of this will have serious consequences for us, but for everyone else in Asia, they will be truly profound." He encouraged me to go on. "We will be expelled," I said. "The Japanese cannot pick up their islands and move, so they will have some hard choices." "What will they do?" he asked, "go nuclear?" "Perhaps," I replied. "They will surely try to resist being drawn competely into the Chinese orbit. The neighbors to the south will certainly not be able to avoid the influence of such a powerful neighbor, and you will be swallowed." He nodded grimly. "But it is the Soviet Union that will feel the greatest unease. The Russians cannot help but view with alarm each passing day. The giant grows bigger and stronger."

And then it was the ambassador's chance to make a rejoinder. He said, "The Soviet Union helped them get started, to its everlasting regret. Will your country now provide them with further assistance to enable them to achieve their goals?" "Not for the time being," I replied. "We haven't offered it, nor have they sought it except in limited amounts." On this inconclusive note, the meeting ended.

Wednesday, May 12, 1976—Monday, May 17, 1976

The President faces his most critical test so far tomorrow in his home state of Michigan. If he fails to win there, the consensus is that he might as well hang up the shoes. The Wednesday Group has been understandably pessimistic. At our meeting on the 12th, Barber Conable said that if Arch Moore hadn't come out for Ford before the West Virginia primary, the President might well have lost that state. As it was, a lot of the Republicans were angry because of the indictment and trial of Moore. They felt that the Justice Department was "out to get Arch." Fortunately, Moore was acquitted in time to give his support to the President.

There was some discussion on why the President had done poorly in Nebraska. Mark Andrews said that the farm vote had cost Ford dearly, that he had carried Lincoln and Omaha but lost the rural areas. He predicted that since Michigan had more of its population concentrated in the cities, the President ought to do better. Garner Shriver of Kansas, who has a lot of farmers in his own district, rebutted Mark, noting that Ford has gotten most of the delegates at the conventions held there. That's somewhat different from a primary, however. Barber struck the most optimistic note of all, announcing that the huge blocks of uncommitted delegates in New York and Pennsylvania were sure to go to Ford by a percentage of 80 to 90. The next day, fifteen delegates in New York announced that they were for Reagan. That didn't destroy Barber's prediction, but it doesn't help Ford's image in New York to have even one of the uncommitteds announce his commitment to Reagan. Pete McCloskey still has his own campaign against Reagan, and apparently the feeling is mutual. Pete said that Reagan had made the observation that, "I should represent the San Andreas Fault." He said that he was in a state of depression. He holds out little hope for Ford in California.

On Wednesday evening, Janie and I went out to the Yermishkins' apartment on Wilson Boulevard in Arlington for dinner. It was an interesting experience. I have been reading Hedrick Smith's book, *The Russians*, which gives an insight into Russian character and mores, based on his three years in the Soviet Union as correspondent for *The New York Times*. Smith writes that the Russians will manifest two personalities, one in public, which is unemotional and dour, and another in private and familiar surroundings, in which they are quite open in their feelings. Both Oleg and Nelly fit the mold, especially Nelly. In public, she has always been very reserved, though friendly. When we entered their apartment, she embraced and kissed Janie on the cheek, as did Oleg, and I got the same reception from her. It surprised both of us, because she has never affected such emotion before. She had prepared a Russian meal, which was served at a modest table in their dinette. Their two sons, fine lads aged fourteen and thirteen, took their meals in their bedroom. Oleg apologized for their shyness and declared that our children are much better in this respect. They did come out to view our China film later.

The meal was complemented by vodka and Georgian wine, both quite good. Oleg invited us to visit them in Moscow next year and promised a picnic dinner with their friends in the woods outside Moscow at their cottage, where we could "drink much more vodka." It was the first revelation we had that they had a dacha, an indication that he has some connections. Most of the evening was taken up with small talk, with the exception of the film, which Oleg viewed with considerable interest. It is certainly a curious relationship, a kind of plaster of paris friendship. On Oleg's part, I suspect he feels the same dilemma. Two fundamentally different social systems create an insuperable barrier, more's the pity.

Friday, May 21, 1976—Monday, May 24, 1976

The House came in at 10:00 a.m. as scheduled on Friday, but managed to do the near-impossible and finish its business by noon, so that those of us who wanted to leave, could. It was Former Members

Day and the former Members were back in fairly large numbers. Besides talking to Porter Hardy, my predecessor, who gets back here regularly for these affairs, I saw some of the more recent ones. Bill Bray was on hand, as was Walter Powell; both of them served on the Armed Services Committee. Walter left after two terms, fed up with a life that left him no time for his family and kept him shackled to a schedule that he felt was suffocating him. A former teacher and elementary school principal, he decided in 1974 not to seek reelection and go back to teaching. Tom Kindness succeeded him. While I was eating a sandwich in the Republican lounge on Friday, he came in and sat down. I was ashamed to have forgotten his name at first, although I made the connection with our committee and our profession. He said that he was back teaching again, junior high school math and history. "I don't miss this place one damned bit," he said. He certainly looked contented. Nevertheless, I like eating on this salary a lot better than on the one I made teaching.

After spending the weekend in Tidewater, we drove back this morning (Monday), arriving in time for me to answer the first quorum call and vote on three bills plus a rule on one. There's a certain vengeance about these Monday votes. With the Leadership gone to get the copy of the Magna Carta in Britain, there was a particular sadism in calling all of those votes. The biggest news was the gossip in the lounge and offices about a girl on the payroll of the House Administration Committee of Wayne Hays, who claimed over the weekend that she can't type, take shorthand, or even answer the phone. For $14,000 a year, she claims, she's been Hays' mistress. Hays has denied it all, but an investigation will get under way, which is sure to keep the thing alive for a few weeks. Whether it will gather the kind of publicity that the Tidal Basin incident involving the stripper and Wilbur Mills did, it's too early to say, but a lot of the fellows were chuckling about it this afternoon, claiming that they had asked all of the girls on their staffs this morning if they could really type. Several said they were sure that Hays would get the geriatric vote, since he's in his sixties and the girl claimed he visited her regularly twice a week.

On a more cogent subject, Ford and Reagan square off in six primaries tomorrow. Jerry did very well in Michigan and Maryland last week, but the opinion around here is that the pendulum will swing back toward Reagan tomorrow. Most of the Virginia delegates went to Reagan on Saturday. No one would have forecast such a horse race a few months ago.

Tuesday, May 25, 1976—Sunday, May 30, 1976

The last few days having been full ones, I have had to delay this narrative until now, Sunday afternoon. The big news is the widening scandal involving Wayne Hays. He made two speeches on

Tuesday, the first shortly before noon, when the House began its session, at which time he stoutly maintained his innocence and damned his accusers. But some time in the next three hours he must have talked to his lawyers or learned of some damaging information, because he decided to go to the Well of the House again, this time with a full House to hear him. The House at the time was debating a bill, but Hays asked to speak out of turn, and a quorum was called to get him an audience. When I walked into the Chamber, Herman Badillo was at the door and said, "Stick around; Hays has a statement to make." Sensing that it was going to be a confession, a lot of the Members did. Hays looked grim and subdued as he waited for the quorum to end. As he was recognized, a hush fell over the House, and the man who has a reputation for inspiring the most fear and dislike among the 435 began to speak. In substance, he admitted that he had had "a relationship" with Elizabeth Ray, but he denied that she had been improperly hired. At the end, he acknowledged that he was regarded as arrogant and mean, but he hoped that no one would ever think him to be dishonest. It drew moderate applause, although I felt that the prevailing mood was not so much one of sympathy as of embarrassment.

At a Whip Luncheon on Wednesday, Bill Frenzel, who sits on Hays' House Administration Committee and cordially dislikes him, said that only the tip of the iceberg was showing. A full-scale investigation has been launched by the Justice Department, some of it no doubt inspired by Hays' vendetta with Thornburgh, whom Hays had charged with playing politics for not prosecuting John Heinz for an election law violation, as Jim Jones had been in Oklahoma. Those who have not been reached by the FBI, *The Washington Post* has or is seeking. Kathy told me that a girl she knew on Ken Gray's staff, and who had later worked for Hays, had called her and asked Kathy to vouch for her having been a bona fide employee. Kathy's name was mentioned by the girl to a reporter, and he tried to reach Kathy through her aunt in Pennsylvania, not knowing her married name. It has caused a stir in every office on the Hill, and has provoked more locker room humor than the Mills episode two years ago.

With Bob Sikes under investigation by the Ethics Committee on the basis of allegations of improper activities in Florida involving abuse of his office, and with Harold Ford of Tennessee under a cloud for having relatives and campaign workers on the payroll, the House is feeling the pressure to take steps to restore public confidence in itself. I heard several of my colleagues on the subway riding in from the Rayburn Building assert that if the Ethics Committee didn't start acting tough in some of these cases, we had better disband it. Editorials and political cartoonists are having a field day roasting the House for failing to police its Members properly.

I've taken some good-natured ribbing about the Hays business since coming home, including the usual questions inquiring if all my secretaries can type. I had to fly to Norfolk for a testimonial speech on

Wednesday evening, and when I rose to speak, I began by saying that while I normally didn't like flying down and back to D.C. in one night, there was a certain benefit in this particular engagment. "Not every Member of the Congress has over 200 witnesses to vouch for his presence on a given evening these days." It brought down the house.

Monday, May 31, 1976—Wednesday, June 2, 1976

With the Memorial Day recess over, we drove back to Washington on Tuesday morning. In the afternoon I attended a meeting of the Military Installations and Facilities Subcommittee to go over our bill prior to going to conference with the Senate today (Wednesday). The staff had already worked out most of the differences, so that we didn't have too much trouble deciding on those projects that we would try to prevail upon the Senate to yield to us. Some question was raised about resisting the Senate cuts of the add-ons of Bob Sikes. Paul Tsompanas, the chief counsel of the Subcommittee, told us that the Senate had cut them out because John Stennis was mad at Sikes for cutting several of Stennis' projects from the Appropriations Bill last year. Now Stennis was getting even. All of us found it a little exasperating to get caught in the crossfire between the two of them. If we acceded to the Senate in their cuts, Sikes might blame us for not holding out for his projects and take it out on us next year—if he's here. Charlie Wilson asked, "Why the hell doesn't Sikes call Stennis and settle it?" The rest of us agreed, and Dick Ichord said that he would call Sikes and tell him to make his peace with Stennis.

The conference today was as painless as it's ever been. It was our year to chair it, so Dick presided and did a good job. He was well prepared, but willing to compromise. Stu Symington was chief spokesman for the Senate. He was flanked by Harry Byrd, Scoop Jackson, and Strom Thurmond. We got into a scrap with Scoop over $11 million for the Trident site in his state, money to be used for impact purposes as a result of the building of extensive facilities for basing the Trident submarine there. We figured that the state of Washington will get enough money from other agencies, to say nothing of revenue from a state tax that is being assessed. But Scoop got mad and felt that we were holding out on him when he had agreed to special projects that either we or other House Members had asked for. He dropped a not-so-subtle hint that Senator Magnuson, his colleague and brother senator from Washington and a member of the Senate Appropriations Committee, might not take kindly to a House-initiated cut. That did it. We yielded. After a two-hour session in the morning, we reassembled in the afternoon for about forty-five minutes and finished the bill. It must have been some kind of record. It is certain that the Defense Authorization Bill will not be so easily resolved. We go to conference on that next week.

King Juan Carlos of Spain spoke to a Joint Meeting of the House and Senate shortly after noon. He continues the parade of chiefs of state who have scheduled Bicentennial visits to the U.S. His message was not weighty, but it was well received, particularly that portion when he mentioned further democratic steps in his own country. Young and handsome, he exuded enough charm to draw prolonged applause, though basically he appears to be a reserved person. I suppose anyone who was in Franco's shadow as long as he was would have some inhibitions, however.

The Hays case continues to give rise to rumors of involvement by other Members, but so far nothing tangible has emerged. A Chicago paper charges that about a dozen congressmen and two senators visited her bedroom, all recorded on a tape recorder under her bed. At least that was the talk at Wednesday Group today. It's just too bizarre to believe, and I became totally skeptical when someone said that Hubert Humphrey was one of the senators! Hays, yes, but not Humphrey. At any rate, the Ethics Committee has voted unanimously to conduct an investigation, and Hays apparently is going to step down from one or more of his committee chairmanships pending the outcome of the charges.

Monday, June 14, 1976—Tuesday, June 15, 1976

Another feverish two days, and the way things seem to be going on the Hill, I feel as though I am experiencing a crazy dream. On Sunday afternoon, Janie and I were driving back and heard the news on the radio that Congressman Howe of Utah had been arrested in Salt Lake City for propositioning a policewoman who was posing as a prostitute. Apparently the evidence is pretty firm, and the senator from that state, Frank Moss, has already called for Howe to quit his race for reelection, that his presence on the ticket is unacceptable to the others running in the state. Then this afternoon (Tuesday), the UPI wire service carried a Jack Anderson story charging Senator Harry Byrd with having a sexual relationship with a woman who had come to him seeking his help in finding her husband. She alleged that Harry had seduced her. If I had to bet on anyone in the Senate sharing his bed with no one but his wife, I would put my money on Harry, and maybe John Stennis. Someone quipped in our lounge that if they didn't pin one of these charges on a Republican soon, all of us were going to be suspected of being homosexuals.

Ironically, Bob Daniel and I were in Harry's office just this morning for a meeting with Army Corps of Engineers officials and representatives from the Tidewater area about the need to develop a water system to provide an adequate supply for the remainder of this century. I suppose that Harry had not yet received word of the story at that point, because he seemed to be in his usual fine fettle. Apparently the Anderson column appeared in the Raleigh newspaper, and it was circulated to the press in Virginia by the Zumwalt campaign people. I hope this isn't an indication of the kind of campaigns we can expect this year.

We did take up the B-1 this morning. Senator Culver, an arch opponent of the plane, had been permitted to attend the House-Senate conference and express his opposition to going forward on a production decision until after the November election. Culver is not a member of the Senate Armed Services Committee, but Stennis and a majority of the Committee voted to let him attend for this purpose. Tony Battista, our head staffer on the Research and Development Subcommittee, made the case for the B-1 and did an excellent job. At the end, he showed a short film of the plane being refueled in the air, then flying 200 feet above the ground with wings contracted at mach .8. The aircraft's stability at this altitude contrasted with another section of film showing a B-52 at the same altitude and somewhat slower speed. The plane bucked visibly, and the pilot had a difficult time flying it. The sequence was actually humorous and provoked some laughter, especially when Culver observed that he thought his home movies were pretty good after all, the cameraman aboard the B-52 not having a very steady hand under those conditions.

Culver's rebuttal of Battista was shrewd. He didn't attempt to turn entirely the arguments about the plane's performance or even the need to go on with a new manned bomber. Instead, he tried to stress that the decision was a major one, one that had suffered more doubt than any other major weapons system in a long time. Therefore, it made sense to delay a production decision until a new President is elected. This is going to be a tough one, and I am by no means certain that the House will stick to its position.

The President spoke at the Southern Baptist Convention in Norfolk, and Tom Downing, Bob Daniel, and I flew down with him. I had had some misgivings about missing recorded votes on the Public Works Bill, but when both Tom and Bob indicated that they were going, I knew that I couldn't very well decline the invitation, especially since the President would be speaking in my district. Luckily, no votes were called during the time we were gone.

I had not been aboard Air Force One since Richard Nixon's first term in 1969. It is still as beautifully appointed as ever. The President came into the lounge where we were sitting after we were aloft. Coatless, he sat next to Bob on the banquette, putting his feet up on the coffee table. He was utterly relaxed and showed no strain from his down-to-the-wire campaign with Ronald Reagan. With Tom, a Democrat, present, we avoided politics and talked instead about Congress and the revelations of recent note. The President agreed that Congress had gotten a black eye. He also noted that the leadership these days is a far cry from the times when Sam Rayburn or Joe Martin was Speaker. In Norfolk, he invited us to share his limousine with him, even though it meant doubling up and using the jump seats. He reminisced about coming to Norfolk as a young naval officer during World War II aboard the carrier *Monterey,* and I told him that he would not recognize the city now. He showed interest in the redevelopment of the inner city, and Scope, the convention center, in particular.

Over 11,000 people heard him in person. Although his message was brief—less than twenty minutes—it was interrupted eighteen times by applause. He struck the right chord with his audience, calling for a stronger code of morality by those who serve, while employing some clever catch phrases like "shifting sands of situation ethics." As I have stated many times, he will never win any forensic prizes, but the crowd was attentive and responded well. The man projects decency, not surprisingly a popular characteristic at a Baptist convention. The trip back to Washington was uneventful, and we were on the Hill by 5:00, in time to make a succession of votes.

Wednesday, June 16, 1976

After taking some calls and signing a few letters, I went over to the committee room for a meeting with several of my House colleagues who are conferees on the Defense Authorization Bill. We went over a list of aircraft differences with the Senate and drew up a counter-proposal to the one they have made for settling our differences. The details are hardly worth setting down here. At 1:30 this afternoon we met with Howard Cannon and John Tower from the Senate side to present our case. Cannon wasn't very much impressed and showed no signs of yielding. He said that they would look at it more closely, and we could meet again in a few days to see if we couldn't come to an agreement. Sam Stratton, our spokesman, told me afterward that he regards Cannon as obstinate, a man who thinks he's a "goddamn expert on airplanes." The full conference goes back tomorrow for another session.

Senator Harry Byrd has made a full denial of any relationship with the woman mentioned in Jack Anderson's column, much to the relief of his Virginia colleagues. The story is so weak that the *Washington Post* would not print it in its issue today. Charlie Thone, a Nebraska Republican, talked to Joseph McCaffrey, who reports on the Hill, and learned that the editors of the *Post* had met yesterday and decided not to run the story, since the woman was not identified and the story could not be substantiated. That's about the most responsible thing the *Post* has done since I came to Congress. Some of the Virginia papers have carried it, however, but have noted that it was distributed by Zumwalt's people after it appeared in the *Raleigh News and Observer.* It could very well backfire on them.

Meanwhile, Charlie Vanik, another Democrat, from Ohio, has been charged by the *Cleveland Plain Dealer* in a story today with having a former prostitute on his payroll. There seems to be no end to it. But to cap everything, each Member has received an invitation to attend a reception on the 25th ostensibly to hear from aggrieved hookers. Given the current climate, I don't think that any Member of Congress would be caught walking his dog in front of the Sheraton Park that night.

> Honorable Person,
>
> Following the formation of the Hookers' Lobby June 21st, 1976, the Feminist Party and COYOTE are holding a co-convention at the Sheraton-Park Hotel, 2600 Woodley Road N.W., to address the issues of prostitution, rape, family violence and the economic exploitation of women.
>
> A Congressional Reception will be held the evening of June 25 from 5:30 p.m. to midnight (no-hostess bar).
>
> A documentary video production will be shown of the organizing and de-criminalizing efforts in the United States and Europe. Florynce Kennedy, Ti-Grace Atkinson, Margo St. James and many more informed people will be present to discuss the issues.
>
> We invite you and your spouses and staff to attend this first American conference and participate in a long overdue civil rights effort.

Thursday, June 17, 1976

Well, the Congressman-for-the-Day today was Joe Waggoner, a Democrat from Louisiana, named as the Member who attempted to solicit a policewoman who was posing as a prostitute on 14th Street last winter. According to the press reports, Joe was chased for five blocks before his car was forced over to the curb. Taken to the police station, he identified himself and was released without being booked. Joe's statement is that he didn't solicit the woman but saw a car trying to block him in and drove away for fear of being the victim of a robbery. Waggoner's troubles will cause no gloating on our side of the aisle. All of us hold him in high esteem.

The fact that no Republicans have been named yet has prompted more humor. Otis Pike clapped me on the knee today and said, "It's clear that you Republicans are a dying breed." "Could be," I smiled. The latest joke has been, "Have you heard about Wayne Hays? He's taken a turn for the nurse."

For those to whom it is happening, it is anything but funny. Harry Byrd came to the House-Senate Conference for awhile today and looked for all the world as if he had lost his best friend. I shook his hand and gave him a friendly pat of reassurance on the arm. Throughout the discussions, he appeared thoroughly distracted.

The real business of the Congress manages to go on. We have spent all of today on the Defense Appropriations Bill, fighting some of the same battles that we fought over two months ago when the Authorization Bill was up—money for another carrier and production money now for the B-1. On these issues, we have managed to hold the line in the bill.

Monday, June 21, 1976—Wednesday, June 23, 1976

We are still battling in conference with the Senate over the B-1. John Culver has sat with us for all three days and has made a heavy pitch to delay production until the new President takes office. His tactic is a ploy, since he and others in the Senate who oppose the B-1 know that it is their last chance to kill the plane. Having failed on a straight up or down choice, they have employed this ruse, and are laying their bet on Jimmy Carter to win in November. Carter has gone on record in opposition to the aircraft. Ergo, if Carter wins in the fall, the plane is dead. However, Jack Flynt of Georgia told several of us yesterday afternoon that he had talked personally with Carter recently, and he said that Carter told him that he regretted having made the statement and now would not be opposed to the plane being ordered into production. He told Flynt that he couldn't say anything publicly, but he had no objection to Jack passing the word quietly. Chalk up one more reason why Carter shouldn't be President. If he feels he didn't have all of the facts before, he ought to have the courage to say so; but that, of course, could make waves before the Democratic Convention in a few weeks. Meanwhile, Culver slashes away at the decision to go forward with the plane, pointing out that testing hasn't been completed, that this is a major weapons decision over which there has been more dispute than on any other weapon in years and therefore the new President in 1977 ought to have a free hand in deciding upon something so momentous. We may find some compromise language tomorrow, but as of now the House side isn't budging.

The Democrats have been having a bloodletting in the House over the proposed reforms of the Administration Committee and the sweeping changes in Member perquisites recommended by the special committee chaired by David Obey. A panic mood has overtaken them, and the recommendations being made would cut sharply the extras now enjoyed by the Members. No more stamp allowance, no cash withdrawals from the stationery account, and the lumping of all funds into a single account. The net result will be a loss in real income for everyone. These have served as a kind of safety valve for Members in lieu of getting a pay increase, and their loss will certainly be an incentive to vote for pay increases in the future, knowing that there is no other source of income to draw from. What fractures me is the psychology of it all. The Democrats are squirming in discomfort over the discredit that has fallen on the Congress as a result of the Hays scandal and the other hijinks of some of their Members. Never mind that they tolerated Hays and even elected him to serve as chairman of the House Administration Committee again last year. Now they are trying to outdo each other in proving their virtue. Renouncing the benefits that Hays gave them is palmed off as an act of purification, but the way it's been done, it looks more like returning stolen goods.

Anyway, the Democrats held a caucus for nearly three hours this morning and then forced the House to rise at 6:00 this evening so that they could go back at it again. Since we Republicans are in the minority, there is little that we can do to influence events. Of course, I am sorry to lose benefits that were already available when I first came here, although Hays certainly made them sweeter. Five years ago, I voted with a minority not to transfer them in toto to the jurisdiction of the House Administration Committee, because I felt it to be a mistake. I have always felt that if we wanted to raise either our salaries or any benefits, we ought to debate the issue and then vote it either up or down in the House in the public eye. None of them have been hidden in any event. To indulge in an orgy of self-denial now strikes me as hypocrisy, and I don't think we are fooling anybody.

Thursday, June 24, 1976—Sunday, June 27, 1976

The conference with the Senate is over, but I missed the wrap-up. I had to leave Washington before noon on Friday to come to Norfolk to speak at the dedication of the mall at Old Dominion University. It has been named in honor of George Kaufman, a good friend of mine and benefactor of the school. On the way home, I heard on the radio that the conference report had been agreed to and the controversial issue of the B-1 settled. Apparently a compromise was achieved which authorized money for the production of the first three aircraft. Should the next President decide to kill the plane, he could do so. I'm sure that John Culver objected to even this concession. He is adamantly opposed to the aircraft, and spoke as forcefully against it as anyone I've heard.

Thursday, July 1, 1976—Monday, July 19, 1976

Back after nearly three weeks, we found the recess all too short. It was time enough, however, for the Democrats to nominate Jimmy Carter for President and Walter Mondale to be his running mate. We watched very little of the proceedings on television, but not out of partisan feelings. We had other engagements. What I read of them, including articles by our local reporters who covered the Democratic Convention, indicated no surprises. I am partisan enough to get a slow burn from the smugness on the other side about their forthcoming victory this fall, probably because deep down I suspect they are going to win. Yet it is hard to believe that Carter can continue to run so strongly without being pinned down on the issues. His selection of Mondale gives the Republicans something of a target to shoot at, in view of his liberal record in the Senate. But Carter must be baited if we are to have a chance. The trouble is that Ford isn't the person to do it. If Reagan gets the nomination, the pressure will be strong on both for a debate. If that happens, the odds are that Reagan will cut him up, though probably not enough to swing the election around. Ford would do well to get John Connally on his ticket. He is by far the most articulate person in the Republican camp and might be able to draw attention to Carter's fuzziness. Carter is a balloon, blown up all out of proportion to his substance, but whether he will be punctured before this fall is another question.

Prior to leaving on the recess, we had an interesting evening at the German Embassy. There were about twenty guests, including two congressmen, Sam Stratton and me. A couple of senators had been invited but had to cancel at the last minute because the Senate was still in session. Besides Georg Leber, the Defense Minister, in whose honor the dinner was held, Don Rumsfeld attended, as did George Meany, who has known Leber for many years. It was the first time I had met the crusty leader of the AFL-CIO. Janie and I sat at a table with Mrs. Leber and Ambassador von Staden. With us was another German and Fred Ikle of the State Department, a bright chap. We spent a fair amount of time talking about China, and I shared some of my impressions from our trip in April. Von Staden said that he had been in the Soviet Union in the 1950s when Adenauer made his visit to arrange for the return of the remaining German prisoners from World War II and restore diplomatic relations. On one occasion there he had attended an outdoor sports rally in the Moscow stadium, to which thousands of participants had come from all over the communist world. As each delegation entered the stadium, they were greeted by loud cheers from the Russians. But when the Chinese marched in, a large group in perfect step, dressed as one, the Russians fell silent. Von Staden noted that this was prior to the break between Moscow and Peking, but even then the Russians were uneasy about their neighbor in Asia. I told him about the reaction of Yermishkin to my comments and his openly voiced fears of the Chinese as a threat to the security of his country.

Thursday, July 29, 1976—Sunday, August 1, 1976

The House reprimanded Bob Sikes on Thursday morning, the first time that it has taken that kind of action since 1922. The late Adam

Clayton Powell was expelled, a much harsher penalty, but his offense was also greater. Nevertheless, for Sikes, a proud and powerful man, it was a humiliating experience. With one exception, it was handled like an execution—something to be gotten over with as soon as possible.

It was made the first order of business. Jack Flynt, the chairman of the Ethics Committee, made a statement declaring that the Committee had carefully examined the charges, a statement as painful as it was necessary. The vote had been decisive, and he recommended that the House approve the Committee's action. Floyd Spence, who anchored the Republican side, made an even briefer statement. It would have been better at that point to move the question, but Andrew Maguire of New Jersey felt it incumbent upon him to take the floor and lecture the House, chastising the Committee for not doing more. Most of the Members regarded this as a piece of demagoguery, and I suspect that it will not be forgotten. Flynt then moved the previous question, and at that point there was some confusion about what kind of vote would be taken. One Member rose to object that a quorum was not present, an indirect way of seeking a record vote. But for this sort of business, a quorum was clearly present, and Albert so stated. When it was evident that a voice vote was imminent, one of the Democrats asked for a record vote. The vote was 381 to reprimand, three voting not to (Hébert, Teague, and Steed, all long-term Democrats) and five voting present, including Sikes and the others, brother Congressmen from Florida. Sikes did not speak in his own defense. He asked permission to "revise and extend his remarks" in the *Record*, but later made a bitter statement, claiming he had been singled out for a minor violation of failing to report certain assets, an offense that other Members have certainly been guilty of at one time or another. Had that been the only matter, I am sure that no action would have been taken. Bob's action in effecting the establishment of The First Navy Bank on the Pensacola Air Station and then acquiring stock in it was the clincher, a clear conflict of interest. It was a regrettable business, but the Hays investigation could make it pale by comparison.

Monday, August 2, 1976—Sunday, August 8, 1976

An interesting week politically, with time running out on the Ford-Reagan contest. In another ten days, it will be resolved for one or the other. The consensus is that bringing Schweiker aboard was a mistake for Reagan, although it was a gamble he had to take. Perhaps there was nothing that he could do to stop the slow but steady Ford gains. But for Ford supporters, like me, there is not much to cheer about. I say this not because the polls show that Carter is so far in front, but rather on the basis of personal observations which are not encouraging.

Late last Wednesday afternoon (August 4), the President hosted a small reception for Virginia delegates who were either pledged to him or were uncommitted, plus some alternates. About twenty-five showed up. The Republican Members from Virginia were also invited, and I went down to the White House at 5:00 to share the President's hospitality. Both the President and Betty Ford moved easily among the group in the State Dining Room, chatting and shaking hands. I watched this scene with some detachment as well as amusement. It was clearly a thrill for all of the delegates and alternates to be a part of an intimate circle that included the President of the United States. They were either gushing or had foolish grins on their faces, all of which reaction was perfectly understandable. For most of these Republican faithfuls, it was a once-in-a-lifetime event, although several had been courted in the last few weeks to win their support at Kansas City. Some had been invited to dinner, others for a private chat.

After meeting and talking with each one, the President asked them to take seats in the chairs grouped around a podium at one end of the room. The President then welcomed them and briefly outlined his accomplishments and how he intended to stand on his record in the forthcoming campaign. He emphasized several points: when he had taken office, confidence in the Presidency was low; he had reversed that. There was still a war on in Vietnam, and 100,000 Americans were still there; now there is peace. Finally, when he had taken office, the nation was in the throes of a recession, and now things were much better. His program was working. The signs and trends that ought to be going up were going up, and those that ought to be going down were going down. It was a low-key, self-confident tack, and it had its impact. The Virginians were clearly impressed, and the President easily fielded the questions which followed. For awhile, I was impressed by the President's skill and misled about his prospects in the months ahead. Two factors led me astray. First, the President is at his best in a small group of this kind. He relates very well in a one-on-one situation, or in the company of a few. Second, the questions weren't tough and most had been raised before, so he had his answers well in hand. Finally, the President sensed that his audience was somewhat awed by the environment and could hardly be hostile. Psychologically, this has an impact on any dialogue.

Three hours later, I sat again in the President's company. This time, the size and composition of the group were different, and the President fared considerably worse than he had in the afternoon. The occasion was a dinner sponsored by the Good Guys, the Republican conservatives in the House. Well over a hundred Members were there, including all of those of conservative persuasion and a number of moderates as well. Three Democrats were also in attendance, Dan Daniel and Dave Satterfield of Virginia and Joe Waggoner of Louisiana. They felt a lot more at home with us than at the Democratic Study Group fund-raiser which was being held simultaneously at the Washington Hilton.

The President arrived toward the end of the cocktail hour, and again circulated among his former House colleagues, posing for photographs with one, having a word with another, and generally putting everyone at ease. "A repeat performance," I thought. It was not to be. Following a hearty steak dinner, Sam Devine, who presided, introduced the President and announced that questions would be taken following the President's remarks. Damned if Ford didn't give the exact speech that he had made to the Republican delegates at the White House a few hours before, even to the same phrases. "Well," I thought, "I've done the same thing. The same words come easily." Everybody listened politely, but it was clear that the President wasn't going to get off with just a few well-chosen words. The "good guys" became the "tough guys."

About the only thing that wasn't brought up was the Panama Canal. Jack Kemp gave the President a hard time about the SALT agreements, and it was evident that he had gotten under the President's skin, because Ford's voice grew hard as he told Jack that he was wrong about SALT clearly favoring the Russians. It might have been worse had the news story in the press the following day been published twenty-four hours earlier—that the Russians have been engaging in underground testing above the level agreed to in SALT.

But on two questions in particular the President was weak in his response. Bill Armstrong of Colorado had been talking at the table about the need for the President to come out with some bold ideas in order to seize the initiative from the Democrats. Now he put it bluntly to the President. He urged him to call for a constitutional amendment on busing, or a single six-year term for the presidency, or offer some new economic ideas, and to have these written into the platform. He said that without this kind of approach, there was just no way we could turn the polls around and beat Carter in the fall. Through it all, the President puffed thoughtfully on his pipe, and then he calmly told Bill that he had people in the White House who were advising him to do these things and that he had them under consideration. The President's lack of enthusiasm for the suggestion was so self-evident that I caught my dining companions looking at each other. The President's answer to Steve Symms was even softer. Admittedly, Steve is a Reagan supporter and one of the staunchest conservatives in the House. However, his question was a legitimate one and not designed to make Ford stumble. Steve noted that there had been an editorial in the *Wall Street Journal* that morning praising Jack Kemp's economic program as an alternative to the Humphrey-Hawkins bill for "full employment." Jack's bill would stimulate and encourage private investment in business and industry, thus making a large amount of capital available for business expansion. The *Journal* editors said that they could not comment fully on how effective the program would be but that it certainly deserved consideration by the Administration. In substance, Steve inquired whether the President had looked at Jack's bill, and since it already had 132 cosponsors in the House, why not embrace it and go with it as an alternative to a bill that has just been exposed as unworkable and inflationary, and take this message to the American people. It was the best question of the night, and Ford's answer was his worst. Instead of saying that he agreed that it deserved immediate attention and he would put Bill Simon to work on it to see how it could be implemented, he lamely told one and all that while he was impressed by the bill, he had to have comments from Simon, Burns, and his other economists, and he couldn't do anything until they told him what their opinion was. He said nothing about his own convictions or initiative, and he left the impression that if Simon or Burns happened to bring it up to him, it might get consideration.

If there was any enthusiasm left for the President's cause, it evaporated with that answer. The President received the expected applause, but the Members didn't even wait for him to leave first, but began filing out of the room for the elevator. The comments that I heard on the way out were almost uniformly of disappointment and discouragement of any chance of winning in November. I recognize that all of this could change, but there is less than three months to go. I find myself somehow wishing that Reagan just might pull it out and get the nomination. At least we might then get the dynamism that needs to be infused into the Ford campaign. Better, we would have the prospect of a debate with Carter, which I am certain would result in a diminishing of Carter's strength. I believe that Reagan, who chewed up Bobby Kennedy in a debate, would make mincemeat of Carter. It might not turn the election around, but we would at least have the satisfaction of drawing blood.

The primaries in Michigan and Missouri took place on Tuesday. Don Riegle surprised a lot of people by winning the Democratic Senate nomination in Michigan, and he will face his House colleague Marv Esch on our side in the fall. However, the most dramatic and tragic event occurred in Missouri. Jerry Litton, a two-term House Member, won the Democratic Senate nomination overwhelmingly, beating both a former governor and Jim Symington, who was trying to succeed his father. On election night Litton, his wife, and both of their children were killed as their private plane was taking off for campaign headquarters, where there was to be a celebration of his major victory. It cast a pall not only in Missouri but here in the House as well.

We had one "first" during the week, attending the dinner in honor of President Kekkonen of Finland. It was held on Tuesday evening and turned out to be both interesting and entertaining. We arrived at the White House at 8:00 p.m. and went up to the East Room for cocktails. Several of my colleagues from the House were there, including John Anderson, Charlie Mosher, and Bill Frenzel and their wives. When the President and Mrs. Ford and President Kekkonen were announced, they stood just inside the entrance to the East Room and the guests formed a line to be received. It was all according to rank, with Cabinet members in front, then Senators and Representatives in order of seniority. The other distinguished guests brought up the rear. Susan Ford, a thoroughly natural young lady, came over to us and immediately engaged us in conversation. It was clear that State Dinners are nothing new to her. Deciding that she could fit anywhere in the pecking order, she moved along with us until we reached the President, where I laughingly introduced the President to his daughter. He laughed and kissed her on the cheek.

The dinner was held in the tent used last month for the first time when the Queen of England was feted. Susan told us that her mother liked the tent so well that she decided to keep it up for other dinners for heads of state the rest of the summer. This was the last occasion that it would be used for. Both the setting and the meal deserve high marks. The entree was tournedos of beef. The wines were American, and while they were not of vintage quality, they were, nevertheless, excellent. My dinner partners were Mrs. Al Unser, the wife of the famed racing driver, and Shirley Temple Black's husband, which is a hell of a way to identify a man, who does, after all, have his own identity. I suspect that he is reconciled to this state of affairs and can take some satisfaction out of the fact that the child starlet of forty years ago now shares one-third of *her* name with him. For all that, he turned out to be an impressive fellow. He had gone to sea as a youth, been in China during the thirties when the Japanese invaded the country, and was wounded during a Japanese attack while he was aboard a ship there. His war career was in PT boats, and he made his business success in commercial fishing. By any measure, he deserves recognition for more than for marrying America's little sweetheart of the Depression days. He communicated intelligence and strength, yet he took pride in his wife's accomplishments as ambassador to Ghana and more recently as chief of protocol in the State Department. He said that she had memorized 500 names before the diplomatic reception for the ambassadors and legation heads which was held a few days ago, an achievement that she had passed off lightly as a result of memory sharpening in her childhood. Since he had lived in Accra with his wife while she was ambassador, I picked his brain for his thoughts on West Africa and American policy in general toward black Africa.

Unfortunately, Mrs. Unser offered little in the way of conversation, although it was easy to see why her husband had first noticed her. She met him through a beauty contest for one of the racing magazines. "I'm just a little girl from a small town in Indiana," she said.

Janie said she had a delightful group at her table, where Shirley Temple Black was the hostess. Al Unser was there, though she never got a chance to talk to him, and she particularly enjoyed a Mr. Tornudd, from the Foreign Ministry in Finland, and a fellow named Tom Carroll, president of Lever Brothers, among other things, who said he really didn't know why he had been invited. She thought it best not to try to explain.

Entertainment was provided in the East Room by George Shearing, the blind pianist. He played beautifully, and fortunately not too long; the concert lasted not longer than twenty or thirty minutes. For the guests who wished to prolong their White House experience, there was dancing afterward, but it had already been a long day for Janie and me, so we left shortly after 11:00.

Wednesday, September 1, 1976—
Saturday, September 4, 1976

The President's chances of winning in the fall are still looked upon as guarded. We had something of an open forum on it at the Wednesday Group meeting, with various Members suggesting positions that Ford ought to take. The President had agreed to see six Members from the House Wednesday Group on Thursday along with a similar delegation from the Senate Wednesday Group. Jim Johnson of Colorado said that the President should be told to indicate that he was going to make wholesale postal reform because of the widespread dissatisfaction over postal service. Mark Andrews was even more outspoken about the unhappiness of the farmers. He doesn't like Butz and says that Butz is just a poor spokesman for the Administration. Mark holds that Ford can't win without the farm states and needs to come out to the Midwest and tell the farmers that they are going to have a free market without restrictions, including sales to the Russians or anyone else.

But it was Joel Pritchard who struck the right chord. He said that all of this was helpful but that the key matter for the President was not to burden himself with a lot of positions right now or wear himself out running around the country on a tight schedule. What Ford needs to do is to prime himself mentally and psychologically so that he can destroy Carter before a national audience. Furthermore, it is vital that the President smash Carter in the first debate, because that is the one that will have the largest viewing. After that, the novelty will wear off fast, and fewer and fewer people will be listening.

On Thursday afternoon, I talked to Joel, who was one of those chosen to see the President that morning, and asked him how the meeting had gone. He said that Ford had talked to them for over an hour and had been very receptive. "Did you tell him what you told us yesterday afternoon?" I asked. "Yes," he replied, "and the President agreed." I have already noticed that the President's schedule of appearances is limited, that he plans to remain in Washington most of the time, with occasional forays into the country. Thus he will have the time for preparation for the debates and will give the impression of minding the nation's business. It may all be for naught, but I believe that he is following the best game plan.

Yermishkin came by on Thursday afternoon, back from a month's

217

vacation in the Land of Lenin. Aside from the weather, which was apparently wet most of the time (while the English have been suffering their worst drought in two and a half centuries!), he looked as though he had enjoyed the reunion with his family and friends. He was anxious to discuss the election and whether I thought that Ford would sign the SALT agreement that is pending. I told him that, given the political circumstances, it appeared to me that the President would not sign anything with the Russians until after the election. He wasn't particularly pleased with that reply, but I suspect that he believes the same thing. "Americans are mercurial about the Russians," I said. "Right now they think that you are aggressive and not to be trusted, and that you are getting the better of us. The President senses this feeling and isn't about to jeopardize himself with the electorate until after November." Yermishkin nodded and smiled wryly.

Wednesday, September 22, 1976

The House has passed an innocuous resolution known as World Adequate Diet, or more popularly, the "Right to Food" Resolution. I have had some lobbying from the Catholic Diocese of Richmond on it, and I had a call Saturday from a constituent urging support of it. The language did little more than pledge American efforts to help nations grow more food and did not commit substantial exports of free food from the U.S. Still, there were some No votes, including, of all people, Millicent Fenwick. Seeing the large majority at the end of the voting period, she went to the Well of the House and changed her vote to Aye. Later, in the Republican lounge, she sputtered about the resolution and her opposition to it. It was clear that only the large margin in favor of it had caused her to switch. One of the fellows reassured her by saying, "Don't worry, Millicent—we all have to rise above principle now and then." She frowned in disgust at herself.

There was one sad piece of news on the wire service yesterday afternoon. Jim Hastings, who came to the House with me back in 1969, and resigned to go into private business the first of this year, has been indicted on several counts of taking kickbacks from his staff while he was a Member. I couldn't believe it until I talked to Lou Frey, who had roomed with Jim for seven years. Lou was devastated by it, but he confirmed it. Jim had talked to him about it. According to the reports, Jim had used the money to pay for his children's education, a boat, a snowmobile, and a car, and to reinstate his New York State retirement. As if the indictment were not enough, Jim's wife is getting a divorce. His whole world is coming apart. I told Lou that it would have been better for Jim if he had never been elected to Congress. Lou agreed.

In the Presidential race, Jimmy Carter has laid another egg with his interview in *Playboy* magazine in regard to committing adultery. While some of his language came from the locker room and may have been intended as such for the readership of the magazine, the thrust of what he said didn't strike me as offensive, but the general reaction nationally seems to have been otherwise. I suppose that most people probably feel that he would have served himself better if he hadn't granted the interview in the first place. The language, while certainly familiar to every American, or nearly every one, is out of place in the minds of most people for a President or a candidate for that office. Republican Members were having a field day on Tuesday afternoon, while Democrats were shaking their heads over their standard bearer's gaffe. It will pass. There is near unanimity that the debates will be the most critical factor in the election.

At the Wednesday Group this afternoon, we made an informal survey of the race. Stu McKinney was positively elated at the turn of events in his district in Connecticut. For one who can almost always be depended upon to be pessimistic, his upbeat note was a surprise. He said that it might be just "Southern prejudice," but that Ford had 34 percent of the vote, Carter 32 percent, and 34 percent were undecided, and this in a district that was Democratic. Thad Cochran said that in his district in Mississippi there was also a shift toward Ford, that loyal Democrats were saying openly that Carter did not appear to be "trustworthy." His conviction is that Southerners will not abide by regional bounds, and that Carter just doesn't look "presidential" to many people. Shirley Pettis, who represents a Republican district in California, noted that Ford is pulling up, but that it is too early to predict. That, of course, would be true in almost every district now. Bill Cohen reported that Carter still has the lead in Maine, but only by 2 percent. Mark Andrews, another perennial pessimist, followed McKinney's lead and gave an optimistic report on North Dakota. He cited the *Playboy* interview as damaging to Carter's image. Ron Sarasin, who has a Connecticut district like McKinney, also reported Ford ahead with 32 percent to 27 percent for Carter and the rest undecided. He added that Bob Giaimo, the dean of their delegation and a strong liberal Democrat, had lamented on Tuesday evening over the *Playboy* flap, "It shows what happens when you back a guy and don't know where he stands."

Peggy Heckler was not very encouraging about her district in Massachusetts, saying that Carter still had the lead, but she cautioned that the debates could sway a large body in either direction. Bill Frenzel described Carter as being "miles ahead" in Minnesota, the one unequivocal statement in Carter's favor.

Friday, October 1, 1976—Monday, November 8, 1976

It is too bad that the Republicans nationwide did not do as well as we did in Virginia. The Old Dominion was one of the few bright spots on election night. For openers, the President carried the state while losing the national election to Carter. My own district went for Carter by a narrow margin. But on the plus side, Bob Daniel held on to his seat by defeating Billy O'Brien in a tough head-to-head race, and Paul Trible fooled the experts by winning Tom Downing's old district, the First, by edging out Bob Quinn by something over 2,000 votes. All of the other races in Virginia left the seats unchanged, so the line-up in the House will be six Republicans to four Democrats. Trible's win was the only new Republican seat gained in the South. At twenty-nine, he shows promise of going far. Janie and I met with him and his wife Rosemary in Yorktown last Friday for lunch and discussed some of the preliminaries to his taking office. He will probably retain most of Tom's staff, a move that I encouraged, and he will open two additional offices in his district, one on the Eastern Shore and the other in Tappahannock. Since Tom never had any need to extend his constituent service so far, this will surely accrue to Paul's favor. I also discussed his sending out a newsletter and using other means to win the voters over. He knows that he has his work cut out for him, and promptly spent the morning after the election shaking hands at the Newport News Shipbuilding yard gate, thanking the workers for sending him to Congress. He asked me if I would write to John Rhodes and recommend him for a seat on the Armed Services Committee. I said that I would, and I did, but I also encouraged him to try to get a seat on the Merchant Marine and Fisheries Committee, in view of Tom's long service on that Committee and its value to the port of Hampton Roads.

All of the hopes that we had in September of picking up a dozen or so seats from the Democrats have been dashed. The Democratic preparations for their freshmen, plus the Carter tide, paid off. Most of the freshmen will be coming back. But as is the case with every election, some veterans went down. On our side, Garner Shriver in Kansas, Burt Talcott in California, and Don Clancy in Ohio lost. All three had been in jeopardy. The Democrats had some surprises, though. Joe Vigorito of Pennsylvania and a neighbor of mine of the fourth floor corridor of Cannon, was defeated. He had been named in a New York off-beat journal as one of the "ten dumbest" in the Congress, hardly an endorsement for reelection, but there were probably other factors as well. Henry Helstoski lost his seat in New Jersey. He is liable to lose much more, since he is under indictment for taking money from aliens in return for securing residence for them through Congressional action. We also picked up Howe's seat in Utah. His conviction for accosting two police decoys for prostitution cost him the support of his own party and ultimately his seat. Bob Leggett squeaked by with a 700-vote margin in his district in California after all the publicity he got siring two children by a mistress, forging his wife's name to a deed, and having a suspicious liaison with a Korean girl who is rumored to have ties with South Korean Intelligence operatives. Any one of these would have done me in here, but they seem to have a more tolerant eye for hijinks in California. Since the Senate races are a matter of record, there's little point in reviewing those, although I was surprised that Bill Brock went down, too. Our hopes of bringing back Vinegar Bend Mizell are gone. He just couldn't overcome the Carter surge in North Carolina. But aside from these few changes, or lack of change, the composition of the Congress remains pretty much the same as it was in the 94th.

Carter remains an enigma for me. I am not prepared to give in to my worst fears, knowing that the office itself tends to have a tempering effect on the holder. That will be far more sobering than the narrow margin of his victory over Ford. The talk of commentators about the 49 percent who didn't vote for him are meaningless. Nixon thought that he had a "mandate" in 1968, and he only had a plurality. I have yet to meet a winner who didn't act as if he had 90 percent of the vote, nor a loser who was consoled by a margin of 49.9 percent.

It would be folly to attempt to implement even half of the promises contained in the Democratic platform. If we try, we will simply be in a race with the British to see who can go bankrupt first. At the same time, I doubt that we will witness much of a diminution in big government, and it will be wishful thinking to look for a substantial drop in deficit spending.

One aspect of it all will be totally new for me. I have yet to serve as a Republican Member in a Democratic Administration. A couple of weeks before we adjourned, Bill Broomfield of Michigan commented in the Republican lounge that it really wasn't such a bad role to be in. By being completely in the minority party, we could attack the Democrats on any program without being saddled with a fraction of the responsibility for anything that went wrong. It's not a position to be coveted, but it's not without its rewards.

1977

Tuesday, January 4, 1977

I took the oath "to uphold and defend the Constitution" for the fifth time this afternoon. While the lustre of that first day eight years ago has dimmed, I reflected today on my survivability with some satisfaction. I never dreamed then that I would make it this far. Indeed, I regarded my initial election as something of a miracle.

Janie and I walked through the tunnel from the Cannon Building to the Capitol shortly before 2:00 and took the elevator up. She had a good seat in the gallery at the rear of the Chamber and was able to see the Speaker as well as the Members sworn in. I met Paul Trible in the Speaker's Lobby, and we shared the ceremony next to each other, along with Caldwell Butler from our delegation. There seemed to be an extraordinary number of small children on the floor today, which is not surprising in view of the increase in younger Members. While normally the privilege of allowing young children to accompany a parent or grandparent to the floor poses no probems, the number today was so large that many Democrats had to find seats on our side of the aisle, and a few Members, arriving late, could find no seat at all. Most children at the age of three or four are restless, and these youngsters were no exception. One little fellow ran across the well just as Tip O'Neill was about to begin his acceptance speech as the new Speaker. I would not be surprised to see a minimum age set for those who are permitted to come to the floor before the next election. It really is getting out of hand.

The proceedings followed the predictable pattern, with Members-elect answering their names when the roll was called by States. The Speaker was then chosen, again by a voice vote, and Tip was escorted in not only by John Rhodes and a representative group from both sides but by two past Speakers, Carl Albert and John McCormack, the latter in remarkable shape for a man of eighty-five. By custom, the Minority Leader presents the Speaker to the House, and John did so with some gentle ribbing, remarking that he knew that Tip would be the best one-term Speaker that the House would ever have. Tip gave as good as he got, beginning his own speech by saying that he knew that the gentleman from Arizona had his eye on the Speaker's seat, and that was all he would ever have on it. In his prepared address, he made it clear that the House would assert its will in the new Administration and that our most important task was to get Americans back to work. It was the clearest signal he could give for the jobs bill about to be hatched. Otherwise, he paid lip service to impartiality, which prompted some quiet snickers on our side, and a barely audible "bullshit" from Caldwell sitting on my left.

Following Tip's remarks, George Mahon, the Dean of the House, gave him the oath of office, then Tip swore in the entire House. Aside from this formality and the confirmation of the various House officials, the only business was the adoption of the new House Rules. Knowing what the outcome of that battle would be, I went back to the office, signed some mail, and returned some telephone calls that were pending. In the recorded votes later in the afternoon, we were rolled decisively by the other side. Procedures have been streamlined, which will diminish what little strength we had to obstruct or slow down the Democratic steamroller. However, as I told a television news team in my office this morning, if their program produces double-digit inflation, we'll know where to place the blame.

It was a quiet day otherwise. Janie and I went up to Paul's office for a small reception, congratulating his parents and his wife Rosemary, who is overdue with their first child. Now that her husband has taken office, I would not be surprised to see nature fulfilled very soon. They are as excited as two kids about being here, which is wholly understandable. Had I been elected to Congress at the age of twenty-nine, my reaction would have been exactly the same.

Wednesday, January 5, 1977— Monday, January 10, 1977

With the Congress marking time until the new Administration takes office, there has been little to hold us in Washington. Accordingly, we drove home on Wednesday morning, omitting the half day we had planned to spend in the office because of an early snowstorm. We had a dinner party to attend that evening at Virginia House, the home of Admiral and Mrs. Ike Kidd at the Norfolk Naval Station, and it was fortunate that we left early. Dozens of cars had skidded into each other and off the side of the Shirley Highway, making driving very hazardous. The Kidds' party was in honor of retiring Navy Secretary Middendorf. Like all of the social affairs at their home, this one was elegant. An added treat was to meet Winston Churchill, II, the grandson of the famed British prime minister. Following in his forebear's footsteps, he is already a member of Parliament, representing a constituency in Manchester. He has won his spurs as a leader in his party, serving in the "shadow cabinet" of Margaret Thatcher in defense. It was this role that brought him to America for conversations with Ike and other defense leaders.

The table conversation was interesting. Bill Middendorf told me that he hoped that he might be of service to the Republican Party as a fund raiser, having filled that role in Connecticut, raising money for Lowell Weicker when he ran for the House and the Senate. Bill has made money in his own right and has the time for it. It was the remarks of young Churchill, however, which engrossed us. He lamented the financial condition of his country and declared that the latest loan guaranteed by the Western powers will be in vain. Not surprisingly, he regarded the socialists as incompetent as well as blind, and he reflected embarrassment over Britain's increasingly weak role in the Atlantic Alliance.

The few days at home were restful, but I managed to fill some engagements and see my constituents too. On Friday I went by one of the shopping malls and signed a petition to the President-elect, asking him not to grant amnesty to those who refused to serve in the armed forces during the Vietnam war. Carter's announcement some weeks ago that he would do this after taking office has aroused considerable opposition, and a nationwide effort has been mounted to dissuade him. I doubt that it will, but the movement has gathered some momentum. I co-signed a letter with over a hundred of my House colleagues which Sonny Montgomery had prepared, and indicated to the local people that I would lend encouragement to their efforts. One of the leaders in Virginia Beach is the wife of a returned prisoner of war, Lt. Commander Mike Christian. To make clear his own opposition to the move, Mike submitted his resignation from the Navy last week and visited a local cemetery to place his medals of valor on the grave of a veteran. It has generated more than an ordinary amount of interest. At the dinner on Wednesday evening, Bill Middendorf told me that he had written a personal letter to Mike and urged him to reconsider his action, telling him that the Navy needed men of his persuasion. I followed up with a letter of my own the next day. Janie and I know Mike and Charlotte Christian well, having had them in our home. Aside from keeping a good man in the service, I would hate to see him resign at this point, since he has only one year remaining before he is eligible to receive his twenty-year retirement pay. For a chap not yet forty, that is no mean sacrifice.

Wednesday, January 12, 1977

The Wednesday Group meeting was held in Bill Cohen's office this afternoon, and although it was sparsely attended, many of the Members having left for home (the President's appearance tonight notwithstanding), it was entertaining. Barber Conable held forth on the Carter program, promising paltry results from the so-called jobs bill which will be forthcoming, and an assurance of a $70 billion deficit which is certain to drive up interest rates and depress the stock market. Furthermore, he is convinced that Carter's program will not be swallowed in toto by the Democrats. Many of the liberals, he believes, are out of sorts with their new-found leader over his solo course in mapping out an economic program. To remind him that they are still around, Barber expects that they will tack on some amendments of their own which will only inflate his program further. Barber also claimed that Phil Burton is alive and kicking, and to prove it, he forecasts that Phil will lead a liberal drive to sack some of the committee or subcommittee chairmen at the Democratic Caucus next week. "They'll need some public executions to get their point across." Bob Sikes looks like the number one candidate to get the axe as Chairman of the Appropriations Subcommittee on Military Installations and Facilities.

I asked what the fate of the proposed salary increase for Members might be. "Well, Ford isn't going to recommend it, I hear," Barber replied. "The reason is that Carter won't agree to back him, so Ford isn't going to make the recommendation by himself. Jerry figured that if he gave the proposed $12,900 raise, Carter would come along behind and cut it by about $4,000 and thus end up letting the Members have an $8,000 raise while looking like a hero to those who are opposed to a salary increase for Members of Congress." With the exception of Chuck Whalen, that brought a collective groan. Chuck has been pushing for a vote that would raise salaries of Members in the next Congress, so that the Members could not be charged with raising their salaries while they were assured of getting the raise. Meanwhile, Brock Adams, Bob Bergland, and Fritz Mondale are reported to have been quietly pressing Carter to go ahead and grant the raise to their former colleagues.

The consensus regarding the President-elect's beginning is not very flattering. Carter sent an invitation to each Member of the House and Senate to attend a reception at the White House on the Saturday following the Inauguration. Apparently not many from our side of the aisle are going. "He's allotted the Diplomatic Corps just thirty minutes," said Chuck Whalen, after Bill Frenzel had noted that the Congressional Reception would only be for an hour. "Do you mean the whole Diplomatic Corps?" asked Barber, and then added, "It will take that long for the Nicaraguan Ambassador to present his credentials."

In many respects, the President's State of the Union Address was his best speech ever. Certainly he never received a warmer reception in the Congress, except possibly when he was sworn in as the Vice President. The Democrats, having won the prize in November, could afford to be charitable, but Jerry brought a strong dose of nostalgia to the Chamber, so it all ended as a love-in.

A larger number of Members showed up than had been expected. Late in the afternoon, word was passed that staff members could accompany Members to the floor. This not only swelled the crowd, it deprived a lot of Members of their seats, and also the Diplomatic Corps, which apparently had 100 percent attendance. Most of the Senate also showed up, including Hubert Humphrey, who looked like death itself. Released last year from cancer surgery, he appeared to have aged ten years.

Some of the wives joined their husbands, Paul Trible's wife initiating it by walking in with Paul. I invited Janie, who was sitting in the gallery, to come down, and when Kit Robinson saw them, she left her seat and came down to sit behind us. It was Rosemary Trible, however, who got the attention. She had started to have labor contractions and wasn't at all sure that she would make it through the President's speech. She did with hours to spare, however, giving birth to a baby girl the next afternoon in Richmond.

We drove home on Thursday morning, attending a dinner party given by Admiral and Mrs. Jerry Denton at their quarters at the Naval Station in Norfolk that night. General Westmoreland was their special guest, since he was scheduled to deliver the address to the graduating class at the Armed Forces Staff College the next morning. He sat across from me and talked about his numerous appearances on television and before various forums around the country, either pushing his book or as a guest in counterpoint to some critic of the Vietnam war. Needless to say, he was outspoken in his opposition to a pardon for the men who dodged the draft. Basically a soldier, he was frank to admit that his excursion into politics in South Carolina was a mistake, and his decision to run for governor there had come only after strong pressures were put on him. He was defeated badly, but philosophical about his loss.

Barber Conable's foreboding regarding the President's recommendation on Congressional pay turned out to be fallacious. Today Ford sent his proposal up to the Hill, and it would raise the salaries of Members to $57,900, unless the Members in an unguarded moment turn it down.

I began the day with a breakfast given by the new Secretary of Defense, Harold Brown, at the Pentagon. My last visit there was nearly a year ago when Don Rumsfeld hosted a breakfast for a few of us to enlist support for an abortive move to supply arms to the anti-communist forces in Angola. Not surprisingly, the change in administrations has in no way diminished the elegance of a breakfast in the dining room of the Secretary of Defense. Crisp linens and sparkling crystal are still the order of the day. I must say, however, that the Secretary is the only person I've ever encountered who drank iced tea for breakfast.

Besides our host, the Under Secretary, and General Brown, the Chairman of the Joint Chiefs, there were about a dozen of the senior members of the Armed Services Committee present, including Mel and Bob Wilson. Although the Secretary answered a few questions about major budget cuts and a slowdown in some programs, his main purpose in asking us over was to make a pitch for his proposed reorganization of the Office of the Secretary of Defense (OSD).

Noting that he is confronted with over two dozen branches with an assistant secretary over each, he declared that there just isn't any way that he can properly oversee their activities. Therefore, he was going to propose that a number of them be combined so that he can meet with a manageable number of heads. Proposals like this are nothing new, and the skepticism that greeted Brown reflected this. Dick Ichord used the monkey-in-the-trees analogy, telling the Secretary that it didn't make sense "to cut down some of the trees if you were just going to put the monkeys on top of each other in the rest of the trees." Charlie Bennett echoed this, saying he had seen it happen before, where the reorganization resulted in another layer going on top of the present ones. But Brown protested that he was determined to reduce the number of people, telling us that unless the total number went down, "I'm not interested in reorganization." I asked him where he was going to send the personnel—"out the gate?" He said that some would probably retire, and those who did not would be sent into field units if they were military personnel, and some civilians, or separated. Apparently he needs authorization legislation from us, and while some skepticism remains, I'm sure that a majority will vote to let him reorganize the Department as he sees fit. Before I left, I told him that he could count on my support. That place is like a hydra.

The Secretary got a little going-over earlier when he was pushed to explain the slowdown in the development of the MX, the new ICBM under development. Brown said that it was better to wait and see what kind of agreement we were going to get in the SALT talks before pushing on with it. He added that we were proceeding on schedule with the tactical cruise missile, but slowing up on the anti-ship sea missile because of target acquisition problems. It was a fairly soft exchange, but I expect that he will have a harder time when he appears formally before the Armed Services Committee in March. The Carter Administration has cut the budget by over $2 billion, and the slowdown on the B-1 as well as other programs is causing friction. I doubt, however, that we will turn much of it around.

In the afternoon, I met with State Senator Marshall Coleman, who is running for the Republican nomination for attorney general this year. He is a very effective debater, makes a strong impression, and promises us leadership for the future. He gave me a list of people at home he wanted to support him and asked me to try to win them over. His opponent in the fight for the nomination is Wyatt Durrette, a Delegate in the General Assembly from Northern Virginia. He is also a good candidate, but I think that Marshall would have the better chance in a statewide race. No matter what happens, if Andrew Miller defeats Henry Howell in the Democratic primary, it is going to be a tough year for Republicans in Virginia. Miller will pull the Democrats together, and the other candidates will "coat-tail" him. I'm grateful to have the year off.

Later in the day, the new Secretary of the Navy, W. Graham Claytor, came by on a courtesy call. He impressed me very much, showing considerable knowledge of the Navy's problems even though he was sworn in less than two weeks ago. We discussed the decision to postpone construction of a fifth nuclear carrier and the need to develop some smaller conventional carriers utilizing V/STOL planes in another decade. His appreciation of the difficulty of making long-term commitments with a very expensive weapon was evident. The same reasoning manifested itself in his discussion of how to deploy Aegis, the Navy's new anti-missile defense system. He made a case for getting it aboard the new destroyers, the DDG-47, and eventually on the nuclear cruisers, so that we will have both nuclear and non-nuclear platforms. He rejected utilizing the *Long Beach,* as we have been pushing for over the past year, saying that while we might get Aegis into the fleet a year earlier, the cost could be great, and worse, we would be putting Aegis on a ship that would have no more than another fifteen years in her. I didn't press him but said that I regarded the deployment of Aegis as an urgent priority, and then I concluded by saying, "Mr. Secretary, if you run the Navy as well as you ran the Southern Railroad, we are bound to be in good shape." He replied with a smile, "Congressman, I'm not sure we'll turn a profit."

Wednesday, February 23, 1977

I finally had an opportunity to spend some time with my Subcommittee on Research and Development. With all of the other meetings going on, I haven't had a chance to sit in for more than just a few minutes. Today, however, I made both the morning and the afternoon sessions and am glad that I could be there. The principal witness was Robert Parker, acting director of research and development of the Defense Department. He had a host of backup witnesses, some of whom were brought into the colloquy that developed. There were not many of us there, but those who did show had a field day, boring in on Parker and his people for the interminable delays that have become a part of the pattern in weapons development. Touching on everything from helicopters to tanks and chemical warfare, Dick Ichord, Jim Lloyd, Tom Downey, and Bill Dickinson all got in their licks. In the afternoon, Larry McDonald pitched in, too, and Tony Battista, the chief staffer, is always feisty.

This thing has been brewing for some time. There has been a growing restlessness over the stretch-out between evaluation and testing of a new weapon and its final delivery to forces in the field or in the fleet. Furthermore, this has not always been the case. The Manhattan Project, which led to the development of the atom bomb, took only four years in World War II, and that was a major effort. The Polaris submarine took four years, the Hawk missile five years. But the SAM-D missile has been twenty years in development, and the renowned Aegis fire control system was initiated in 1961 and won't get into the fleet until 1981!

Lloyd delivered what bordered on a tirade against the "think tanks" and other institutions that have grown up in the Defense Department, closing his remarks by saying that he regarded systems analysts as a "pain in the ass." It brought a round of laughter in the room, but when Dick asked him if he didn't want to strike the comment from the record, Jim replied, "Not at all—that's how I feel."

There's no doubt that too many programs have been reevaluated so many times, and the goal of absolute technical perfection pursued, that we have unnecessarily delayed the deployment of vital weapons. The value of prolonged evaluation and testing is questionable, especially considering Soviet advances in equipment in recent years.

In the afternoon session, it reached a point where Lloyd and McDonald asked the witnesses for an example of a thorough study paying commensurate dividends. One chap volunteered that they had done a comprehensive study over a two-year period of the effect of two warheads impacting successively on a missile site and the possible "fratricidal" result, where the first explosion might nullify the following warhead's effect. Battista threw up his hands in exasperation. "We've known that since Grant was a cadet," he said. It was clearly a long day for the boys from R&D, but if it helps light a fire under them, the roasting will have been worth it.

The House met this afternoon to consider the Third Concurrent Resolution on the Budget, and we Republicans got rolled as expected. A substitute amendment by John Rousselot to get a tax reduction in for business went down overwhelmingly. The inflationary fears on our side of the aisle show no sign of being shared by the other side. If there isn't an impact—an inflationary one—on the economy by next year this time, I'm going to believe that we have a new set of economic laws.

This was one of the lightest days I've had in recent weeks. Janie and I got to the office about 9:15 this morning, and I did a little filming for Vic preparatory to recording our weekly television show tomorrow. My R&D Subcommittee met at 11:00, and I went by for that to engage in some discussion with my colleagues on a $200 million cut in R&D funds, a minor reduction for the benefit of the Budget Committee, which still gives us maneuvering room to reduce further, as we probably will.

What provoked more verbiage was the perennial tug-of-war between the Army and the Air Force over roles and missions of the air service in a tactical combat situation. The Army has gotten around the prohibition on having fixed-wing combat aircraft by developing the helicopter. Whenever their representatives come to the Hill, they are careful to delineate between the two types of craft, and each supports the other for the record, apparently in the belief that by doing that they are more likely to gain approval for their requests. Our experience with combat forces in the field, however, and in particular in Vietnam, showed that the soldiers on the ground placed greater reliance on helicopters flown by their own branch types. Bill Dickinson said that the American advisers at An Loc, which was besieged for weeks, appreciated the Air Force strikes against the enemy, but got more respite from the helicopters, which they could vector better and which stayed in the area longer than fixed-wing planes did, which usually dropped their loads and flew away.

We have found ourselves in a serious issue that touches this question of roles and missions. An enormous amount of money has been spent on an advanced helicopter, and we have reached the point of having to decide whether to proceed with production or cut the thing off and cease further tests and evaluation, which only accumulate more debt. Some of the Members have grave doubts about its effectiveness. They feel that if the Army had a choice of going for the helicopter or a fixed-wing airplane, a less expensive and long-time loitering aircraft called "The Enforcer," they would opt for the fixed wing. Since that isn't likely to happen unless we change the basic policy, the Air Force will retain the A-10, which is tagged as a tactical support plane, and the Army will struggle along with its helicopters.

Tony Battista told us of some interesting findings about the effectiveness of helicopters as tank destroyers in the European environment, where we would be most likely to use them. He said that recent maneuvers showed that when the helicopters were used in an attack role, the ratio of loss was eighteen helicopters for every tank destroyed. Conversely, in a defensive situation, it was eighteen tanks destroyed for every helicopter lost. So how the bird is used obviously makes a great deal of difference. Tony also had some harsh words about the A-10. The joke being told is that it will break all records—for hits it will take!

At the end of the meeting, we voted to call for hearings on the roles and missions issue. I said that the matter had been argued ever since I had been in Congress, and had obviously preceded that. The time has come to reconsider a decision that was made thirty years ago when the Air Force was created. If the Army can manage its own tactical role, then it ought to determine and acquire whatever aircraft are needed for that purpose. I'm not sure how far we are going to get with this, but at least it will move the debate to the proper forum—the Armed Services Committee and finally to the Defense Department itself.

Tomorrow, we take up the new ethics legislation, which is sure to stir some impassioned words and long debate, but which is certain to pass. After the pay raise, few people around here are likely to vote against a measure which supposedly keeps the Members more honest. For myself, I regard much of it as a charade, and the denial of the right of a Member to earn money honestly and legitimately outside the Congress, an unwarranted interference with his private life. I think we are becoming more concerned with form than with substance.

Wednesday, March 2, 1977—Sunday, March 6, 1977

The Armed Services Committee opened its first full hearings on the Defense Authorization Bill on Wednesday with the two Browns in attendance—Harold, the Secretary of Defense, and George, Chairman of the Joint Chiefs. The Secretary demonstrated that he knows how to handle a hearing. While he didn't actually orchestrate it, he managed to avoid being painted into a corner. I got the distinct feeling that he knew that the five-minute rule, which restricts every Member's time to five minutes, could be employed to his own advantage just by prolonging his answers. It was impossible to go into depth with him. Dr. Larry McDonald, our John Bircher urologist from Georgia, scorned the whole business. He calls these hearings "waltzing with the witness."

Sam Stratton began it all by criticizing the decision to cut off funds and close down the new Armed Services Medical School. He reminded the Secretary that Congress had specifically mandated that the school be created. Wasn't the Administration's action an infringement on the power of Congress? Brown said that it was a proposed action, and Congress could put the money back in and keep the school in operation if it wanted to. Sam had his hackles up and pointed to the constitutional provision posted in front of Brown and asked him if he understood it. Brown then adjusted his glasses and read it aloud and agreed that Congress indeed had the power "to raise and support Armies and provide and maintain a Navy," but that the Defense Department could recommend. It was a stand-off. Even though he isn't here to defend it, Eddie Hébert's dream isn't going to succumb without a fight.

I had three questions for the Secretary. I briefly reviewed the growing problem of standardization for NATO and asked what steps were going to be taken by the Secretary of Defense to set a positive course for eventual standardization of most NATO arms and equipment. Brown replied that he regards this as an important priority and that he was now getting together plans to move decisively toward adopting a common system in arms. He added that it was going to be difficult, especially with the resistance that sectors of the American defense community would put up. I interjected that he could expect the same from contractors and Members of Congress who would be affected.

Later on, when Dave Emery of Maine, a new member of our committee, got recognition, he pursued this further. He reminded Brown that the Maine company producing machine guns for the M-60 tank had lost its contract to Fabrique National in Belgium last year. He declared that the price of standardization was paid in lost jobs and abandoned technology, and he questioned whether it was worth it. In this instance, Brown showed his mettle. He manifested sympathy for Dave's particular problem but wouldn't back off from his goal. If the feelings were strong in the United States, he said, "They are even stronger in Europe." The Europeans resent the current disproportion of arms sales in favor of the U.S. Any standardization program will result in some loss of jobs for a nation. What will probably occur, he noted, would be the manufacture of lower technology arms by European firms, while high technology materiel, such as sophisticated combat aircraft, would be sold by the U.S. The impact of all this at home might have to be softened by varying industry items, keeping some domestic capability and stretch-outs in purchases.

The best and quickest answer I got from the Secretary was in reply to my question on continued funding for the commissaries. The current defense budget provides for continuing the subsidy. So unless the Senate moves to cut it out this year, we should be spared that annual battle.

The last question that I posed pertained to the recommended expenditures for civil defense. I reminded the Secretary that we were spending less on that than for one B-1 bomber. "Well, that's still a lot of money," he answered. He said that the Soviet plans were not so fully developed as to guarantee safety from an American attack, and that our best hope lay in our own strategic forces. Jack Brinkley took up the question when he was recognized and pressed Brown even further, citing recent studies of what the Russians have done. Brown said that he would review it, but I have the feeling that his promise was only lip service. Any real initiative will have to come from the Congress.

Since a vote on whether to fund a fourth nuclear carrier of the *Nimitz* class was to come on Thursday, along with putting Aegis aboard the *Long Beach*, in the Third Concurrent Resolution on the Budget for FY '77, a number of the Members pushed the Secretary hard on a decision to cancel both projects. Brown gave the same reply that I had gotten from Secretary of the Navy Claytor a couple of weeks ago. He said that it all boiled down to a subjective judgment on whether it was better to build another large attack carrier for over a billion dollars or go ahead for two smaller ones from which V/STOL aircraft could operate. He repeated what I had heard from Claytor, that there would be some cases where the nuclear carrier and its attending strike force would be needed and others where the small carrier would fill the role.

As for the *Long Beach*, he simply felt that it was a mistake to make that kind of an investment on a ship that would be twenty years old by the time the work was done and the vessel was back in the fleet. His preference was to place Aegis on the destroyer designed for that purpose, the DDG-47. Nor did Brown show much enthusiasm for the nuclear strike cruiser which has been proposed as the platform for the Aegis.

All of these decisions are fundamental ones which will affect the path our Navy will be taking from now until the end of the century. Clearly, the oppressive costs of shipbuilding have overtaken the planning, if not the thinking, in the Defense Department. To be sure, the development of cruise missiles, which pose a grave threat to surface forces, has also influenced these decisions. But I think that it is the shrinking dollar that has been the principal factor in terminating the line of nuclear carriers. Brown is right about one thing: it is a subjective judgment. With the cost of oil bound to rise again, and the cruising constraints on a conventionally-powered ship, the decision to go back to oil-burning carriers, albeit smaller ones, may not prove to be so wise. Nor is placing Aegis on the DDG-47 without peril. A number of the Members and staffers have voiced fears over the vulnerability of this ship. In giving up weight to the Aegis system, aluminum has been substituted for steel in many critical places. Again, such a ship must be refueled frequently, especially if driven at high speeds.

I think that what disturbed many of the Members about the Secretary's decision was the knowledge that the design of a new carrier, to say nothing of a new V/STOL plane, will take years, thus delaying deployment into the fleet of needed air strength until the late 1980s, or even the 1990s.

All of these new arguments were raised on Thursday, when the House debated an amendment by Bill Chappell of Florida to restore the funds for the fourth nuclear carrier. But they were for naught. The amendment was beaten decisively, while the move to put funds in for the conversion of the *Long Beach* went down by an even wider margin. I voted for both, although I was less enthusiastic about the *Long Beach*.

The House took up the Ethics Bill on Wednesday afternoon, struggling with it until nearly 10:00 that night. Most of the attention was focused on the title relating to the limit on outside earned income. It brought the Speaker out of the stable, and Tip took the floor to bring all of his forensic powers to bear, as well as the not-so-subtle influence of his office, to get his people in line. Using the recent pay raise, for which he had taken most of the heat, as a club, he reminded the Members that the nation expected that the Congress would now remove any incentives for seeking additional remuneration beyond a modest amount over their salaries.

While I am unaffected by the limit, since I have no other source of income outside of a few small honoraria each year, I can well understand the resentment of a number of the Members at this restriction. For one thing, I don't believe that the shortcomings of this body have often been the result of non-Congressional enterprises. We may well preclude some highly qualified people from becoming candidates because of this move. Nevertheless, I was not so strong in my convictions that I felt that I should vote against the bill. Like most of my colleagues, I obeyed the herd instinct, especially after the margin on the board grew to such lopsided proportions. So now we have an Ethics Bill. After the Senate acts, we'll put the two together, but I have the feeling that we are going to succeed in raising the level of self-harassment without really changing our character.

On Friday my Committee heard from the new Secretary of the Army, Clifford Alexander, Jr. As the first black appointed to this position, he has gotten a little more publicity than appointees would normally receive. Aside from whatever image it gives the Carter Administration, he showed that his appointment was not a mistake. There was little of the abrasiveness that marked some of the interrogation of Harold Brown, and Alexander offered a generally optimistic picture of the Army. While there are some significant shortcomings, especially in equipment, the trends are favorable. Vice Chief of Staff General Walter Kerwin, Jr., accompanied the Secretary, and I raised the roles and missions issue that had been the subject of discussion in the R&D Subcommittee earlier in the week. General Kerwin defended the current arrangement, which didn't surprise me, but he didn't object to my suggestion that a thorough review by our Committee might be helpful. I may be wrong, but I can't help but believe that the Army stubbornly holds on to its relationship with the Air Force for fear that any departure from it might jeopardize its helicopter option.

Monday, March 7, 1977—Sunday, March 13, 1977

An uneventful week, this one, unless one happened to be among the unlucky who were at the B'nai B'rith Headquarters, the Islamic Center, or the District Building when the Hanafi Muslims arrived, weapons in hand, for an armed takeover on Wednesday. There is certainly no point in recapitulating all of that here. It ended, fortunately, with the lives, if not the nerves, of the hostages intact. The death of a young reporter and the wounding of other innocents either by gunfire, knives, or beating at the outset of it all lent credence to the threats of the terrorists. Nothing else in this town could compete with this distraction, whose ripple effect lapped against the high and low, official and unofficial alike. Whether you were a harassed commuter forced to detour around

234

the roadblocks that cordoned off the besieged areas, or the British prime minister, obliged to be received on the White House lawn without the customary nineteen-gun salute (for fear of triggering more serious shooting a few blocks away), the presence of armed terrorists in the heart of the city was manifest. The Hill, of course, was not immune either. The legislative schedule was shortened, so that the Members rapidly concluded the nation's business early Thursday afternoon, prudently putting the abrasive Rhodesian chrome question over until the following week. All of this was to the relief of the Capitol police, who earned some unsought overtime by doing double duty manning the House Office Buildings in extra strength. Someone quipped that the Hanafis had a better sense of priorities than to seize a portion of this maligned body. With the outrage still sputtering over the pay raise, the terrorists would have been encouraged to do their worst.

We began the week by driving up to Richmond on Monday to attend a kickoff luncheon for John Dalton's campaign to become the next Governor of Virginia. It was held at the venerable John Marshall Hotel, which has hosted more political functions and pow-wows than any other hostelry in the state. There was a pretty fair attendance. Over 550 showed up, including the Governor, who introduced John; four of the six Republican congressmen from Virginia; and three aspirants for Bill Scott's Senate seat; Dick Obenshain; Linwood Holton, our last Governor; and John Warner, whose commendable record as head of the American Revolution Bicentennial Administration, and before that as Secretary of the Navy, has been totally overshadowed by his most recent exploit, his marriage to Elizabeth Taylor. They flew in from Washington with my House colleagues, arriving shortly after the luncheon had begun. Neither John Dalton nor Mills Godwin caused the rubbernecking in that ballroom that Liz Taylor did. Political audiences are seldom sophisticated, even Virginia Republicans. Those faithful who had plunked down $25 apiece for gravy-laden hamburger were obviously determined to get more for their money than indigestion and an earful of conservative rhetoric. They did. There is an awful lot of Liz Taylor. A beauty in her youth, she has suffered from the propensity of many women in their forties. In a word: she is fat. Nevertheless, if she has not shed any pounds, neither has she lost her magnetism. Throughout the speech-making, the audience stared alternately at her and at the speakers.

Janie and I drove back to Washington in the middle of the afternoon, arriving in time to sign all of the mail and clear off our desks. There was a reception in the Rayburn Building, sponsored by the Virginia Association of Housing and Community Development officials. In the past, they have hosted a breakfast, using the occasion to make a pitch for a generous portion of the federal housing funds for urban development. In the thought that a cocktail reception might bring out more of the Members, they tried the new format. It was a disaster. What they had not counted on was the novelty of an open bar for those of their own number who make this annual pilgrimage to Washington regarding it as an oasis in the desert of the mundane routine in their own cities. For congressmen, a late afternoon cocktail reception is about as exciting as a second dish of breakfast oatmeal. I counted two of my colleagues present, plus several staffers. The rest represented the lobby itself. The euphoria of two days away from their offices and the free booze (the reception having been charged to their urban contingency funds) was too much.

The presentation by their officers to persuade us of the need to secure adequate funding to prevent further urban decay in the Commonwealth was lost in a babble of voices, laughing, and general good humor which made the program itself a distraction rather than the focus of attention. My own role was limited, albeit necessary. Someone has to act as an official host in order to reserve the room. That was my fate, which meant that I was obliged to remain throughout the affair. I managed to keep a straight face afterward by suggesting that it might be more effective if they scheduled individual appointments next year with the Members in their offices. The party could be held afterward without any interruptions.

Monday, May 2, 1977—Tuesday, May 3, 1977

Things are back to normal this week, with nothing earthshaking in the House so far, although we'll have a go at the Budget Resolution again either tomorrow (Wednesday) or Thursday. There have been a few minor suspensions, and today I voted against the Public Works Jobs Bill for the umpteenth time; this time it was the conference report.

My Subcommittee on Military Installations and Facilities met yesterday to mark up the Military Construction Authorization Bill. We managed to get through most of it in about two and one-half hours, and will probably end up a little lower than the recommended budget figure offered by the Defense Department. We had the inevitable add-ons by several Members to consider after we had covered the line items. In fact, most of these Members appeared before us one morning last week to make a personal pitch for their pet projects. Although he has been deposed as chairman of the Appropriations Subcommittee on Military Construction, Bob Sikes showed up and submitted ten additional projects for authorization. That showed real cheek, or perhaps he believes that his clout lingers on. When we reached his add-ons, a self-conscious chuckle went through the Subcommittee. Lou Nedzi, our chairman, asked us that our pleasure was. The first group dealt with projects at the Naval Air Station at Pensacola. I can't remember now what each one pertained to, or the total figure, but it was substantial. One was listed as a "Survival Training Facility" for over $2 million. Another was for a chapel addition, and another, an enlisted men's club. The only thing we approved was the purchase of some land near one of the landing fields, for less than half a million dollars. With some lingering respect for Sikes' former power, I tentatively raised the possibility of authorizing the Survival Training Facility. After all, that sounded as if it would be important for training naval aviators. "Just what is it?" I asked the staff. It turned out to be a euphemism for a gymnasium. When he started listing basketball and squash courts and a swimming pool, I suggested that we rename the House gym and call it a Survival Traning Facility. That ended any further discussion, and we ended up approving only the land purchase, knowing that it was vital as a noise zone. We then turned to five projects at Tyndall Air Force Base. Sikes did a little better there, picking up support on a motion by Jack Brinkley which was seconded by me for construction of a technical center costing in excess of $3 million. That plus a minor facility was the sum of his acquisitions. A year ago, he would have gotten at least half of his requests. "The king is dead, long live the king," Nedzi muttered to me. "He didn't do too badly," I said. "I haven't brought up any add-ons at all." Robin Beard heard me. "You don't need any," he said. "You can't squeeze anything else into Norfolk anyway."

The full Armed Services Committee met today to hear requests from the Navy and Air Force for some reprogramming of funds. Everything went their way until the end, when Admiral Turner requested some minor reprogramming of funds for the CVV, the new aircraft carrier to succeed the Nimitz line. Although the sum asked for was small, the proposal to build a conventionally-powered ship with limited capability touched a raw nerve on the Committee, especially after we had fought unsuccessfully to secure approval of a fifth nuclear carrier earlier this year. The proposed ship is somewhat larger than the Essex class of World War II. Its speed is less than thirty knots, which is totally inadequate to modern carrier task force operations. It has only two elevators, which would make it very vulnerable to enemy action, and it lacks sufficient ability to protect itself from enemy weapons. This plus its dependence on oil would make it an unsatisfactory follow-on to the nuclear carriers we have been building. The cost will run between $1.2 and $1.3 billion, or about $.6 to $.7 billion less than the Nimitz nuclear vessels. It just doesn't make any sense. Adding the cost of fuel oil, in the long run it would be better to go with the current nuclear carriers, which can carry more planes and sail indefinitely.

The Navy, of course, would also prefer to continue to build the Nimitz class ships, but failing in that they want some new seagoing platforms for their aircraft. They didn't get one today. Bob Wilson, Sam Stratton, Charlie Wilson, and I lit into them for coming up with a vessel which I described as a "step backward." When the vote was called for, it went down. I'm not sure what will happen now. It may be that the Navy will now reapply pressure within the Defense Department in an attempt to refloat the nuclear carrier concept. Whether or not the Administration will buy that is another matter.

Not too much doing during this period, although the House did pass the First Budget Resolution the second time around. That happened on Thursday. Although a valiant effort was made by some of our people on the Armed Services Committee to have the Burleson Amendment adopted again, restoring the money cut from defense, it failed. The Budget Committee had come back with a "compromise," putting back about $1 billion of the $4 billion that they had originally cut. The Democratic Leadership then did a thorough lobbying job with their Whips to get their people in line, and it worked. Some subsequent moves to set the figure first at $119 billion and then at $118 billion also failed. Any hope of further restoration rests with the Senate at conference. I hope that they stand firm, because the conferees from our side will be loaded with liberals of Giaimo's ilk.

The only other major piece of legislation passed by the House during the week was the Foreign Relations Authorization Act. That came up on Wednesday, and since we didn't go into session until 3:00 p.m., we stayed here until 7:30 before passing it. We got into the usual fracas over whether or not any funds in the bill would be used to negotiate away our rights in Panama, but managed to retain the compromise language proposed by John Buchanan last year, protecting our "vital interests." All of the rhetoric uttered on this subject is totally superfluous, since once the new treaty is negotiated, it will have to be approved by the Senate anyway.

As a result of remaining in session into Wednesday evening, we had an opportunity to watch the first half of the Nixon-Frost interview. There is a television set in the Republican lounge which normally gets little attention from the Members, but on Wednesday night the place was jammed. All of the chairs were filled, and those who weren't standing sat on the floor. There were the expected wry comments before Nixon and Frost appeared. "Son of Watergate," Jack Kemp called it. It brought back a lot of painful memories for most of us. Bill Gradison of Cincinnati swore a soft oath and said he would not have lost his first try for his seat in 1974 had it not been for the scandal. Nixon came off poorly in the exchange with Frost. The media the next day were practically unanimous on this. So were the Republican Members in the lounge Wednesday night. I didn't hear or see the last half of the program and thus didn't witness Nixon's plea at the end that he had let the nation down. But what I did see made it clear that he was guilty of dissembling in his answers.

We were here for about half a day on Friday. The House took up the Rule and general debate only on the Housing and Community Development Act of 1977. There being only a vote on the Rule, we were able to leave shortly after noon for home. The weekend, such as it was, was busy but not exceptional. I had office appointments in Norfolk on

Saturday morning, opened the Little League Baseball season in Kemps-ville in Virginia Beach in the afternoon, and attended a Republican fund-raiser banquet with John Dalton as the speaker that night. This morning (Sunday), I spoke at a Mother's Day ceremony at a nursing home in Virginia Beach, a rather depressing affair. Sitting listlessly in the dining room, the frail old women and few men present sat mute while I recited the needs of older Americans (as if they needed me to remind them of what they were). To mark the occasion, each had been pinned with a pink carnation, a well-meant gesture by the management but which only seemed to compound their sadness. The few who had relatives present reflected what little joy there was. At the conclusion of my remarks, I was asked if I would present a special flower to the oldest person in the home, a little black lady in a wheelchair. Ninety-five and senile, she was rolled forward by three of her children. But the recognition of her longevity did not move her. I gave the flowers to her daughter and leaned over to gently kiss the face of her mother, who had remained asleep through it all, her chin resting on her chest.

We drove back to Arlington this afternoon and then in to the office this evening to sign the mail from Friday and prepare for the coming week's events.

Thursday, June 30, 1977

The last day of business before the July 4 recess, and the House managed to spend it wisely, finishing up the Defense Appropria-tions Bill. I did not stay for much of the debate, preferring instead to wind up all of the business on my desk so that I could leave it clear before our departure.

The big news of the day was the President's announcement that he had decided not to go into production of the B-1, a decision that came as a surprise to nearly everyone. The general feeling was that he would permit a partial buy, perhaps over a hundred of the aircraft, but not the 244 that had been planned originally. The next move of the Congress will occur when he sends us a rescission request. If the Congress refuses it, which is unlikely, at least in the Senate, the President can still stall and wait for another opportunity to kill the funding.

My own feeling is that he is making a mistake. The Russians are sure to continue building the Backfire while we continue to rely on the B-52, some of which are over twenty years old. Carter did say that increased attention would be given to the cruise missile. I would hope so, even though that weapon will not give us the capability of the B-1. No one can say that they weren't forewarned. Carter said during his campaign that the B-1 shouldn't be built.

Tonight at the Chinese Liaison Office, we sat with Bob and Shirley Wilson and Sam Stratton discussing it. Sam had his B-1 necktie on, a gift from either Boeing or Rockwell, a blue tie with B-1 silhouettes on it.

"You wore it in vain, Sam," I said, "he still killed the buy." Sam agreed, and said he should be wearing a mourning band on it. Carter's decision was supposed to be the best-kept secret in Washington. Neither Byrd in the Senate nor O'Neill in the House knew about it beforehand. Somebody got the message, however, because Rockwell stock opened two points lower on the New York Stock Exchange this morning before Carter even made the announcement.

The reception at the Chinese Liaison Office was heavily attended this evening, even though a lot of Members had already left the city. Many of the people there were from the State Department, and several sat at our table. The dining room featured a long table groaning with Chinese dishes which the guests attacked voraciously. I chatted with Madame Shen briefly. Ever the little steel bird, she asked me what I thought about Carter's decision on the B-1. I confessed to disappointment. She pressed me on the course the Congress would take, and I replied that the battle wasn't completely over, although the President was likely to have his way.

Thursday, July 14, 1977

We had a full house at the Armed Services Committee meeting this morning to hear General Brown, the Chairman of the Joint Chiefs, testify. While the subject was supposed to be the President's decision to withdraw U.S. ground forces from South Korea, the Members pressed the general on the B-1 decision, the killing of two U.S. officers at Panmunjom last year, and even the war in South Vietnam. General Brown was clearly nettled by it, and made some wry asides. His temper wasn't improved by Sam Stratton, who presided at the hearing and gave Brown a hard time about the opinions of the field officers on the Korean decision being withheld from the Committee. I felt that Sam badgered the general unnecessarily about the communications system, implying that it was being used improperly. At length, Brown said that he would meet with the Committee counsel and go over the messages that were pertinent to see which ones might be made available.

We then got into discussions on the ability of the South Koreans to defend themselves, the repercussions of our own withdrawal, and the failure of the Joint Chiefs to have their own decisions prevail with the Commander-in-Chief. I regarded much of it as superfluous. Larry McDonald got the worst of an exchange with Brown. Citing Brown's own convictions about the troop withdrawal and the B-1, plus an earlier statement that he would always feel badly that we had never used all of our resources in Vietnam, Larry asked him why he and other top-ranking officers didn't resign in the face of these unpopular decisions. By this time, Brown was nearly out of patience, and he looked at Larry and said that he had always been trained to obey civilian leadership, that it was ingrained in him since he had been at West Point. Furthermore, he added, he didn't believe that his resignation would have any more of an effect upon the decision to withdraw our troops from Korea "than if you resigned from this Committee." The audience and the committee broke into laughter.

At the end of the questioning on the troop withdrawal, we went into executive session to hear General Brown brief us on the incident of last night when an American helicopter strayed into North Korean airspace and was shot down with the loss of three men and capture of a fourth. There is a disposition from the President down to remain calm about it.

Monday, July 18, 1977—Tuesday, July 19, 1977

Although I made no mention of it in this journal, the increasing attention and revelations regarding the activities of Tongsun Park and other Korean lobbyists is making larger and larger waves in the House. For several months, the House Ethics Committee has had the matter under investigation but has made little progress. The press and a number of younger House Members have charged that Jack Flynt, the chairman, is deliberately dragging his feet. This past weekend, the chief counsel of the Committee resigned in protest over the delays and failure to follow up on the specific suggestions that he had made to push forward with the investigation.

The newspapers, however, have shown no reticence. I have received calls from reporters from the *Washington Post,* as well as from others at home and also from the *Richmond Times-Dispatch,* asking me if I received money from or had any contact of any kind with Park or the other Koreans. Fortunately I have been able to reply in the negative. The Ethics Committee circulated a questionnaire to every Member, asking pretty much the same questions and even whether or not we had visited South Korea and under what circumstances. However, responding to the questionnaire was put on a voluntary basis, so one may assume that only those who had no dealings with the Koreans will reply.

While both Democrats and Republicans have been recipients of Park's donations, the preponderance of Members involved come from the Democratic side. Still, my personal feeling is that while many of them showed poor judgment in accepting contributions from a foreign national, it does not necessarily follow that they agreed to influence legislation as a result of receiving the money. The same would hold true for contributions made by a union or a business group to a campaign fund. I talked to Floyd Spence this afternoon about this. He's a member of the Ethics Committee and has been badgered for the last few weeks by reporters seeking information on the investigation. I told Floyd that I doubted that it could be proven that anyone had agreed to provide some service or a vote, although acceptance of a large donation might presume some friendly inclination toward South Korea. Still, stranger things have happened around here, and I may be premature in making such a charitable judgment.

Last night we attended a private screening of the film "MacArthur," at the Motion Picture Association headquarters at 1600 I Street NW. We were the guests of the president of the association, Jack Valenti, and the showing was preceded by cocktails and a buffet supper. The approximately fifty guests included Members of the House and Senate Armed Services Committees and some high-ranking officers from the Air Force. It wasn't a bad film, although a little long at two and one-half hours. What was distracting was the running commentary in back of me by Scoop Jackson of Washington. He kept telling his wife about each campaign and identifying the major characters as they appeared. He talked as though he had been on MacArthur's staff, but I suspect that his role in World War II was just about as significant as mine.

This evening we attend a dinner party at the quarters of Admiral James Holloway, the Chief of Naval Operations. The dinner is in honor of Rear Admiral Joseph Barkai, Chief of Staff of the Israeli Navy. Several Israeli naval personnel will be in attendance, along with some of our senior officers and defense officials. Janie and I are the only political ingredients, and a literary flavor will be provided by the presence of Herman Wouk, the author, and his wife. Having read *The Caine Mutiny* and *The Winds of War,* I am rather curious to meet him.

Wednesday, July 20, 1977

The weather continues to be hot and humid, and the air stagnation level in Washington is reflected in the smog that envelops the city in a suffocating blanket. At the Carter White House family picnic this evening, those congressmen and senators who came directly from the Hill quickly shed their coats and loosened their ties. Unfortunately, little relief appears to be in sight.

The picnic itself was not nearly the mob scene that I had thought it might be. Someone said that the Carters have scheduled three of them for the Members and their families, which would explain the moderate-sized crowd. The large outdoor stage that was erected several weeks ago for the concert entertaining Helmut Schmidt was still in place. This evening, the fare was pure country culture, with a heavy accent on Georgia. Not even the heat diminished the enthusiasm of the square dancers. Most of the guests, however, paid little heed to the activities on the stage, but occupied themselves instead with the food and drink: frankfurters, hamburgers, cole slaw, and baked beans, washed down by either iced tea or the Georgia national drink, Coca-Cola. Bob Bauman arrived with his family, looking absolutely wilted by the heat, and when Janie told him that in the absence of Billy Carter there was no beer, he retorted, "Why do you think I worked so hard to elect the other guy?"

The President, in a cocoon of news- and cameramen, moved about the grounds, taking time to watch his daughter Amy in a free-style volleyball game with some other children and several of the Washington Redskins. A magician was warming up at another spot on the grounds, so there was something for everyone.

Insulated as he was by the ubiquitous newspeople, who could easily double as a bodyguard, the President was impossible to get near, so Janie and I didn't even try to penetrate that cordon to shake the President's hand but settled instead on a brief but personal chat with Mrs. Carter. She is attractive and has a natural friendliness.

I overheard several of my colleagues in the House today say that they weren't going to bother to attend the picnic, but I think that those of us who did go rather enjoyed it. There were clowns and balloons for the children, and an 1890 pipe organ to generate a festive air, yet it wasn't the kind of unintentional circus we've been exposed to elsewhere in this city. So I ate my initial words of reservation about the picnic along with the President's hamburger.

Last night's engagement was totally different, but a delightful and stimulating evening. The Holloways are excellent hosts. Janie noticed how Jim and Dabney moved among their guests to insure that no couple was left alone or isolated with one person. As a result, we enjoyed conversations with all of the Israeli visitors, and I had an interesting and extended discussion with Admiral Barkai, a slight, bearded, animated man. Born in Romania, he came to Israel in 1948 at the age of thirteen. Now he commands their small, but highly effective, navy.

At the dinner table I had the opportunity to talk with Herman Wouk. I complimented him on his historical research in providing the backdrop for *The Winds of War*. He said that he knew he had engaged in historical license in placing his principal character at so many major scenes, but declared that that was an author's privilege. Someone spoke up to say that it wasn't totally impossible, that Chip Bohlen had been a witness to a remarkable number of major events. I asked Wouk if he was going to write a sequel to *The Winds of War*. He replied that he had almost completed it. He expects to have it out by late next year. "And what will be the title of it?" I asked. "I don't know," he replied. "I haven't thought of one yet." And then he went on to say that he didn't settle on the title, *The Winds of War*, until he had the galley proofs of the book. He said that he came up with about forty possibilities, none of which his wife liked, until he settled on the final one. He is an entertaining conversationalist and showed a quick wit, which is not too surprising, because he told us that he had been a gag writer for Fred Allen, the radio comedian of forty years ago, an unusual beginning for a man who has achieved success as a writer of historical fiction.

In between these two social events, I managed to put in a day for the taxpayers. The House spent most of the afternoon on the Agriculture Bill, and it looks as though we'll be at it all day tomorrow, and possibly even Friday. Next week is also heavy, and the week after has been blocked off for the Energy Bill. I learned today that the Speaker has scheduled a noon to 8:00 p.m. session every day in order to complete it before the recess begins on Friday evening, August 5, and he's threatened to hold us here until the middle of August if we don't finish it by the 5th. Shades of Sam Rayburn, but this place needs a prod.

Thursday, September 8, 1977

The House met at 10:00 this morning and spent the day on the Defense Appropriations Conference Report and the Second Concurrent Budget Resolution. It was a day of drama and some close votes. Anyone who believed that the B-1 was a dead bird got a surprise when Joe Addabbo offered an amendment to adopt the Senate language to void the funds for the B-1 as the President wished and use the money for other aircraft procurement and cruise missile development. For awhile, the B-1 was revived. The same spirited arguments were made that we heard earlier this year. When the vote was called for, the feeling even on the part of the supporters of the B-1 was that it would lose, but when the time had expired for voting, it was tied at 197 apiece. There was a scramble in the well, with Tip O'Neill doing some arm-twisting. In the end the Democratic Leadership found enough votes, and the amendment carried by three votes. We had some key people missing: Jack Kemp, Shirley Pettis, Jimmy Quillen, and Bill Ketchum were absent. With their votes, we could have carried the day. Ketchum in particular will be hard-pressed to explain his absence. He has several thousand workers from his district in California employed at the Rockwell plant. It was a tough one to lose; I say this because the Air Force, which always wanted the B-1, is now making a pitch to the Armed Services Committee to authorize the development and construction of a stretch version of the FB-111 as a substitute bomber to penetrate Soviet air defenses. There are strong indications that we will end up spending as much, or almost as much, on this plane, which will have neither the range nor the capability of the B-1.

This afternoon, General Slay, head of Air Force R&D, was before our committee to testify on behalf of this option and to fill us in on cruise missile development. He had the misfortune to appear within an hour after the B-1 vote in the House. Charlie Wilson of California, who shares Rockwell International with Ketchum, was on hand and vented his spleen on the general. He took him to task for not having the Air Force make a stronger effort on behalf of the B-1, telling him that if the Air Force had not run "at the first shot," they would have carried the day in the House. Frankly, I think that Charlie is right. After Carter came out against the B-1, the Air Force frantically looked around for an alternate and immediately began promoting the stretched FB-111. Charlie scorned that, asking Slay, "Well, what have you got? A nose and a tail and nothing else. You've got to fill in with a new fuselage and a completely new avionics system, as well as adapt the B-1's F-101 engine to it." General Slay lamely replied that they also had the wings of the

244

FB-111 which they could use. That prompted some wry chuckles. Not surprisingly, Sam Stratton got in some licks, too. I noticed that he was wearing his B-1 necktie again, but his talisman failed him today.

Later in the afternoon, the House considered the Second Budget Resolution. Smarting from the unwillingness of the government in Seoul to send Tongsun Park back to the United States, Bruce Caputo of New York, the Republican gadfly on the Ethics Committee, offered an amendment to make substantial cuts in aid to South Korea. It lost by twenty-four votes, but it was interesting to see the split among the Members. Liberals and conservatives were on both sides of the issue. I voted No, feeling that denying aid to South Korea doesn't serve American interests. Furthermore, I haven't seen a nation yet that reacts to such tactics except with hostility. An amendment by Andy Jacobs that would have made an even bigger cut was rejected even more decisively.

Thursday, October 6, 1977— Tuesday, October 11, 1977

With the House adjourned for the Columbus Day recess on Friday and Monday, there is little to record for this period. On Thursday, the House completed work on the Labor Reform Act and some minor legislation, and we were able to leave for home early in the afternoon. Today was also light, with general debate only on a couple of bills, all of which leads me to believe that we are going to be here until the middle of November. There is a minor logjam making up, and it is bound to be compounded by the House and Senate energy bills, which are miles, indeed light years, apart. Resolving them will take the wisdom of Solomon and the patience of Job. Theoretically, our leaving here was supposed to hinge on Tip's having his prostate operation. That was to have occurred this week, but we're still here. So the legislative process goes on, and one can assume that the Speaker continues to piss.

I had a full time of it at home: two speeches on Friday, a breakfast with the Home Builders in the morning, and a luncheon with the Boy Scout executives at noon. On Saturday, Janie and I had appointments at my Beach office; then attended a Lions District luncheon in Norfolk at which I introduced Paul Trible; then went on to a punt, pass, and kick contest in Virginia Beach, where I handed out the trophies to the winning youngsters; and finally ended the evening with a speech to a dinner meeting of Merchant Marine Academy alumni. It was a long day. On Sunday morning I drove over to the Bide-A-Wee golf course in Portsmouth to participate in the opening ceremonies of the World Seniors Golf Championship Match. I had thought that a steady rain might bring a postponement, but I had forgotten how tenacious golf aficionados can be. Besides the two contenders, Boros of the U.S. and O'Connor of Ireland, there were some 300 spectators on to splash from hole to hole with them. I left after the playing of the national anthems.

We attended a breakfast for Joe Canada, the Republican candidate for lieutenant governor, on Monday morning in Norfolk. Over a hundred showed up, and Joe gave what I feel was his best speech to date. It reflected a maturing on the hustings, a honing of his political talents. Unfortunately, he's running against a chap with unlimited funds, Chuck Robb, LBJ's son-in-law. Joe has neither the money nor the name identification to compete with the challenger, especially when Lady Bird, Luci, and Lynda are all stumping the state on Robb's behalf. He told me privately that his chances are slim, but he has managed to shave Robb's edge some. I think that the best he can hope for is a respectable showing. On the other hand, he said that he believes that Henry Howell has peaked and that John Dalton will come on to win. The flap over the cancellation of the debates has died, and John seems to be picking up strength from many of the uncommitted voters. The Governor and I are co-hosting a breakfast at $10 a head at Omni in Norfolk on Friday morning, November 4. It is more a rally of support for John than a fund-raiser. We are issuing a jointly-signed letter this week. It ought to draw at least a thousand people and maybe more.

Wednesday, October 19, 1977—
Monday, October 24, 1977

The four-day recess enabled us to catch up on some personal business at home with time left over to relax as well. It is pretty certain now that the Congress will conclude regular business on November 4, leaving the House and Senate conferees in Washington to resolve the differences in the Energy Bill. Once they have done that, we will then come back for a vote on passage. None of the conferees are particularly happy about this arrangement, but they just don't have much choice. I told Bill Steiger, one of our conferees, that they ought to pay him time and a half for this assignment. "I wouldn't have it for time and a half," he grumbled.

We had a busy time of it the last two days before adjourning. My Military Installations and Facilities Subcommittee met on Wednesday morning to hear from the director of the Defense Civil Preparedness Agency, Bardyl R. Tirana. He asked us not to pass Jack Brinkley's bill, because they are in the process of overhauling the agency now. The reorganization plans will be presented early next year. For us to mandate additional duties in the form of responsibility for natural disaster to localities would muddy their own efforts. I'm not sure that the bill would interfere that much, but I can understand why Tirana and his organization prefer no congressional action until the plan has been reviewed.

The full Committee met on Thursday afternoon to hear from General Brown, Chairman of the Joint Chiefs, on the Panama Canal treaties. We had a fraction of the Members present, most of them having gone over to the House to listen to and participate in the debate on the effort to restore funds for the B-1 in the Supplemental Appropriations Bill. About a half dozen of us stuck around to hear General Brown, and even that number had declined before the meeting ended. Not surprisingly, Larry McDonald came on like a locomotive. There's no love lost between the two of them anyway, and both pull no punches in their exchanges. McDonald began by saying that he had conducted about 200 autopsies in his career as a physician but had never wanted to throw up so much as he had after reading Brown's statement. I saw the general's jaw muscles tighten, but he held his tongue. Later, he declared that he supported the treaties because he regarded the Canal as "the last vestige of colonialism" in this hemisphere. At that McDonald asked him what he regarded the U.S. Navy base as at Guantanamo Bay, Cuba. It was a telling thrust, and Brown tried to argue that the two properties were totally different. I thought that he got the worst of it. He was followed at the witness table by Congressman George Hansen of Idaho, who has been in the thick of the fight against the Canal treaties. He got wound up like a Baptist preacher, but he made some good points all the same. Had the rest of the Members been there, including the liberals, we would have had a lot more fireworks.

The debate over the Supplemental Appropriations Bill was very extensive, stretching from Wednesday to Thursday, and we are still not finished with it. The fight over the B-1 amendment wasn't concluded until late Thursday afternoon. There was a lot of jockeying, with the supporters determined to stay and force a vote rather than put the matter over until Tuesday of the following week. The Democratic Leadership was worried that it didn't have enough votes to kill the amendment and tried unsuccesfully to have the Committee of the Whole rise. Bob Michel and others on our side ran around arm-twisting Republican opponents of the B-1 to at least vote with us to stay in session until a vote could be taken. All of this strategy came to naught, however. Although the vote to rise was defeated, the vote on the Chappell Amendment to restore funds for the B-1 was negative by a margin of ten votes. There may be another attempt to save the airplane on Tuesday, when a motion to recommit the bill with instructions to restore the money will be offered. My guess is that it will lose, too, and that will be the death plunge for the B-1.

Thursday, October 27, 1977— Sunday, October 30, 1977

I had a most interesting visit from Ambassador Addou of Somalia on Friday morning. Not surprisingly, he was on a mission related to his country's desire to secure arms from the United States. What did surprise me was the degree of candor he manifested in sharing with me both the confidential messages he had received from Siad Barre, his

President, and the substance and tenor of the Russian response to Somali representatives.

Normally reserved and in control of his feelings, he made what amounted to a plea for help, the emotion and bitterness in his voice spilling out with his words. He began by reviewing the events that had transpired since their revolution eight years ago—the latent quarrel with Ethiopia which had led them to seek unsuccessfully a supply of arms from the West, how the Russian ambassador in Mogadishu had come forward and offered to fill their needs, and the reciprocal awarding of naval and communications facilities by the Somali government to the Soviets. He protested defensively that none of this would ever have occurred had the West been sympathetic to Somalia's needs, although he recognized that the U.S. had long been friendly with the old Emperor in Addis Ababa, Haile Selassie. The recent turn of events in Ethiopia had changed everything, he said. The overthrow of the monarchy and the assumption of power by Colonel Mengistu had led to persecution and oppression of Ethiopian minorities, in particular their Somali cousins in the Ogaden. Allowing for the fact that rule from Addis Ababa was seldom benevolent or enlightened, I thought that he was painting a pretty subjective picture. Nevertheless, few nations behave altruistically toward their neighbors, and Somalia's concern about the state of things in Ethiopia mixed with a little covetousness for the Ogaden is understandable. If Haile Selassie had still been on the throne, the Somalis would have gotten all the military equipment they wanted from the Russians, and the Ambassador would not have been baring his diplomatic soul in my office. Mengistu's professed Marxism made Ethiopia the newest candidate for the Soviet East African Club, and the fat was in the fire.

Listening to this summary of events, I couldn't help but smile inwardly at the political swindling in which nations indulge. The Russians, according to Addou, tried to pacify the Somalis by declaring grandly that they believed the solution to the Ethiopian-Somali quarrel was a confederation embracing not only their two countries but eventually all of East Africa, including the Sudan and Kenya. It was a scheme worthy of the late Cecil Rhodes. Marx and Lenin, who spent their careers fulminating against this very sort of thing, would have been mortified. The Somalis weren't taken in by any of this and rejected it out of hand. Now, declared Addou, the Russians are going to be told to get out of Berbera and the other facilities from which they've been operating in Somalia. When he told me this, I remembered my own visit to Berbera in the touchy two days we spent in that country in July 1975. My most vivid memory is the searing heat, with temperatures consistently over 100 degrees. They may be unhappy in Moscow when they get the word to go, but the Russians in Berbera will break out the vodka.

It is hardly surprising that with the loss of their chief arms supplier, the Somalis are now so desperate for another source. It is public knowledge that Carter has told the Somalis that we are not going to be a party to the conflict between them and the Ethiopians. Addou said that Vance had told his government that the U.S. would supply arms later. "We need the arms today, not tomorrow," he wailed. "If someone is dying of thirst, you don't tell him that you will give him a drink of water tomorrow." He sounded positively desperate, possibly because he confided that he had received several personal messages from Siad Barre himself to press their cause with us. And then he added, "Our representatives talked to Gromyko in New York, and he told us, 'The West will not help you. Sooner or later you will come on your knees to us.'"

"Did he really say that? Was he that coarse?" I asked.

"Yes, those were his words."

I felt constrained to tell the Ambassador that there was precious little that I could do to get him arms. He said that he knew that, but he had taken note of the fact that the Chairman of the House Armed Services Committee and a number of Members are due to visit Africa after the House adjourns. He asked me if I would press Mel Price to include Somalia in the itinerary. I said that I would be most happy to do so, and I emphasized that if Siad Barre could make his case with the delegation, he might generate enough support in the Congress to loosen up the Administration position. "Thank you, thank you, my good friend," he said, seizing my hand.

The truth is, I really don't blame Carter for not wanting to become embroiled in an East African dispute. However, I am also aware that if Soviet success in dominating that part of the world is to be thwarted, the U.S. can funnel some support, through the Saudis if necessary, to prop up the Somalis and stabilize them outside the Soviet orbit. The Soviet-dominated confederation is not so wild a dream if the West does nothing. Numeri of the Sudan has been sounding the alarm for the past year about Soviet efforts to penetrate and control East Africa. He would surely have seconded Addou's fears. The Saudis across the Red Sea are similarly concerned and have tried to woo the Somalis away from Russian influence for some time. The best opportunity appears to be at hand.

Thursday, November 3, 1977— Sunday, November 6, 1977

The major event on Thursday was the welcome extended by the House to Senator Hubert Humphrey. The Senate had already given him an emotional homecoming the week before, when Humphrey returned from cancer treatments in Minnesota, flying back to Washington on Air Force One as a guest of the President. Since his illness is terminal, both bodies wished to honor him not only while he is still alive but while he is able to be physically present. The House was jammed with Members and guests, and short speeches were made by Jim Wright, Mo

Udall, Paul Simon, and Yvonne Burke on the Democratic side, and by Bob Michel and Bill Frenzel on ours. For the most part, they were humorous, with some gentle ribbing and an affection that stopped short of being saccharine. The Senator enjoyed it all. At the end, he took the podium just below the Speaker and responded with an equal degree of humor and good will. How much longer he will live, no one can say. His hair is now white, and his weight loss is terribly visible, yet his color is good and his voice is strong.

We drove home Thursday night so that we would be able to attend the breakfast in honor of John Dalton at the Omni Hotel on Friday morning. That turned out to be a rousing success. About 1,000 people were in the dining room to hear principally from John and Governor Mills Godwin, with some short remarks from Mayor Vince Thomas and me. My pessimism of several weeks ago has diminished, and I am now cautiously optimistic about the outcome. A number of polls and mock elections in the area have been favorable to John. I think that he will carry Virginia Beach and lose Norfolk, with the Second District going for Henry Howell by 60 percent or less. Should that happen, John should make up the shortfall of votes elsewhere in the state and take the election. Tuesday's the day.

Monday, November 7, 1977— Sunday, November 13, 1977

John Dalton has been elected Governor of Virginia. The victory on Tuesday was a surprisingly easy one, made possible by an exceptional turnout, excellent organization by the Republicans, and a substantial assist by conservative Democrats. Mills Godwin's vigorous participation in the last few weeks gave the Dalton campaign the kind of momentum that every candidate hopes for on election day. I had despaired of John's chances in September after he cancelled his debates with Howell, but all of that gloom was dispelled in the week or two preceding the election. It was clear that Dalton had edged ahead. Furthermore, the steam seemed to go out of Henry's campaign. Virginia Beach went for Dalton, and Howell's margin in Norfolk was not as large as it had been four years ago when he ran against Mills. We were very pleased by the Republican showing here.

In addition to John's win, Marshall Coleman won the attorney general race. Joe Canada's loss to Chuck Robb was not unexpected, though Joe had kept his hopes up till the end. At least he carried his home city of Virginia Beach.

We are back in Washington, the House having reassembled today (Tuesday) for the purpose of passing a number of conference reports and receiving a progress report on the Energy Bill. That measure is proceeding at a snail's pace. Charlie Vanik, one of the conferees, observed wryly that we would have a Middle East peace before we got an agreement with the Senate. Meanwhile, the House Leadership is talking boldly about recessing at the end of this week and coming back on December 19 to take up the compromise Energy Bill. I haven't talked to anyone who believes that's going to happen. Bill Steiger, one of our Republican conferees, told me at lunch today that he doesn't think they will be finished then, and he really didn't know when the measure would be wrapped up. It could go well into next year.

As if that impasse weren't enough to keep us at odds with the other body, we deadlocked again today on the abortion amendment language. I stayed in the Chamber to listen to all of the debate, and was disposed to vote for the compromise. The language appeared to be as categorical as anyone could wish, but the opponents, led by Henry Hyde and Dan Flood, with a strong assist from Bob Bauman, exposed the loopholes that might be taken advantage of by physicians who favor abortion on demand. I thought that Bob Michel expressed it well when he noted that neither Califano, who heads HEW, nor the President favors abortions paid for by the government, and they would surely put restrictions in the regulations that would prevent widespread circumvention. If indeed large numbers of abortions occurred, we would have plenty of evidence next year before we took up the HEW Bill again, and we could write in tougher language at that time. But the language was rejected again, 205 Nays to 183 Yeas. I could have gone either way, but Paul Trible came up and urged me to go along with a No vote again. He said that he wasn't happy either, but felt that we ought to uphold the House position one more time. That means that we will have to pass another Continuing Resolution tomorrow to insure that the affected federal employees are paid the first of the month. This cannot go on indefinitely. Billions of dollars for funding for educational and other programs are being held up by this one issue.

I saw John Ford, chief counsel for the Armed Services Committee, yesterday, and he filled me in on the Africa trip by the chairman and those who accompanied him. I asked in particular about their visit with Siad Barre in Mogadishu. He said that the Russians had been expelled the day before they arrived. Furthermore, the Somalis vented their displeasure with the Russians by making them open their baggage at the airport and examining it thoroughly and minutely, as well as putting them through the time-consuming routine of filling out endless forms before they let them depart. It must have been pretty humiliating. But John said that Mel made no promises to Siad Barre. While it is well to have the Russians out, John declared that we need to move with caution in helping the Somalis. Acknowledging that the people in the Ogaden are akin to the Somalis, he pointed out that, nevertheless, the frontier lines that exist among the African states are those left by the old colonial boundaries, which were seldom drawn along ethnic lines. To insure stability, the Organization of Africa Unity (OAU) declared years ago that the old boundaries are inviolate, knowing that if this declaration was not made, many of the new states would be tempted to move against neighbors whose frontiers included ethnic minorities of their own population.

Thus, the OAU has looked askance at the Somali incursion into Ethiopia on behalf of the Ogaden rebels, even though many of the African states aren't particularly keen on Mengistu, the Ethiopian strong man. "Still, it would be a mistake to do nothing," I said. "Well, you're right," John replied, "but it ought to be done indirectly. The Saudis could put up the money, and the French make a good airplane, and the British a good tank. The Somalis could make their purchases from them."

"That's exactly what I told the Somali ambassador," I said.

I'm not sure what will follow out of all this, but at least for the time being the Soviets are out of Berbera. John added that the Somalis apparently found them just as galling as guests as the Egyptians had. They took their aid, but they did not suffer their presence gladly.

The rest of the trip was a success. They had meetings with Begin in Israel and Sadat in Cairo and served as an informal conduit for the exchange that led to Sadat's visit to Israel two weeks ago. They also called on several African leaders in Zambia, where they had breakfast with Kenneth Kaunda, and in Zaire with Mobutu, and finally a visit to the Ivory Coast.

Among my appointments this morning was Lin Holton, now actively seeking the Republican nomination for the U.S. Senate. I told him of my efforts to line up a number of key people in Virginia Beach among the Republican stalwarts there to assure him of carrying the Second District delegation at the convention in Richmond next June. He is going down later this week to make some converts on his own, and I encouraged him to call me when he got back to let me know if I could follow up for him. It is a laborious way to get a nomination, but it is the only way to lock up a convention ahead of time. Countless calls and flattering attention have to be paid to hundreds of party faithful, the lieutenants and spear-carriers who fill the convention delegations. Knowing that Lin must do this in nine other districts besides mine, I can appreciate his desire to go to the Senate. I am glad that I am not motivated to try for it. It's all that I can do to remember the names of key workers in the Second District. I shudder to think of trying to sort out the Republicans in the other nine.

Wednesday, November 30, 1977

Not much of a schedule today. There was a Republican conference in the morning, at which time Bud Brown took the floor to review the progress to date of the House-Senate conference on energy. A paper was handed out enumerating the points that have been resolved so far, but the big issues of deregulation of natural gas and the wellhead tax are far from settlement. Like Bill Steiger yesterday, Bud has little hope that the package will be ready for us before Christmas. What also rags our people is the fact that the Senate is not going to treat the final product as one bill, but five, in the same manner that they passed the segments in their body. Thus, five votes will occur in the Senate but only one in the House. Recalling what old Page Belcher of Oklahoma used to say about agriculture bills when they were before us, Bud said that we could apply Page's standards to the Energy Bill: it was always best to vote for an agriculture bill that was going to be defeated and not vote for one that was going to pass, because you could be certain that the farmers would always blame their troubles on the failure or passage of a bill, no matter what happened.

Friday, December 2, 1977— Wednesday, December 7, 1977

The abortion controversy has at last run its course. Late this afternoon (Wednesday), the House took up, for the second time during the day, compromise language, the key feature of which was the certification by two physicians that a woman's life would be imperiled, or that she would face severe prolonged physical health problems if she did not have an abortion. There was another clause allowing abortion for rape or incest when reported promptly to a law enforcement or public health service agency, but that didn't raise the questions that it has in the past.

For most of the Members, the battle had become one of semantics, and as such got a little preposterous. On Tuesday, the proposed amendment failed because some of the liberals teamed up with the anti-abortionists to kill language that some of the pro-abortionists thought was too restrictive. Earlier this afternoon, one word was removed from yesterday's language. Instead of abortion permitted for "forcible rape or incest," it became "rape or incest," the word "forcible" having been stricken. Most of the pro-abortionists got back on board, but the language failed by just seven votes. That prompted the leaders to go back and try again. The formula of two doctors was trotted out, and by this time enough Members were weary of the deadlock to go for it. It carried by 181-167. The Senate concurred an hour or so later, and the bill has gone to the White House to be signed into law. Thousands of employees of HEW across the country will breathe a collective sigh of relief tomorrow. Their paychecks will now be uninterrupted, at least until next October. Hopefully, we will not have a repeat performance then. I had a number of employees call me, and several weeks ago three girls who work in the Social Security office came to see me, to protest the anguish and uncertainty they were being put through. I assured them that they wouldn't miss a paycheck, but this afternoon I wasn't so sure.

Having broken ranks with the anti-abortionists in the House yesterday, I got a flurry of phone calls and telegrams today, pressing me to stand firm on the Hyde Amendment. They ranged from pleas to threats of political reprisal, yet those that I was able to answer personally, I succeeded in mollifying by making it clear that their position wasn't being completely sacrificed. The Catholic Bishop in Richmond, Bishop Sullivan, called me just prior to our second vote of the day. He had previously phoned Paul Trible, and gotten the same reply, that Paul and I, having been faithful to the Hyde Amendment until Monday, felt that the time had come to break the impasse, and in supporting the new House language, were not abandoning our conviction that the Federal government should not finance elective abortions.

The House, which reassembled itself after a long weekend, has been busy with assorted conference reports since Tuesday at noon. The B-1 has proven to be a phoenix arisen from the ashes and got a new lease on life late Tuesday in a House vote. There were a lot of absentees, including me because of my speaking engagement in Norfolk, but my vote wasn't needed. Bob Dornan put on a furious lobbying campaign, and it must have paid dividends.

Tuesday, December 13, 1977— Wednesday, December 14, 1977

My confidence in personally adjourning sine die was premature. Although we did indeed leave for home yesterday afternoon (Tuesday), we drove right back up today after hearing that the conferees had ended the deadlock on the Social Security Bill and will have it ready for consideration by both houses tomorrow. There is no chance that the energy measure will be finished before next year, however, so it really looks like a sine die adjournment tomorrow, with the Second Session due to convene on January 19.

Although the House has not been meeting these past two days, I have managed to stay busy. On Tuesday morning I had a number of callers, including Ambassador Addou of Somalia and one of the ministers from his country's cabinet. I got another earful of the most recent developments in East Africa. According to Addou and his colleague, the Russians are pouring in weapons for the Ethiopians. The latter are now starting to employ MiG fighters, two of which were shot down this week near Hargeisa in northern Somalia. When they told me this, I recalled our stopover there on the way to Berbera back in July

1975.

The Somali minister has obviously been sent here to bolster Addou's efforts to soften up the Carter Administration to supply Somalia with arms. They have already talked to Brzezinski and Vance. "What kind of reception did you get?" I asked.

"Brzezinski was sympathetic, but noncommittal," he replied.

"I'm not surprised. He advises, he doesn't make decisions."

They had also been to see Mel and Sam Stratton, both of whom were friendly and apparently more willing to see an arms delivery program instituted. They agreed that little could be done in the Congress until after we reassemble in January.

What really caught my attention was the account of the minister of his visit to Moscow several months ago, when the Somalis made a final attempt to dissuade the Russians from aiding the Ethiopians. The Soviets by that time had decided not to waste any amenities on the Somalis and bluntly told them that they were going "to teach them a lesson." They accused the Somalis of having "splashed water in their face in front of the Third World." From the accounts of the humiliating way the Russians were kicked out of Somalia in November, it appears that the Somalis did a lot more than splash them. They dunked the Russians' heads in the water.

Just what the Carter Administration will do remains to be seen, but I feel certain that some military aid from the West will be forthcoming. Only yesterday the Egyptians and Sudanese indicated their willingness to ally themselves with Somalia, and while that does not spell intervention in the war with Ethiopia, it surely could complicate matters for the Russians and Addis Ababa.

Thursday, December 15, 1977— Monday, December 19, 1977

This will probably be my last entry for 1977, since we are now home for the recess that will run until January 19, 1978. For the rest of the month, my time will be spent as it has in the other extended periods I have had in my district, with visits to the various Navy facilities, speeches, office appointments, and other meetings with constituents, plus some time with my family and friends.

On January 2, I will fly to New York to spend the night preparatory to flying to Europe the next day for an eight-day stay. I'm taking two staffers from my Subcommittee on Military Installations and Facilities with me to have a look at some dependent housing in Torrejon AFB, Spain, and some Army housing in Germany, with a side trip for myself to Hamburg and Kiel to see Captain Wiese and Captain Steindorff and some other German acquaintances. It should be interesting and will give me a breather from the mundane schedule that often marks a recess.

Our last day of the First Session was Thursday, December 15. The principal business was, of course, the Social Security conference report. I had had misgivings about my vote in favor of the measure when it passed the House some weeks ago, but decided to reserve judgment until I had had the opportunity to listen to all of the debate after we got it back from the Senate. My fears about the bill only deepened as I listened to the proponents and opponents make their arguments in the well.

The taxes represent the worst features of the bill. As the critics pointed out, they are the highest peacetime taxes ever levied in our history. Al Ullman was at pains to defend them and tried to make them more palatable by telling everyone that he hoped that before the burden of those taxes fell in the early 1980s, the Congress would be able to revise the law and find alternate resources of revenue. It seemed to me that he was whistling in the dark. Furthermore, he admitted that no new taxes would be levied next year. If that is the case, I wondered, why are we in such a hurry to pass this bill now? Why not wait until next year and explore those "alternate sources" rather than put such an onerous load on the backs of the American middle class which by statute would have to be assumed within three to four years? Ullman made much of the fact that this corrective action by the Congress would restore the financial health of the trust fund well into the next century, but Bill Ketchum came back with the argument that the formula for retaining solvency has been predicated on an inflation rate of no more than 4 percent. Anyone who believes that we will succeed in holding inflation to that figure just hasn't looked at the record for the last few years. The Congress, which has been the worst offender in busting the budget and adding to deficit financing, shows no signs of changing its ways. My guess is that long before this century is out, the trust fund will be in jeopardy again. The debt so long postponed is falling due. It is only a milestone along the road to the financial crisis that is our inevitable destination.

Bob Daniel and Ken Robinson joined me in switching our votes from Aye to No, but Paul Trible and Bill Wampler stuck with Harris and Fisher in support of the bill. The rest of the Virginia delegation were in the No column, but the bill passed comfortably and has gone to the President for his signature. Once that measure was out of the way, there was no other business to hold us, and the First Session was adjourned sine die. The Energy Bill becomes 1978 business.

The only other event of note that day was a visit from John Warner, the only major unannounced candidate for the Republican nomination for the U.S. Senate, Linwood Holton having gone public today (Monday), and Dick Obenshain a short time back. John would undoubtedly make an attractive nominee, with or without Liz Taylor. He has the looks, the poise, and the self-assuredness that are the marks of a good contender. On television he would be the most effective of anyone in either camp, but in spite of all this, I made it clear to him that I had made a commitment to Linwood Holton and could not break it.

He was philosophical about that and asked only that I not apply undue pressure on members of the local city committees on Linwood's behalf. I replied that I always made my views known but had never tried to force them on my supporters. He asked for the names of a number of key individuals in Norfolk and Virginia Beach who would hold the balance among the delegates from the Second District to the Republican convention next June. That convention could well end up in a three-way deadlock, which could make it the most interesting and dramatic Republican Convention in memory. I wouldn't miss it for all the tea in China.

Afterword

That Republican Convention proved to be every bit as exciting as I had anticipated. John Warner, with Liz Taylor beside him, brought the convention to its feet in a dramatic bid to win the Senate nomination. But the nod went to Dick Obenshain, an intelligent, articulate spokesman for conservatism.

Political fortunes have sometimes hinged on tragedy. Dick Obenshain's untimely death in an airplane crash revived Warner's political career. Chosen almost by default, he plunged into the Senate campaign against Andrew Miller and overtook him in a race that went down to the wire, the final outcome undetermined until a recount of the votes was completed after the election.

The same year, 1978, took me back to the Soviet Union for the first time since I had visited there as a tourist in 1966. This time, as part of a congressional delegation, I met with members of the Supreme Soviet and spent an afternoon with Marshal Ogarkov, chief of the Soviet General Staff, a man largely unknown in the West, seen only in the company of the dour leaders standing atop Lenin's Tomb on ceremonial occasions.

The ensuing years saw the triumphs and failures of the Carter Presidency, much of which I had an opportunity to view close up. On the Hill, I continued to gain seniority on the powerful Armed Services Committee, and I added a new dimension to my career through my appointment as a U.S. delegate to the North Atlantic Assembly, an organization of parliamentarians from all of the NATO countries. This gave me the opportunity to further expand my horizons and to build friendships and associations with my counterparts in such bodies as the House of Commons and the Bundestag. I found international debate to be just as stimulating as the exchanges in the House of Representatives.

In 1979, I picked up an additional committee assignment, the Permanent Select Committee on Intelligence, a six-year appointment that will terminate at the end of 1984. Much of what I have heard and learned in that Committee will never appear in these pages, but enough can be divulged to give the reader an intimate look at several intelligence ventures, among them the ill-fated hostage rescue operation in Iran and U.S. efforts in Central America.

In 1983, with my elevation to senior Republican in the Virginia House delegation, I became a member of the Committee on Committees, the group responsible for committee assignments, and learned a great deal more about the inner workings of the House.

Finally, the advent of the Reagan Administration brought a new chapter to my journal and even a visit to Camp David. Personal meetings with Lee Kuan Yew of Singapore, Indira Gandhi in New Delhi, and Anwar Sadat at his home in Aswan provided me with memories that will last a lifetime.

I will be sharing these experiences, and others, with you in my second volume, which will cover the years 1978 to the present, a time without the sorrow and despair that plagued our country in the years in this first book, but nevertheless a period of great excitement and vitality, and some frustration, six years of change and maturation.

Appendix

All those listed were Members of the House of Representatives at the time their names appeared in this journal, except as otherwise noted.

Abzug, Bella—Democrat, New York
Albert, Carl—Democrat, Oklahoma
Anderson, John—Republican, Illinois
Andrews, Mark—Republican, North
  Dakota (subsequently a Senator)
Arends, Les—Republican, Illinois
Armstrong, William—Republican,
  Colorado (subsequently a Senator)
Ashbrook, John—Republican, Ohio
Aspin, Les—Democrat, Wisconsin
Aspinall, Wayne—Democrat, Colorado

Badillo, Herman—Democrat, New York
Bafalis, L. A. "Skip"—Republican, Florida
Baker, Howard—Senator—Republican,
  Tennessee
Bartlett, Dewey—Senator—Republican,
  Oklahoma
Bauman, Robert—Republican, Maryland
Beall, Glenn—Senator—Republican,
  Maryland
Beard, Robin—Republican, Tennessee
Bell, Alphonzo—Republican, California
Bennett, Charles—Democrat, Florida
Biester, Edward "Pete"—Republican,
  Pennsylvania
Bolling, Richard—Democrat, Missouri
Boyles, Blanche—Manager,
  Congressman Whitehurst's Virginia
  Beach Office
Brademas, John—Democrat, Indiana
Bray, William—Republican, Indiana
Brinkley, Jack—Democrat, Georgia
Brock, William—Senator—Republican,
  Tennessee
Broomfield, William—Republican,
  Michigan
Brown, Clarence "Bud"—Republican,
  Ohio
Broyhill, James—Republican, North
  Carolina
Broyhill, Joel—Republican, Virginia
Buchanan, John—Republican, Alabama
Buckley, James—Senator-
  Conservative/Republican, New York
Burke, Herbert—Republican, Florida
Burke, Yvonne Braithwaite—Democrat,
  California

Butler, Caldwell—Republican, Virginia
Byrd, Harry F., Jr.—Senator—
  Independent, Virginia

Camp, John N. "Happy"—Republican,
  Oklahoma
Cannon, Howard—Senator—Democrat,
  Nevada
Caputo, Bruce—Republican, New York
Carter, Tim Lee—Republican, Kentucky
Cederberg, Elford "Al"—Republican,
  Michigan
Chappell, William—Democrat, Florida
Clancy, Don—Republican, Ohio
Clausen, Don—Republican, California
Cleveland, James—Republican, New
  Hampshire
Cochran, Thad—Republican, Mississippi
  (subsequently a Senator)
Cohen, William—Republican, Maine
  (subsequently a Senator)
Conable, Barber—Republican, New York
Conlan, John—Republican, Arizona
Conte, Silvio—Republican,
  Massachusetts
Conyers, John—Democrat, Michigan
Coughlin, Lawrence—Republican,
  Pennsylvania
Crane, Philip—Republican, Illinois
Culver, John—Senator—Democrat, Iowa

Dalton, John—Governor of Virginia,
  1978-82, Republican
Daniel, Robert—Republican, Virginia
Daniel, W. C. "Dan"—Democrat, Virginia
Davis, Glenn—Republican, Wisconsin
de la Garza, E. "Kika"—Democrat, Texas
Dellenback, John—Republican, Oregon
Dellums, Ronald—Democrat, California
Dennis, David—Republican, Indiana
Derwinski, Edward—Republican, Illinois
Devine, Samuel—Republican, Ohio
Dickinson, William—Republican,
  Alabama
Dirksen, Everett—Senator—Republican,
  Illinois
Dorn, Kathleen—Receptionist—
  Appointments Secretary in

Congressman Whitehurst's Washington office
Dornan, Robert—Republican, California
Downey, Thomas—Democrat, New York
Downing, Thomas—Democrat, Virginia
Drago, Charles "Buddy"—Legislative Assistant to Congressman Whitehurst, 1969-72
Drinan, Robert—Democrat, Massachusetts
DuPont, Pierre—Republican, Delaware

Emery, David—Republican, Maine
Esch, Marvin—Republican, Michigan
Fenwick, Millicent—Republican, New Jersey
Findley, Paul—Republican, Illinois
Fish, Hamilton—Republican, New York
Fisher, Clark—Democrat, Texas
Flood, Dan—Democrat, Pennsylvania
Flowers, Walter—Democrat, Georgia
Flynt, Jack—Democrat, Georgia
Fong, Hiram—Senator—Republican, Hawaii
Ford, Harold—Democrat, Tennessee
Foreman, Edward—Republican, New Mexico
Forsythe, Edward—Republican, New Jersey
Frelinghuysen, Peter—Republican, New Jersey
Frenzel, William—Republican, Minnesota
Frey, Louis—Republican, Florida
Froehlich, Harold—Republican, Wisconsin
Fulbright, William—Senator—Democrat, Arkansas

Giaimo, Robert—Democrat, Connecticut
Godwin, Mills—Governor of Virginia (As a Democrat, 1966-70, and as a Republican, 1974-78)
Goldwater, Barry—Senator—Republican, Arizona
Goldwater, Barry, Jr.—Republican, California
Gradison, Willis—Republican, Ohio
Gross, H. R.—Republican, Iowa
Gubser, Charles—Republican, California
Gude, Gilbert—Republican, Maryland
Guyer, Tennyson—Republican, Ohio

Hall, Durward "Doc"—Republican, Missouri
Hansen, George—Republican, Idaho
Hansen, Orval—Republican, Idaho
Harsha, William—Republican, Ohio

Hastings, James—Republican, New York
Hays, Wayne—Democrat, Ohio
Hébert, F. Edward—Democrat, Louisiana
Heckler, Margaret—Republican, Massachusetts
Heinz, John—Republican, Pennsylvania (subsequently a Senator)
Helstoski, Henry—Democrat, New Jersey
Hogan, Lawrence—Republican, Maryland
Holt, Marjorie—Republican, Maryland
Holton, Linwood—Governor of Virginia, 1970-74, Republican
Holtzman, Elizabeth—Democrat, New York
Howe, Allan—Democrat, Utah
Hunt, John—Republican, New Jersey
Hutchinson, Edward—Republican, Michigan
Hyde, Henry—Republican, Illinois

Ichord, Richard-Democrat, Missouri

Jackson, Henry "Scoop"—Senator—Democrat, Washington
Jacobs, Andrew—Democrat, Indiana
Javits, Jacob—Senator—Republican, New York
Johnson, James—Republican, Colorado
Jonas, Charles—Republican, North Carolina
Jones, James—Democrat, Oklahoma

Kelly, Richard—Republican, Florida
Kemp, Jack—Republican, New York
Ketchum, William—Republican, California
King, Carleton—Republican, New York
Koch, Edward—Democrat, New York

Lahey, Patrick—Senator—Democrat, Vermont
Landgrebe, Earl—Republican, Indiana
Leggett, Robert—Democrat, California
Lehman, William—Democrat, Florida
Lennon, Alton—Democrat, North Carolina
Lloyd, Jim—Democrat, California
Long, Clarence—Democrat, Maryland
Lowenstein, Allard—Democrat, New York
Lujan, Manuel—Republican, New Mexico
Magnuson, Warren—Senator—Democrat, Washington
Maguire, Andrew—Democrat, New Jersey
Mahon, George—Democrat, Texas

Mann, James—Democrat, South
  Carolina
Mansfield, Mike—Senator—Democrat,
  Montana
Mathias, Charles "Mac"—Senator—
  Republican, Maryland
Mayne, Wiley—Republican, Iowa
McClory, Robert—Republican, Illinois
McCloskey, Paul "Pete"—Republican,
  California
McClure, James—Senator—Republican,
  Idaho
McCormack, John—Democrat,
  Massachusetts
McDade, Joseph—Republican,
  Pennsylvania
McDonald, Larry—Democrat, Georgia
McEwen, Robert—Republican, New York
McGee, Gale—Senator—Democrat,
  Wyoming
McKinney, Stewart—Republican,
  Connecticut
McMillan, John—Democrat, South
  Carolina
Mezvinsky, Edward—Democrat, Iowa
Middendorf, J. William—Secretary of the
  Navy in the Ford Administration
Milford, Dale—Democrat, Texas
Mizell, Wilmer "Vinegar Bend"—
  Republican, North Carolina
Montgomery, Gillespie "Sonny"—
  Democrat, Mississippi
Moorhead, Carlos—Republican,
  California
Mosher, Charles—Republican, Ohio
Myers, John—Republican, Indiana

Nedzi, Lucien—Democrat, Michigan
Nichols, Bill—Democrat, Alabama

Obey, David—Democrat, Wisconsin
O'Hara, James—Democrat, Michigan
O'Neill, Thomas P. "Tip"—Democrat,
  Massachusetts

Parris, Stanford—Republican, Virginia
Passman, Otto—Democrat, Louisiana
Pastore, John—Senator—Democrat,
  Rhode Island
Patman, Wright—Democrat, Texas
Percy, Charles—Senator—Republican,
  Illinois
Perry, Gwen—Military Liaison in
  Congressman Whitehurst's
  Washington office
Pettis, Shirley—Republican, California
Peyser, Peter—First elected as a

Republican from New York, switched
  parties, and ultimately returned as a
  Democrat
Philbin, Philip—Democrat,
  Massachusetts
Pickle, J. J. "Jake"—Democrat, Texas
Poff, Richard—Republican, Virginia
  (preceded Caldwell Butler as
  Congressman for the 6th District)
Powell, Victor—Press Aide for
  Congressman Whitehurst
Powell, Walter—Republican, Ohio
Price, Melvin—Democrat, Illinois
Pritchard, Joel—Republican, Washington

Quie, Albert—Republican, Minnesota
Quillen, James—Republican, Tennessee

Railsback, Tom—Republican, Illinois
Randall, William—Democrat, Missouri
Regula, Ralph—Republican, Ohio
Reuss, Henry—Democrat, Wisconsin
Rhodes, John—Republican, Arizona
Riegle, Don—First elected as a
  Republican from Michigan, switched
  parties in 1973, now a Democratic
  Senator
Rivers, L. Mendel—Democrat, South
  Carolina
Robinson, J. Kenneth—Republican,
  Virginia
Robison, Howard—Republican, New
  York
Rodino, Peter—Democrat, New Jersey
Rogers, Paul—Democrat, Florida
Rousselot, John—Republican, California
Ruth, Earl—Republican, North Carolina
Ryan, William Fitts—Democrat, New
  York

Sandman, Charles—Republican, New
  Jersey
Sarasin, Ronald—Republican,
  Connecticut
Satterfield, David—Democrat, Virginia
Saylor, John—Republican, Pennsylvania
Schneebeli, Herman—Republican,
  Pennsylvania
Schroeder, Patricia—Democrat,
  Colorado
Schulze, Richard—Republican,
  Pennsylvania
Scott, William—Senator—Republican,
  Virginia
Shriver, Garner—Republican, Kansas
Sikes, Robert L. F.—Democrat, Florida
Simon, Paul—Democrat, Illinois

Smith, Henry—Republican, New York
Snyder, Gene—Republican, Kentucky
Spence, Floyd—Republican, South
  Carolina
Staggers, Harley—Democrat, West
  Virginia
Stanton, J. William—Republican, Ohio
Steed, Tom—Democrat, Oklahoma
Steele, Robert—Republican, Connecticut
Steelman, Alan—Republican, Texas
Steiger, William—Republican, Wisconsin
Stennis, John—Senator—Democrat,
  Mississippi
Stratton, Samuel—Democrat, New York
Symington, James—Democrat, Missouri
Symington, Stuart—Senator—Democrat,
  Missouri
Symms, Steve—Republican, Idaho
  (subsequently a Senator)

Talcott, Burt—Republican, California
Teague, Olin "Tiger"—Democrat, Texas
Thompson, R. Burnett—Administrative
  Assistant to Congressman Whitehurst,
  1969-74
Thone, Charles—Republican, Nebraska
Thornton, Ray—Democrat, Arkansas
Thurmond, Strom—Senator—
  Republican, South Carolina
Trible, Paul—Republican, Virginia
  (subsequently a Senator)

Udall, Morris—Democrat, Arizona

Vanik, Charles—Democrat, Ohio
Veysey, Victor—Republican, California
Vigorito, Joseph—Democrat,
  Pennsylvania

Waggoner, Joe—Democrat, Louisiana
Waldie, Jerome—Democrat, California
Wampler, William—Republican, Virginia
Warner, John—Republican, Virginia—
  formerly Secretary of the Navy and
  Administrator of the American
  Revolution Bicentennial
  Administration, now a Senator
Wasserman, Rena—Manager,
  Congressman Whitehurst's Norfolk
  office
Whalen, Charles—Republican, Ohio
Whitten, Jamie—Democrat, Mississippi
Widnall, William—Republican, New
  Jersey
Wiggins, Charles—Republican, California
Wilson, Bob—Republican, California
Wilson, Charles—Democrat, California
Wolff, Lester—Democrat, New York
Won Pat, Antonio—Delegate—
  Democrat, Guam

Yates, Sidney—Democrat, Illinois
Yermishkin, Oleg—Second Secretary,
  Embassy of the USSR
Young, Bill—Republican, Florida